UNITED STATES ARMY

TRAINING CENTER

ARMOR

FORT KNOX, KENTUCKY

All Rights Reserved, ALBERT LOVE ENTERPRISES, INC., Doraville, Georgia

History of United States Army Training Center, Armor

The history of the United States Army Training Center, Armor, dates back to 1940, when Europe was overrun by Naziism and the United States initiated its first peacetime draft in history. The Training Center had three names in that first year. It was entitled the Armored Force School and Replacement Center on 1 October, 1940, and changed to the Armored Force Replacement Center 25 days later. In April, 1941, the title became the Armored Force Replacement Training Center.

The Armored Force Replacement Training Center grew considerably in size and function during World War II, with the title being changed again in 1943 to the Armor Replacement Training Center. After the war, when the United States demobilized portions of its huge wartime forces, the Armor Replacement Training Center was placed on an inactive status. This occurred in July of 1947 when the Third Armored Division was reactivated at Fort Knox and assumed the training mission of the Armor Replacement Training Center.

In 1955, the Third Armored Division was ordered to "combat ready" status for eventual shipment to Europe. This brought the Armor Replacement Training Center back to active status in March of that year to carry on the training functions. The name of the Training Center was changed to its present title in March of 1956.

As of 31 December, 1963, more than 550,000 trainees had completed training programs in the Training Center since its inception.

There are four training brigades in the United States Army Training Center, Armor. The First Brigade is responsible for Advanced Individual Training in Armor and Reconnaissance and Basic Unit Training in Armor and Reconnaissance. The Second Brigade trains men to be specialists in fields such as cooking, radio operation and clerical work. The Third and Fourth Brigades give Basic Combat Training.

The Training Center also maintains two separate companies—Headquarters Company and Service Company—and two attached units, the Noncommissioned Officers Academy and the 113th Band. USATCA has the capability of conducting training for about 18,000 men at one time. Its training and administrative personnel, both officers and enlisted men, number about 4,300. The total strength of the Training Center is approximately 22,000. Over 85,000 trainees graduate from various programs in USATCA each year.

Gold Vault

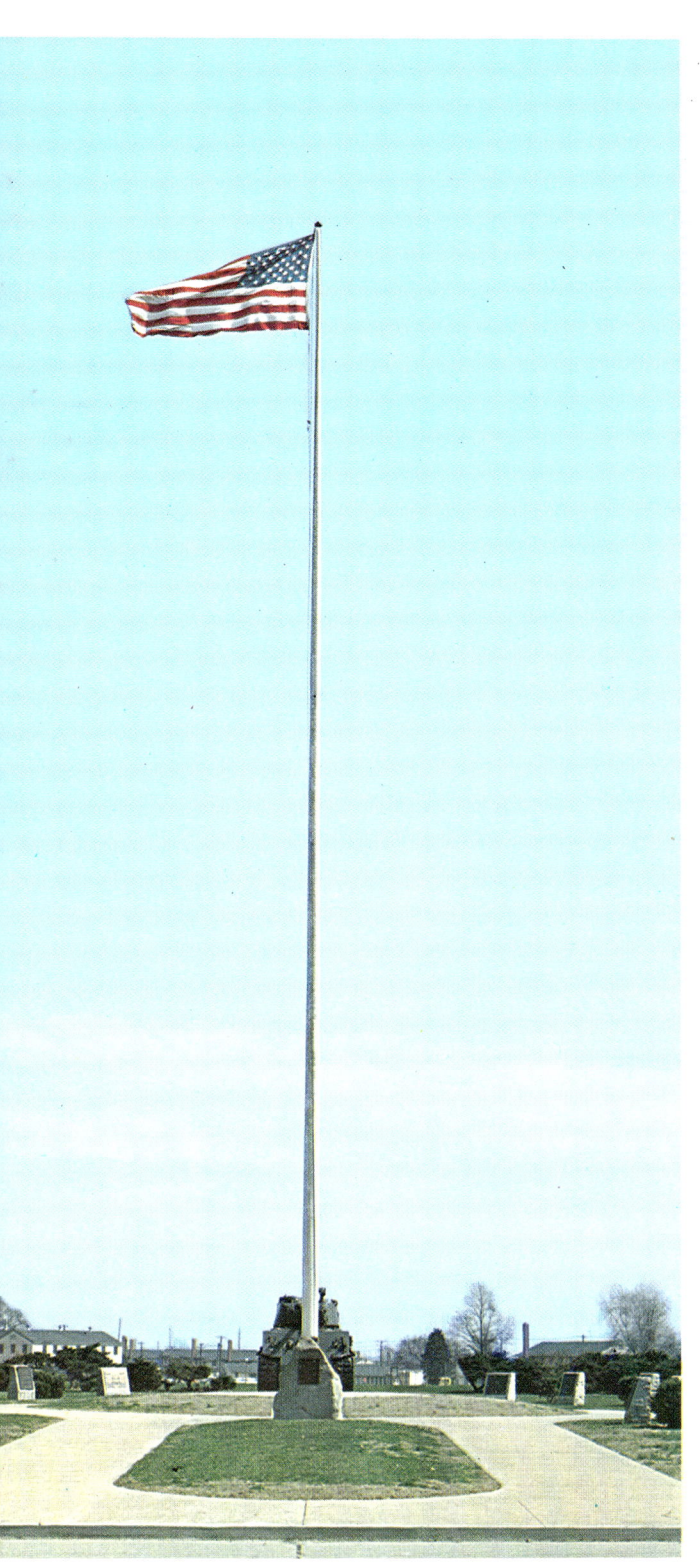
Colors—Post Headquarters

Entrance to Fort Knox

Service Club

Chapel

BRIGADIER GENERAL WILSON M. HAWKINS
Commanding General
U. S. ARMY TRAINING CENTER, ARMOR

BRIGADIER GENERAL HAWKINS

Brigadier General Wilson M. Hawkins was commissioned as a second lieutenant, Infantry Reserve, in 1931 after participating in the ROTC program at Louisiana State University. He then attended graduate school at Harvard University and received his masters degree in Business Administration in 1934. In 1939 he won a regular Army commission as a second lieutenant, Cavalry, and was assigned to the 6th Cavalry Regiment.

In 1942 he was reassigned to the 67th Armored Regiment, 2d Armored Division and fought with that division during World War II in North Africa and Europe.

General Hawkins returned to the United States in 1946 and graduated from the Command and General Staff College in 1947. He then served as an instructor of tactics in the Armor School at Fort Knox and in the Artillery School at Fort Sill.

Upon the outbreak of hostilities in Korea in 1950, General Hawkins was dispatched to the Far East where he was assigned to the G-3 Section of the Far East and United Nations Command. In early 1951 following the Chinese entry into the war, General Hawkins was requested for command of the 64th Tank Battalion, 3d Infantry Division, which he commanded through four campaigns against the communists.

In 1953 General Hawkins once again returned to the United States and attended the Armed Forces Staff College. Upon graduation he came to Fort Knox where he served as Chief of the Combat Vehicles Section of what is now the Armor Board. General Hawkins attended the Army War College in 1955-56.

For the next two years he commanded the 14th Armored Cavalry Regiment in Germany and in 1958 he moved to Seventh Army Headquarters as Deputy G-3.

Returning to the United States and Fort Leavenworth in 1959 General Hawkins served in the Command and General Staff College until 1963 when he became Deputy Commander, Combined Arms Group, Combat Developments Command. He assumed command of the US Army Training Center, Armor on 3 September 1965.

General Hawkins has been awarded the Silver Star with Oak-Leaf Cluster, Legion of Merit with Oak-Leaf Cluster, Bronze Star Medal with Oak-Leaf Cluster, Air Medal, Army Commendation Medal, and Purple Heart. He has 12 campaign stars and arrowhead for D-Day amphibious landings.

HEADQUARTERS US ARMY TRAINING CENTER, ARMOR
OFFICE OF THE COMMANDING GENERAL
Fort Knox, Kentucky

This book records a new and important period in your life—the start of a military career. You arrived here over eight weeks ago as a civilian; now you depart as a soldier.

The value of basic training can be measured only in terms of how the new soldier uses the knowledge and skills he has acquired. We have aimed at making you look and act like a soldier, at qualifying you in your basic weapon, making you physically fit, knowledgeable in military subjects and proud of your own abilities and of the Army.

As you go to Advanced Individual Training and a permanent assignment, or return to your civilian community, you will look back upon these weeks as some of the most significant in your lives.

You have proven your mettle in the crucible of basic training. The officers and enlisted men of your cadre are proud of you. As a soldier, walk with pride, for you are now responsible for the reputation, tradition and history of the finest Army in the world.

To all of you I extend my congratulations on your accomplishments and my best wishes for your continuing success in the years ahead.

WILSON M. HAWKINS
Brigadier General, USA
Commanding

COLONEL WILLIAM S. HUFF
Deputy Commander

COLONEL RUSSELL W. ERNST
Chief of Staff

Cavalry Chapel

Religious Services

Mess Hall

PCPT

Basic Marksmanship

Retreat

Reception Station

Field Inspection

Basic Marksmanship—Zeroing In

Basic Marksmanship—Off Hand

Basic Marksmanship—Night Firing

Marches

Basic Marksmanship—Record Firing

Chow in the Field

Basic Marksmanship—Record Firing

Color Guard

USATCA Headquarters

Drill Competition

Physical Training

Basic Marksmanship

Hand to Hand Combat Training

Dismounted Drill

Present Arms

Commanding Officer's ReviewDismounted Drill

Hand Grenades

Hand to Hand Combat

Inspection

Graduation

Parades and Ceremonies

Colors Passing in Review

Awards

Passing in Review

In Processing

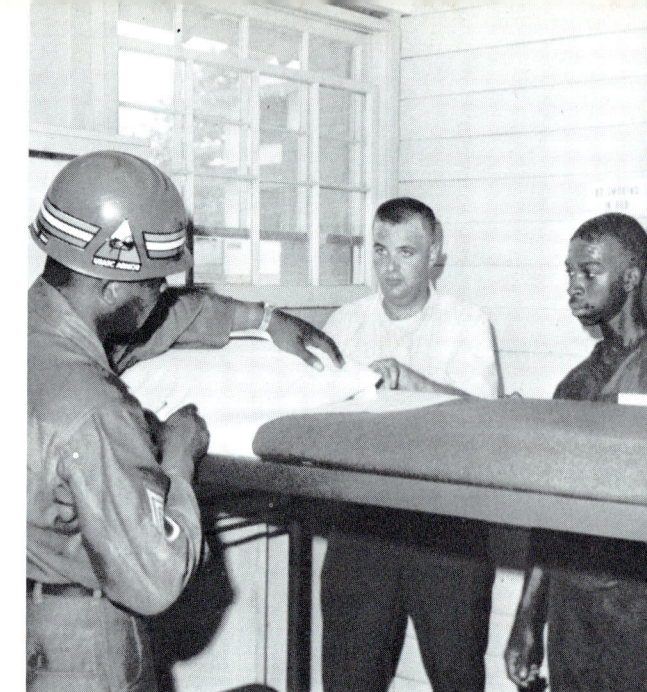

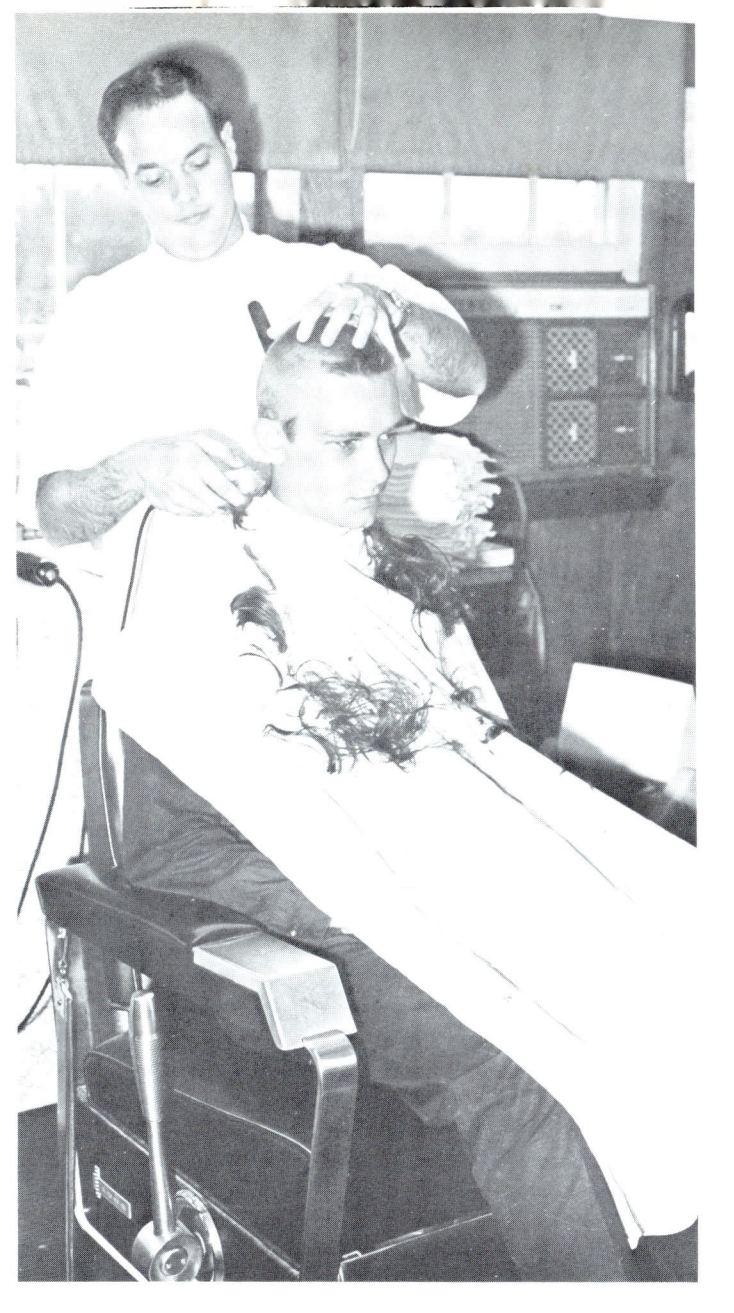

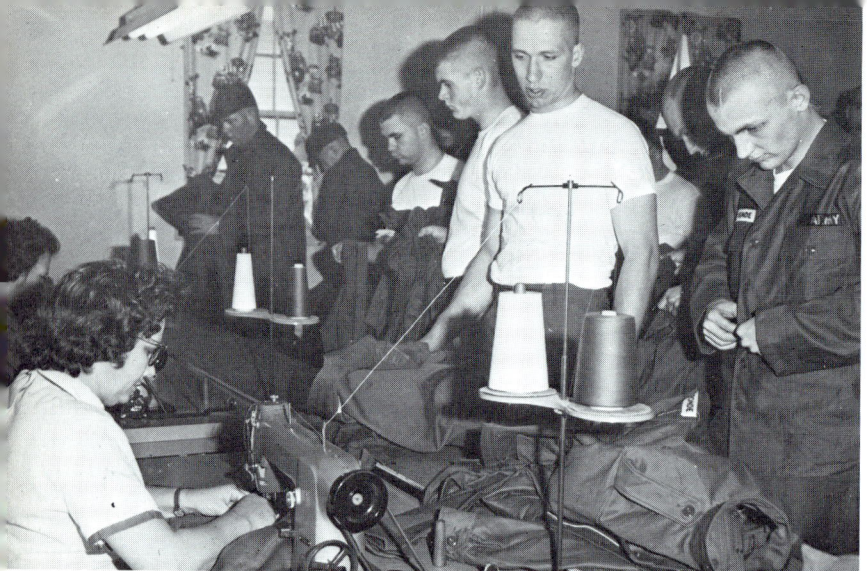
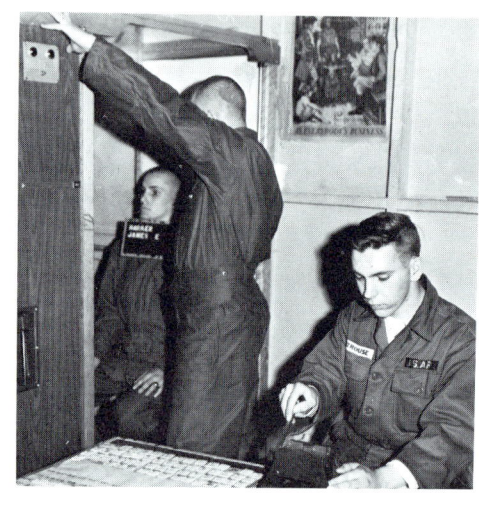

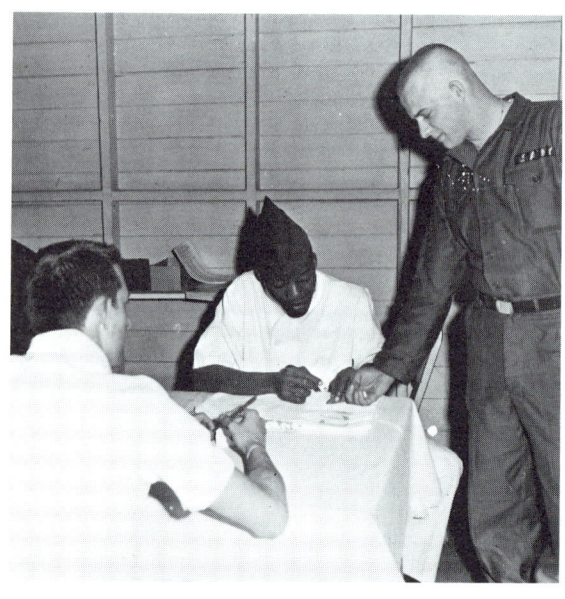
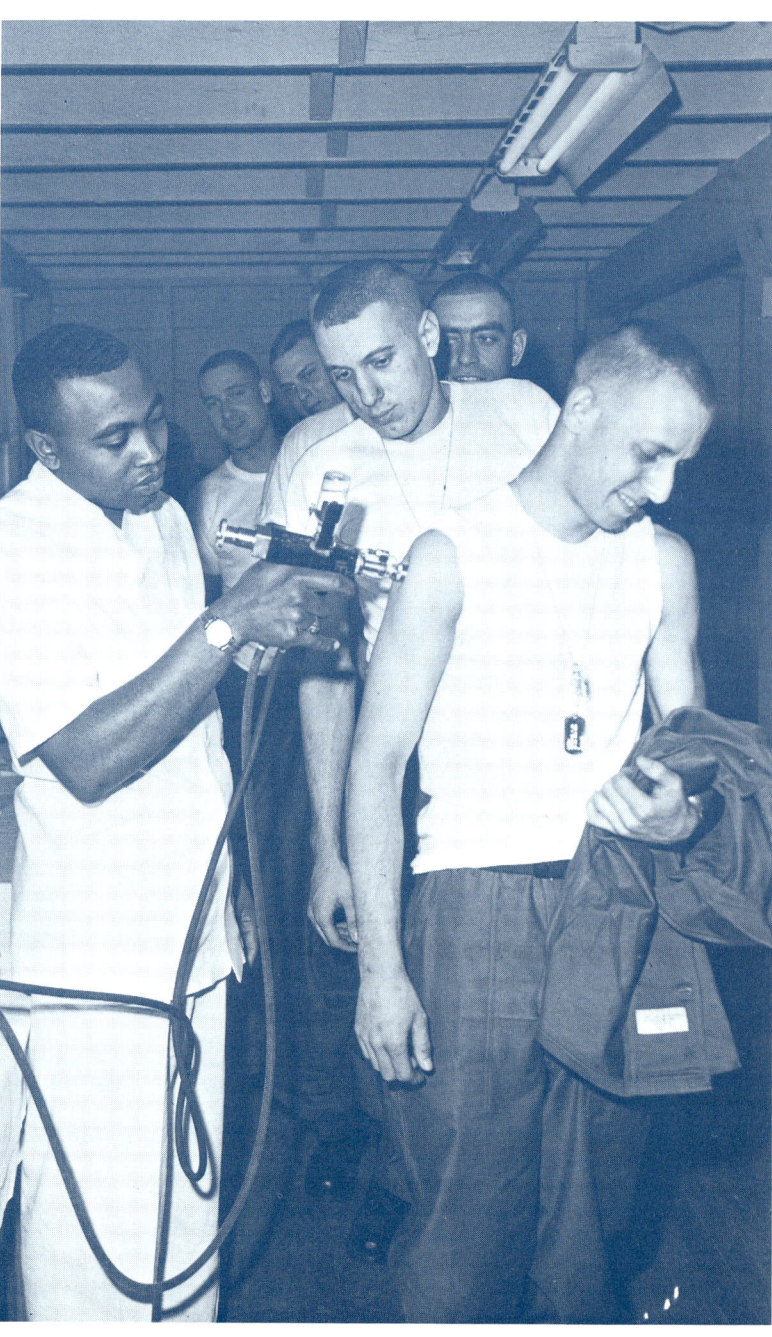

Pick Up

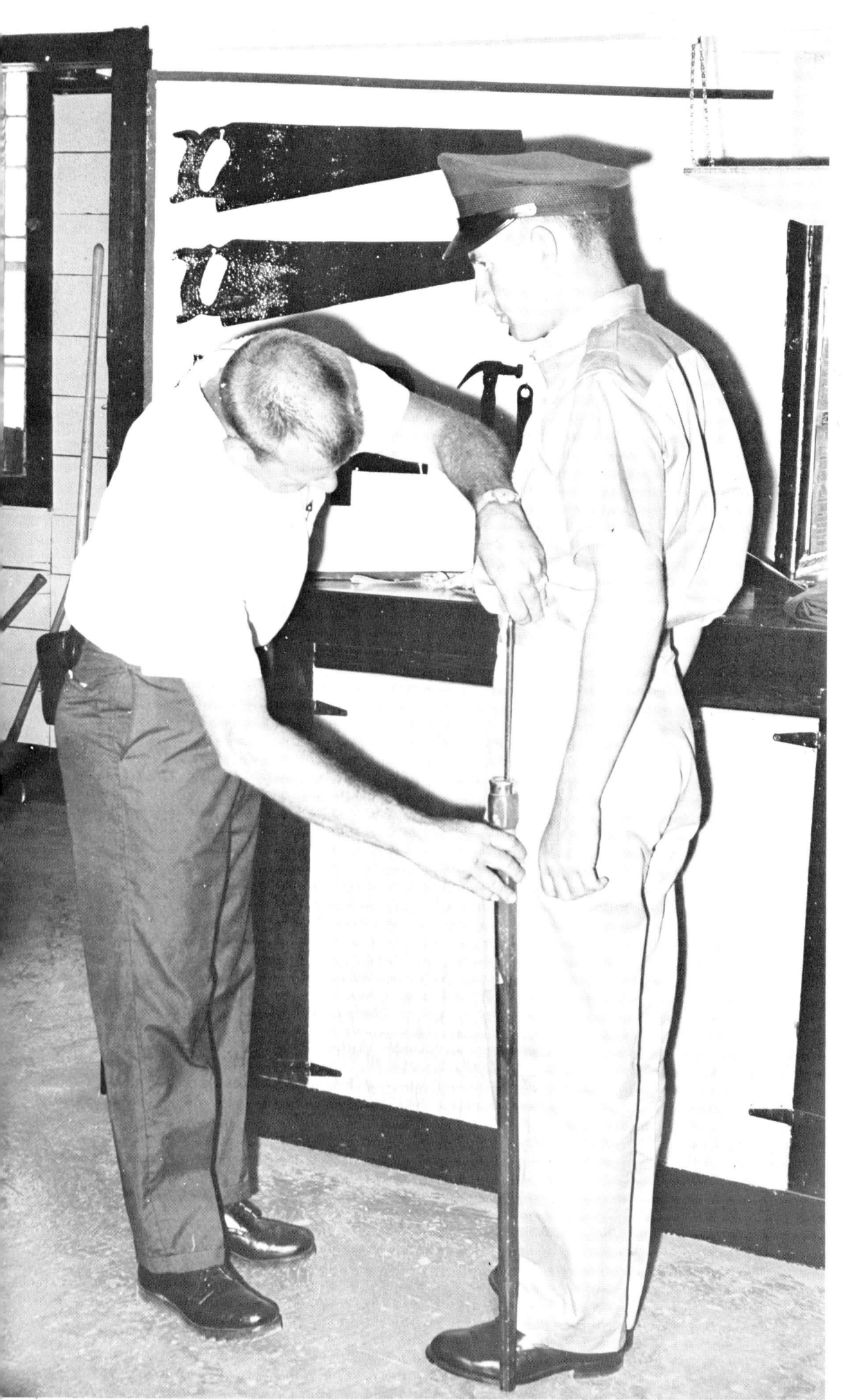

Uniform Check

Dismounted Drill

Manual Of Arms

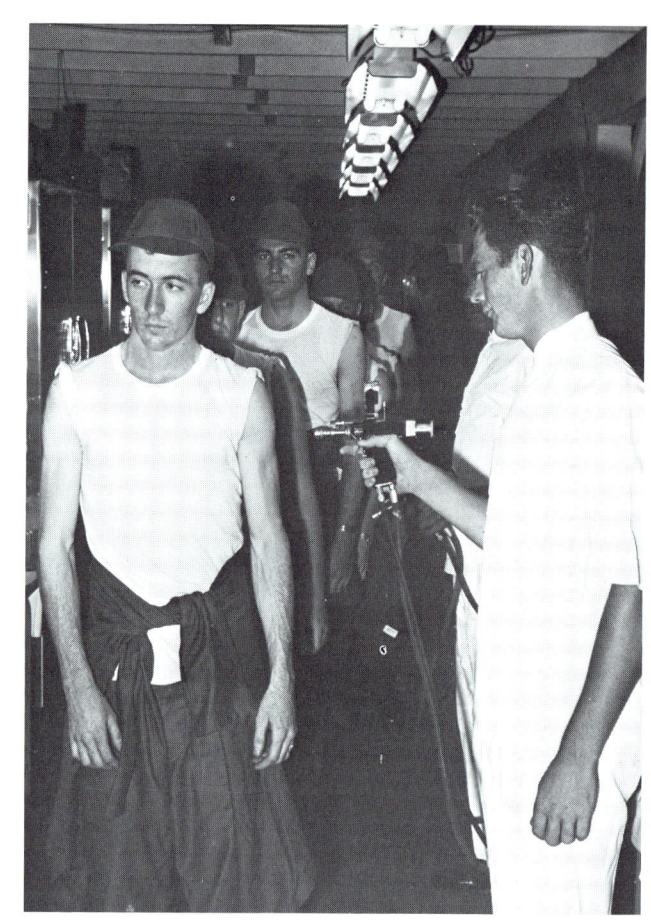

Shots

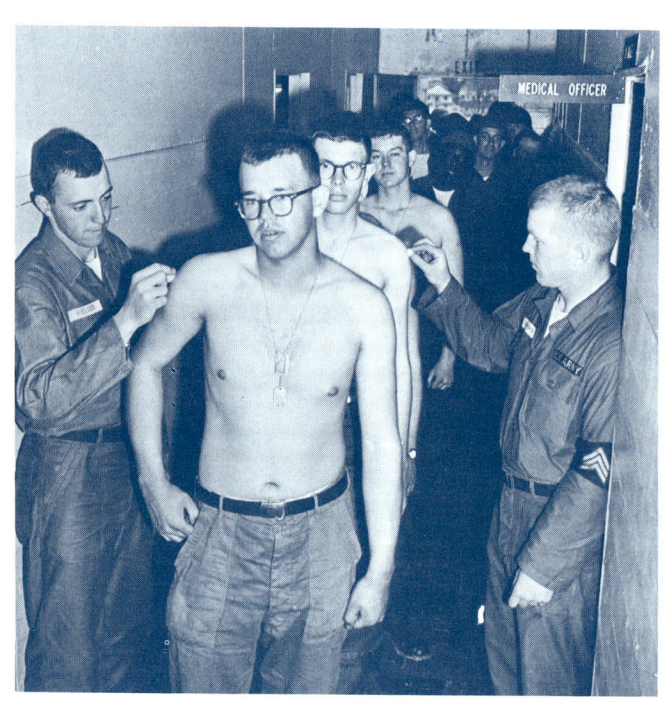
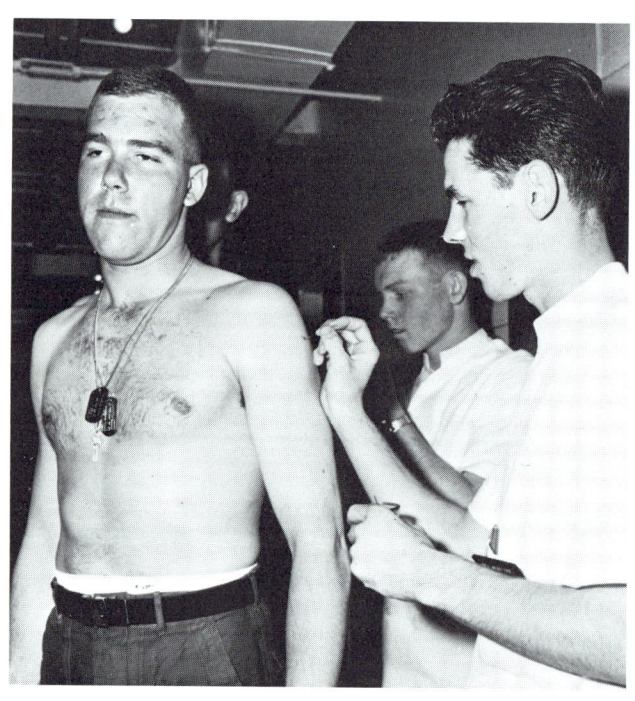

NO SMOKING
PHARMACY
SCREENING

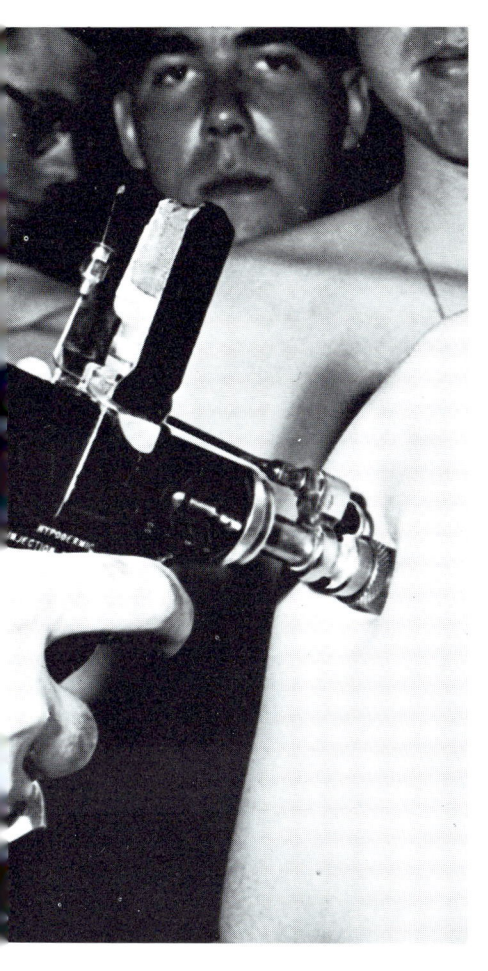

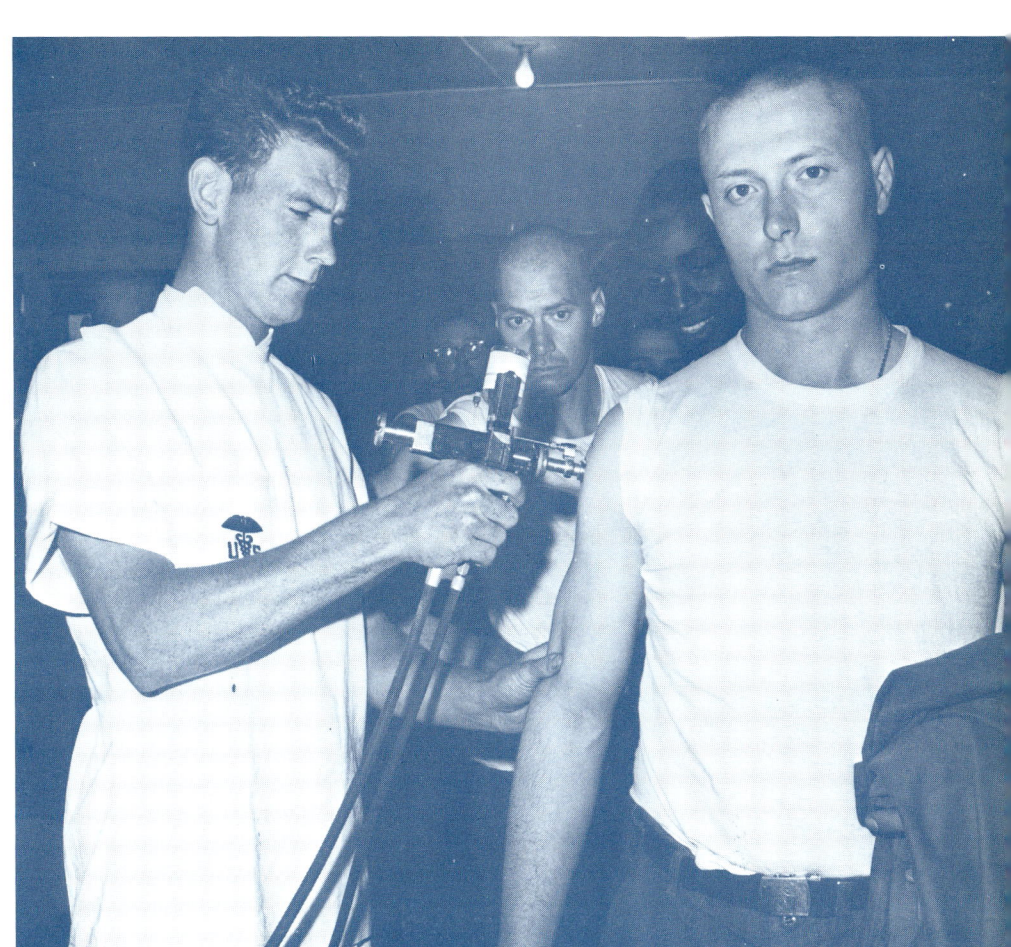

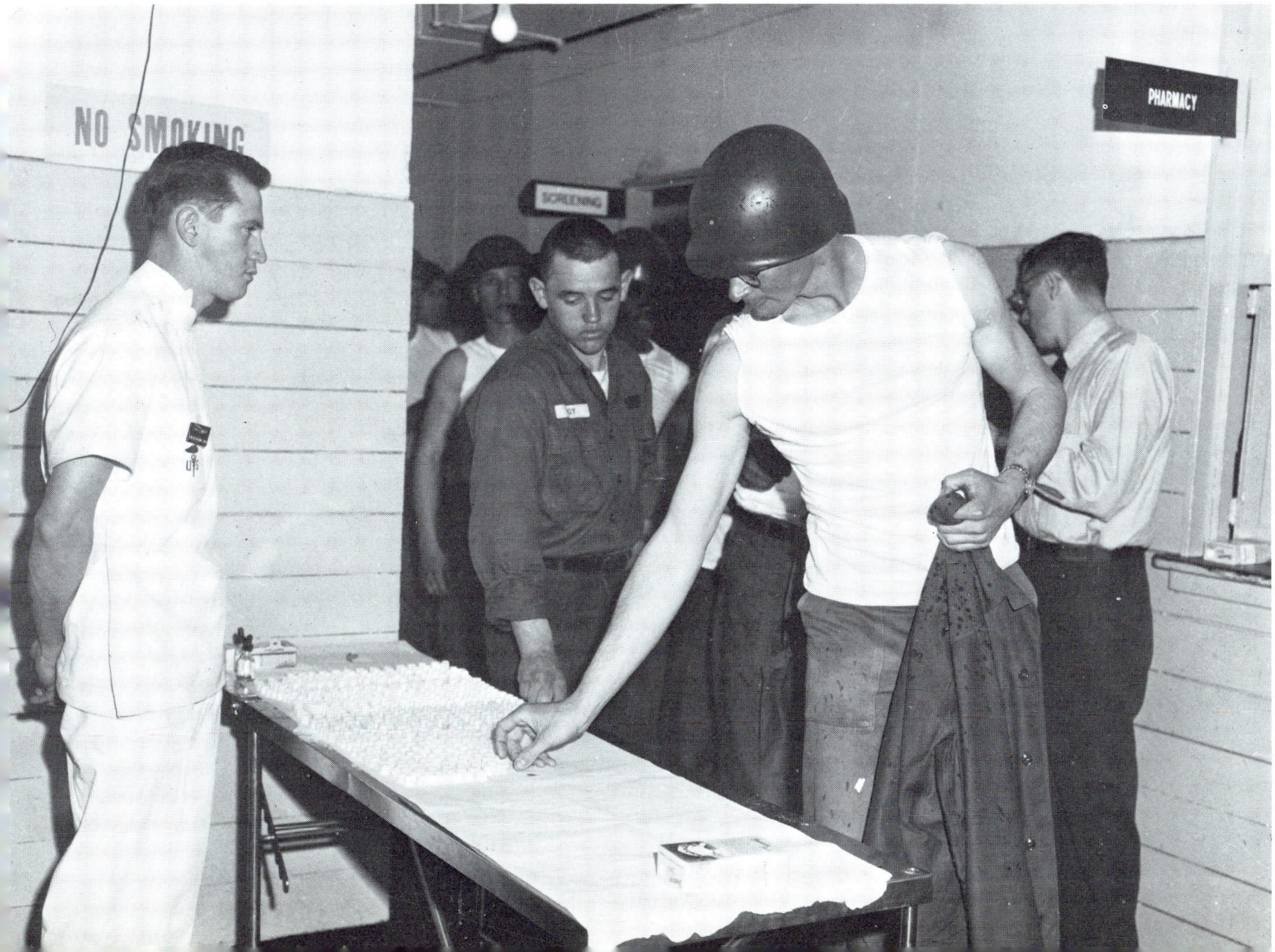

Dental Check

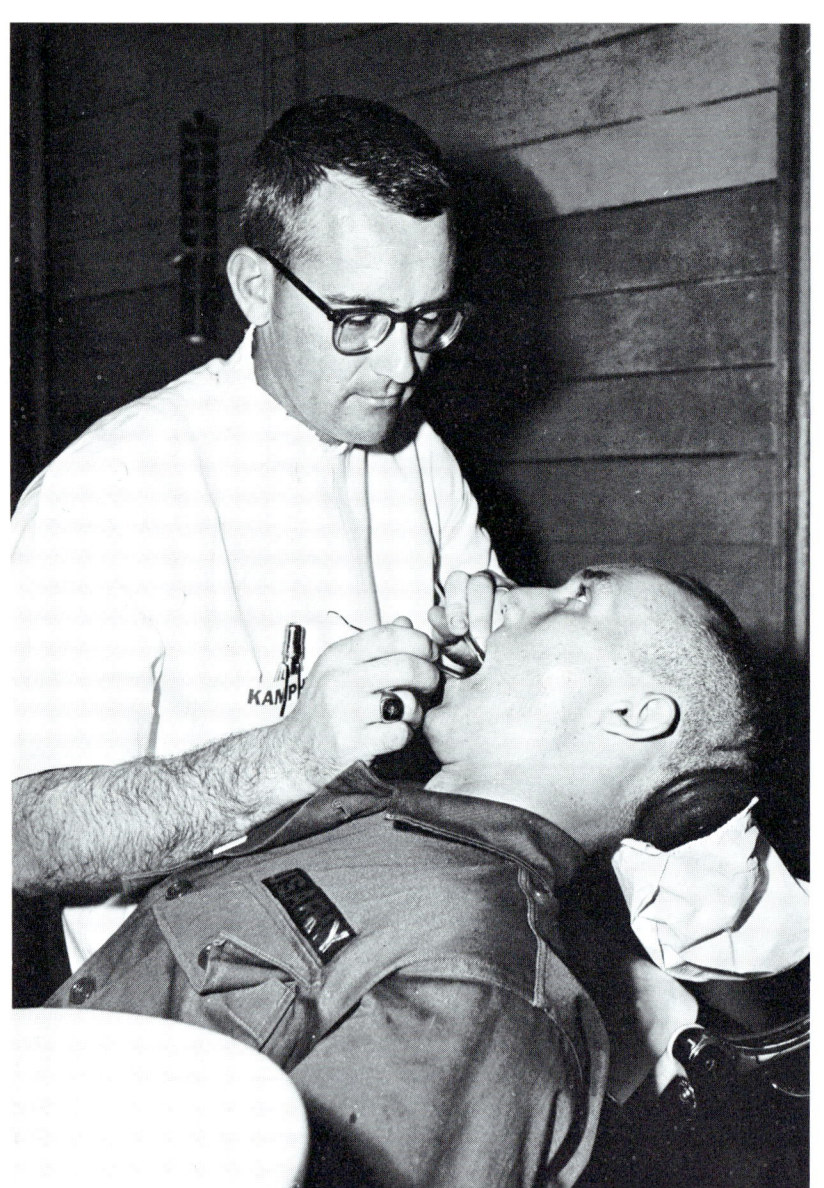
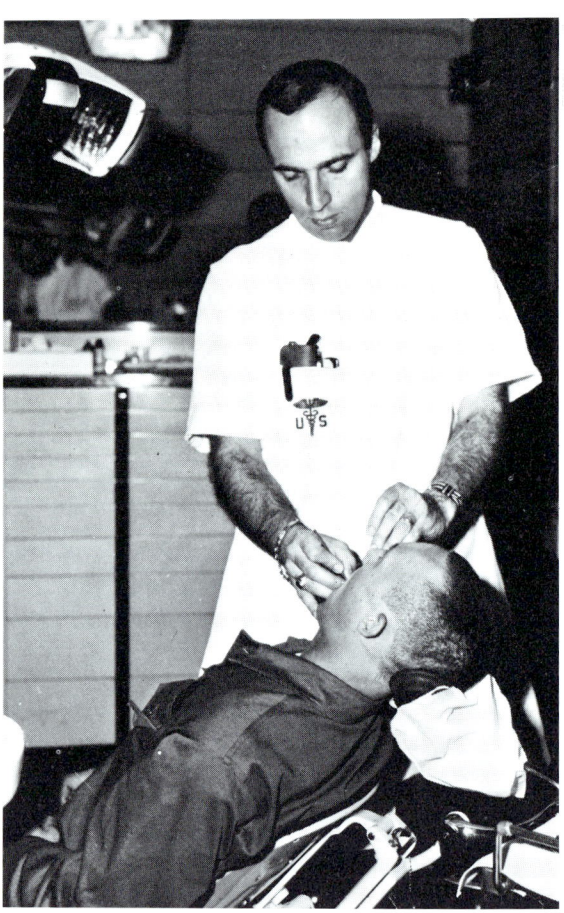
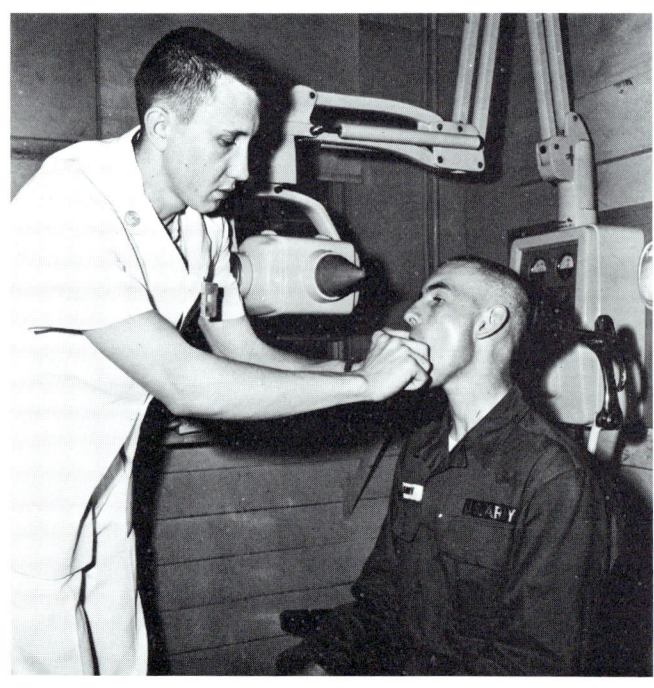
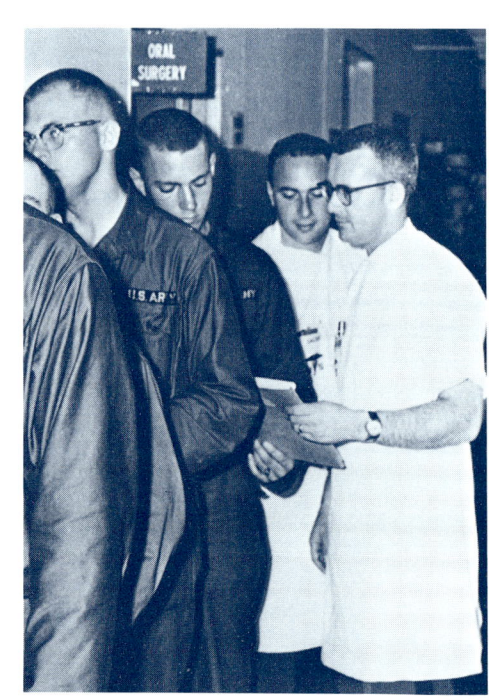

Eye Examination

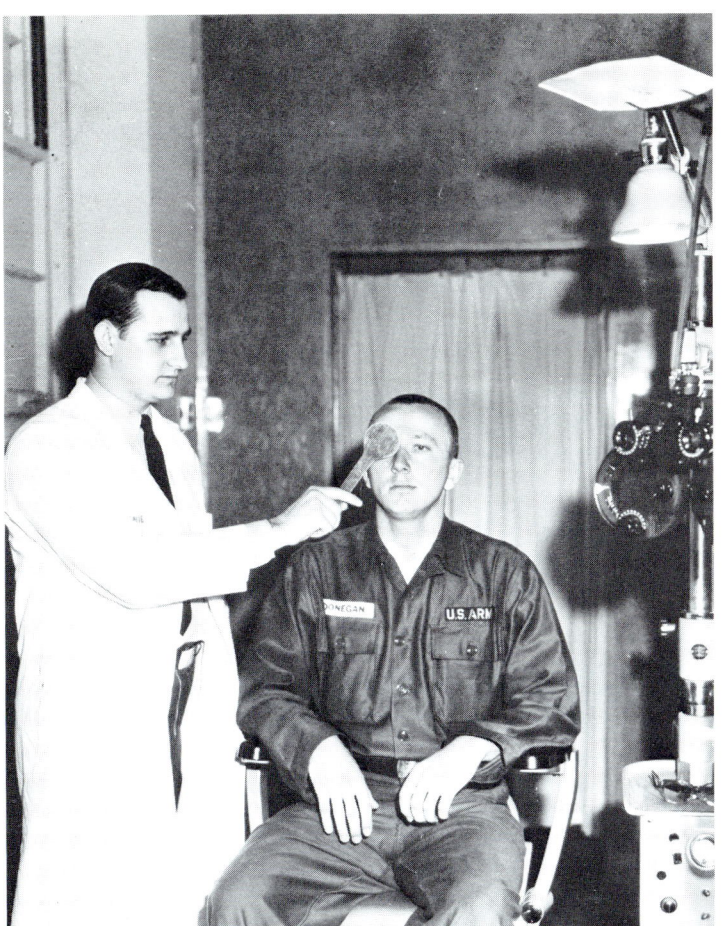
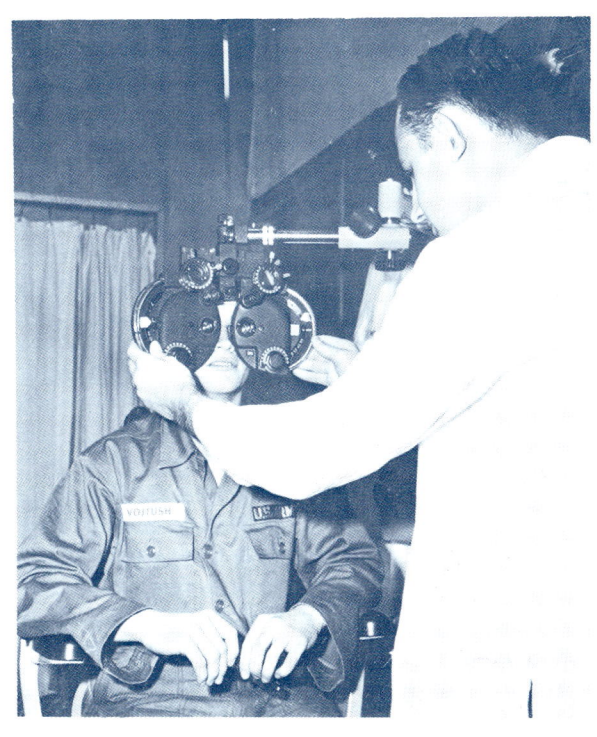
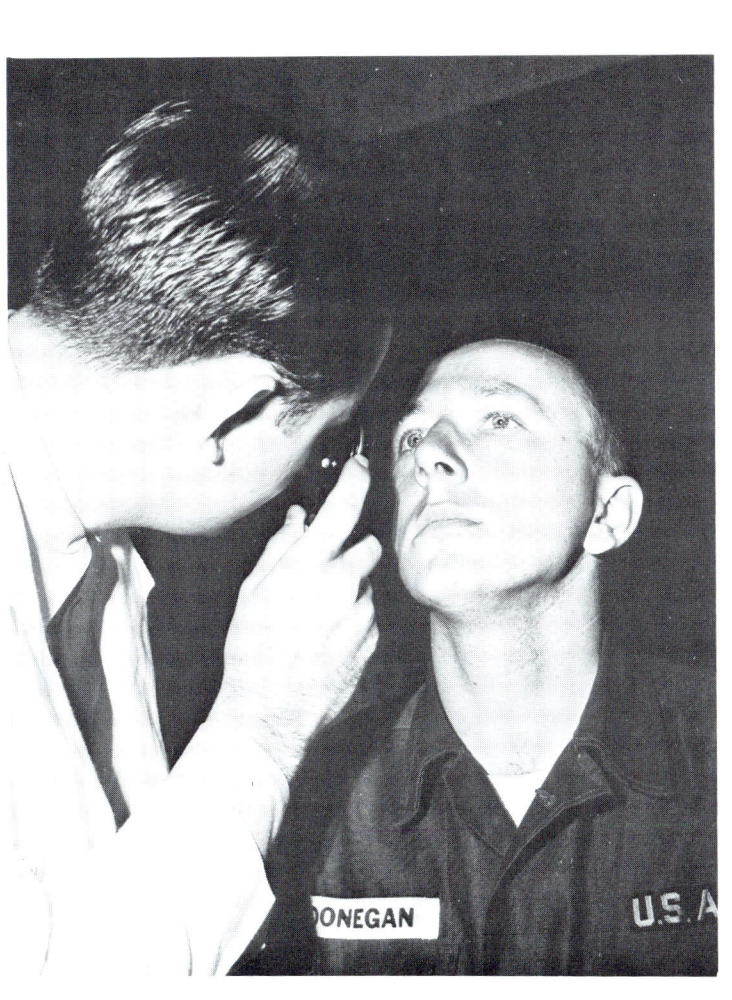

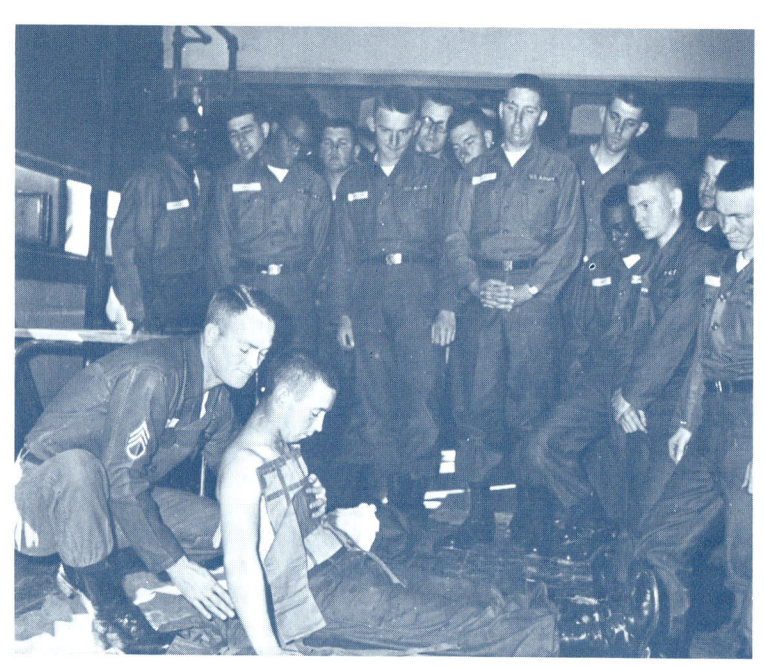

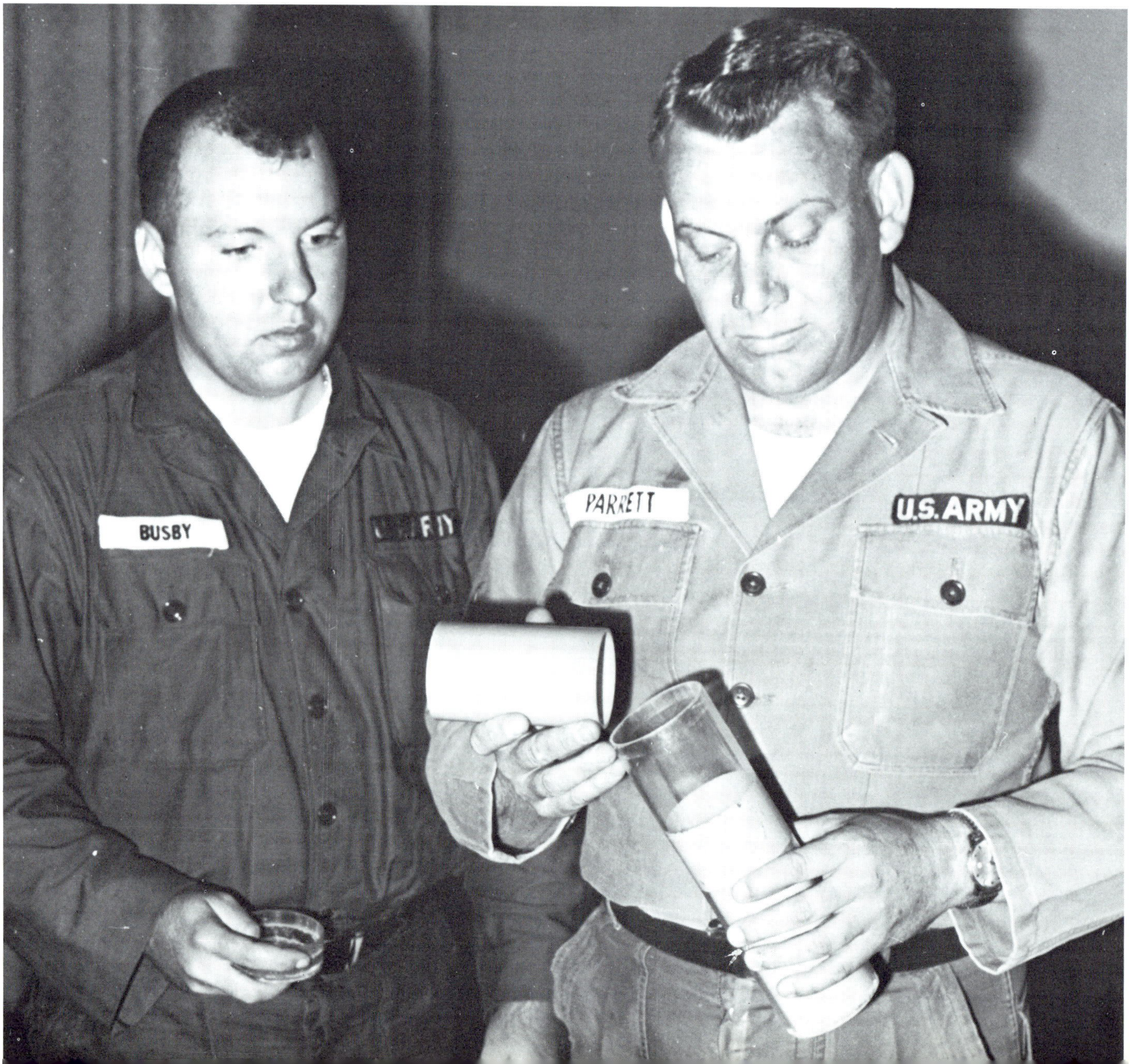

First Aid

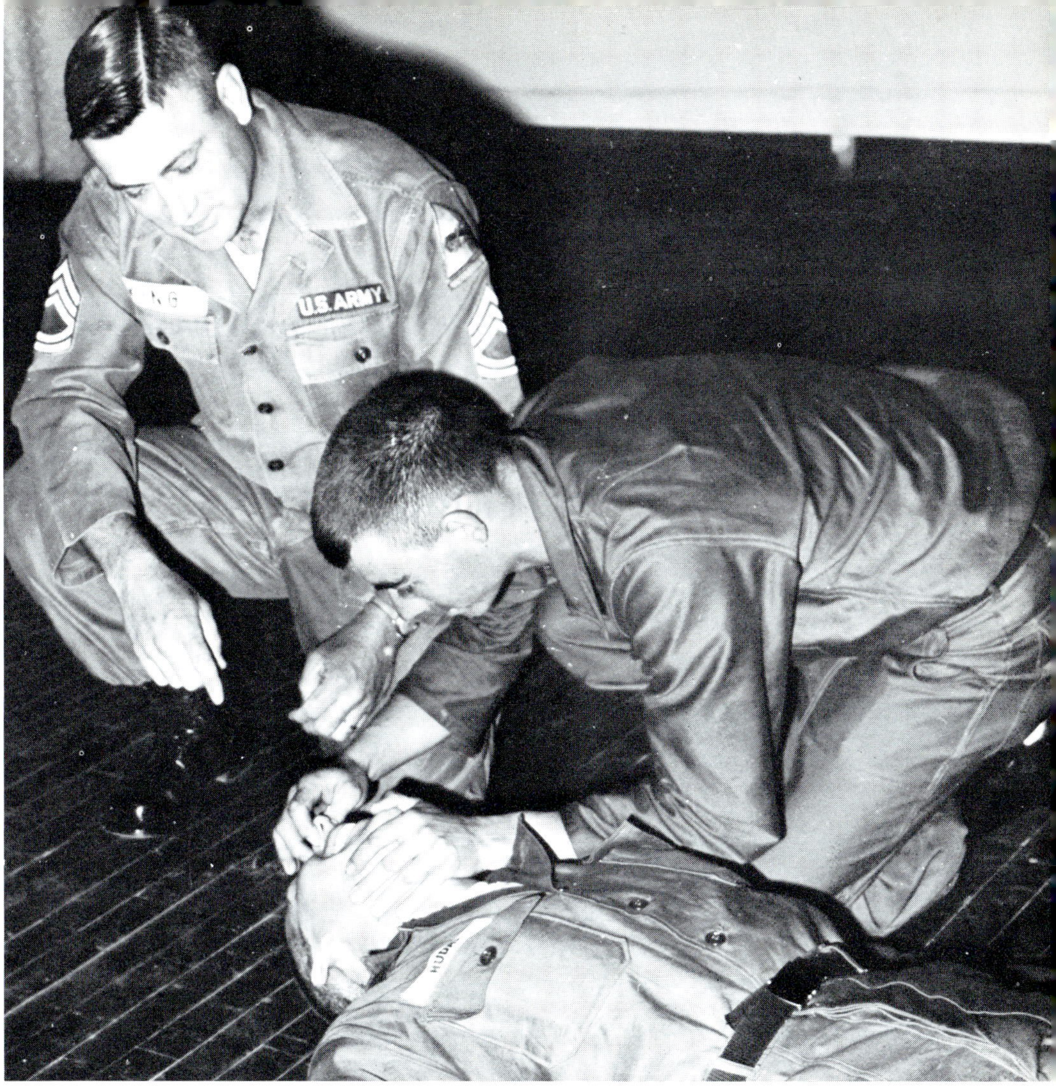

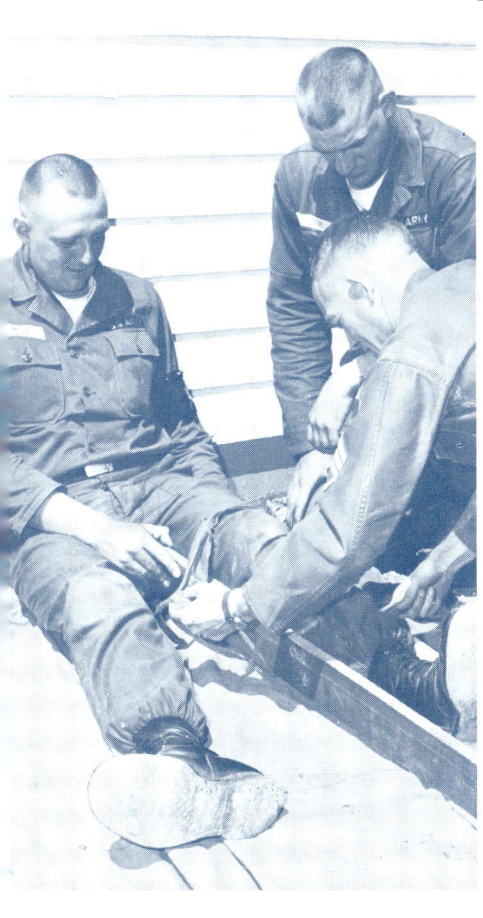

Physical Training

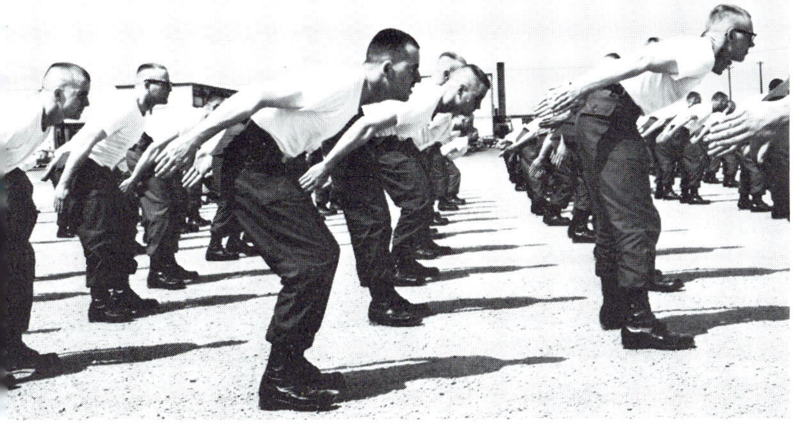
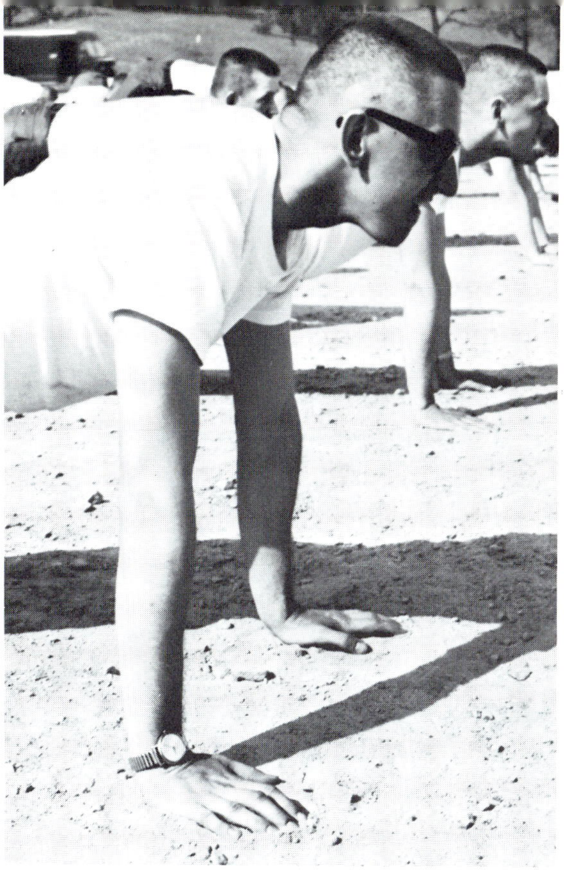
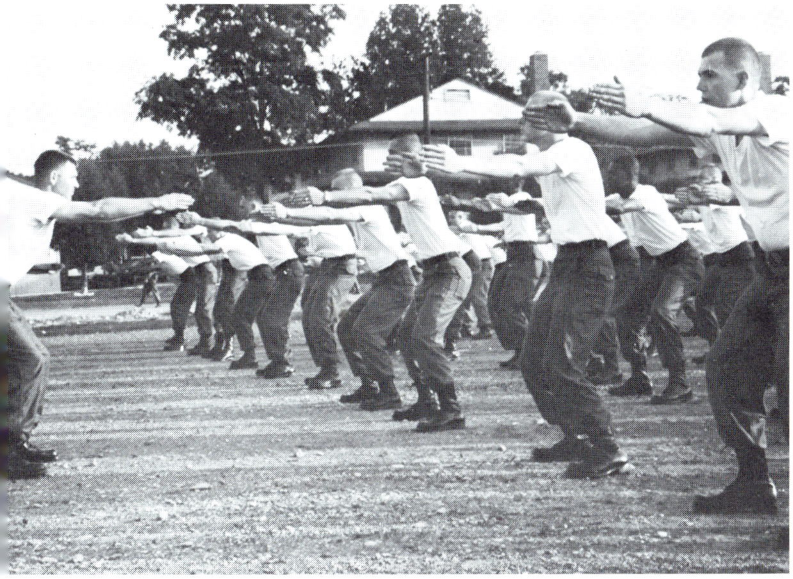
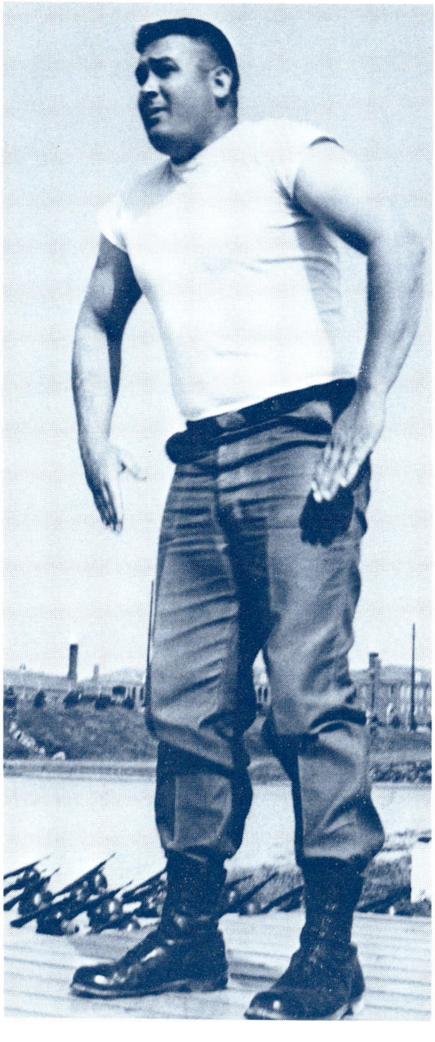
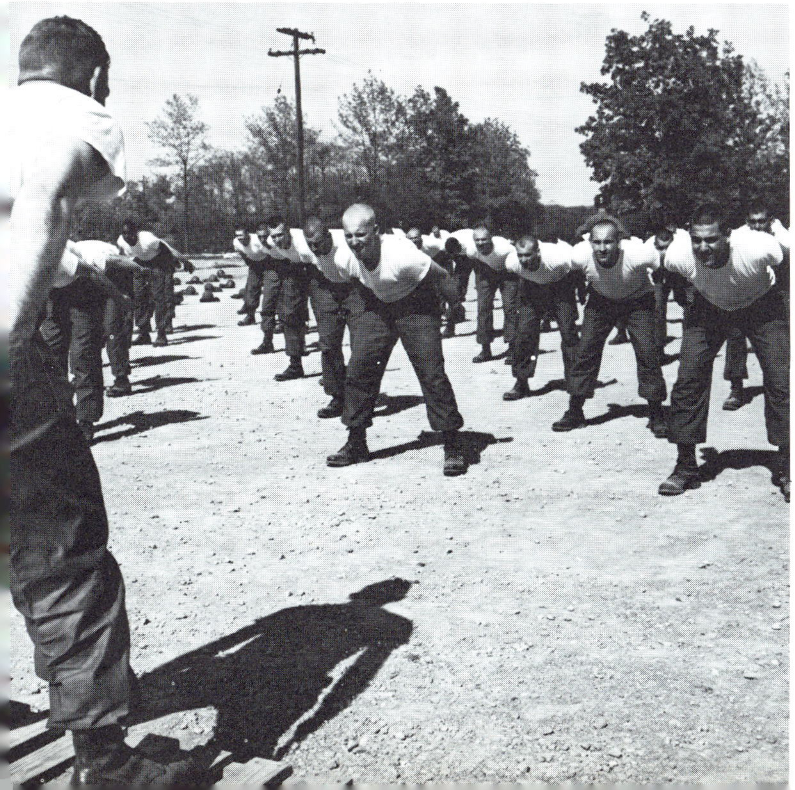

Guard Duty

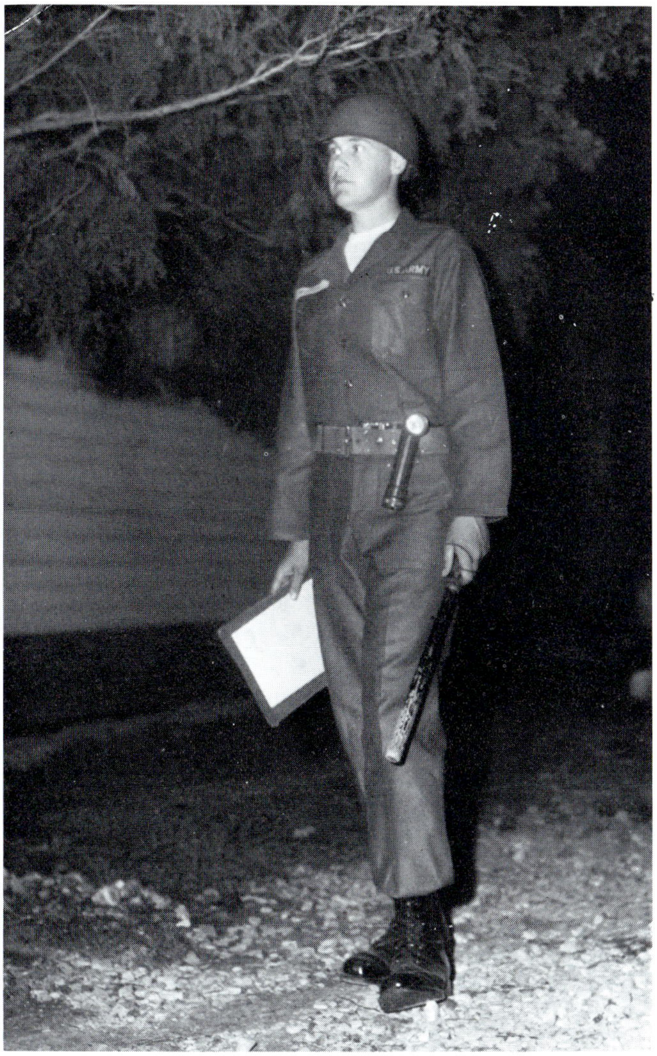
U.S. ARMY

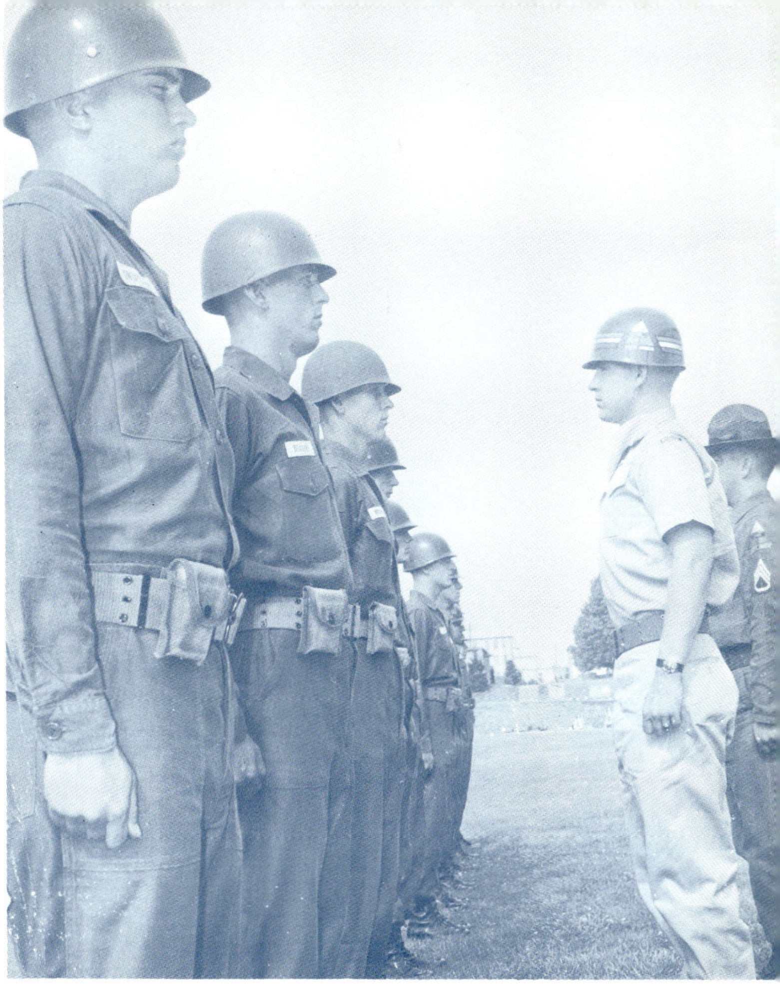

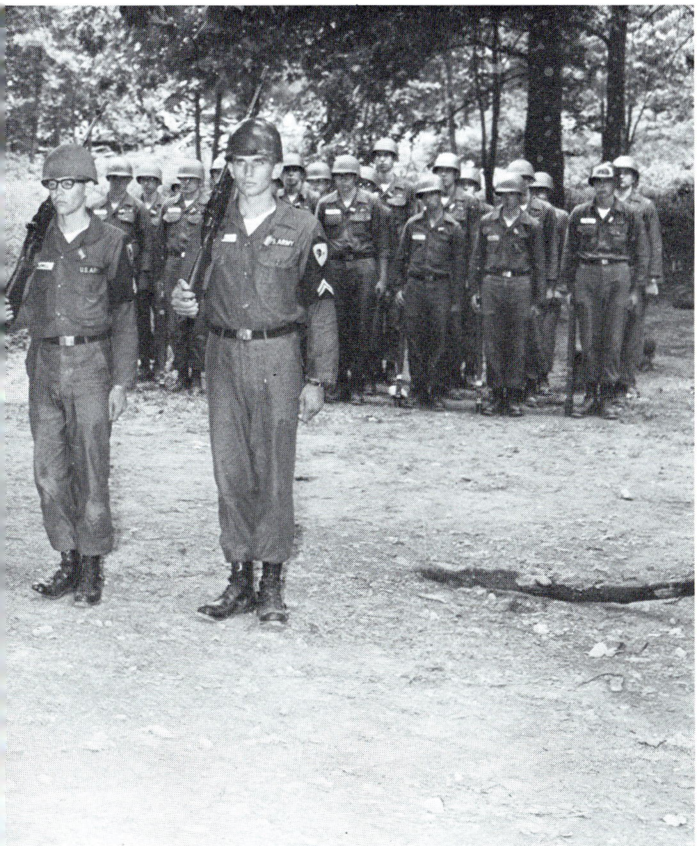

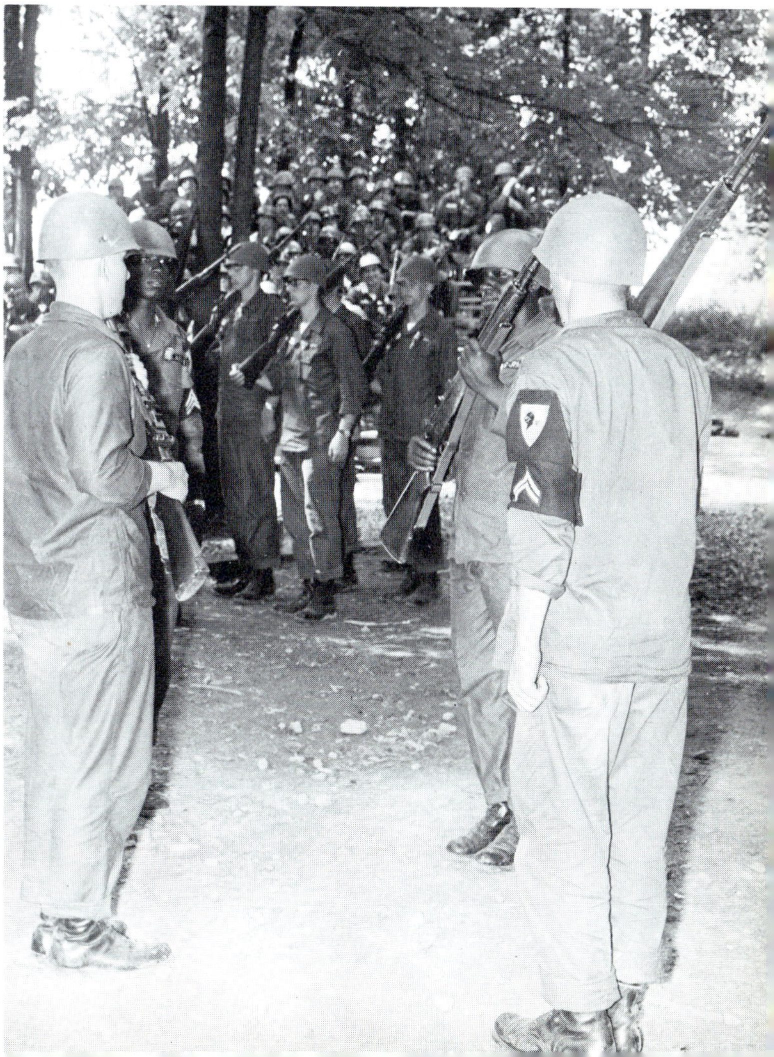

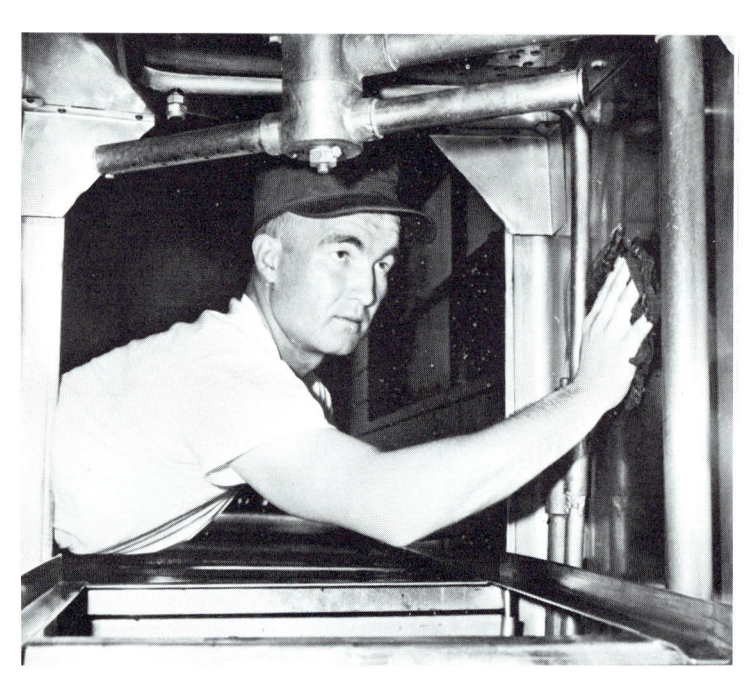

KP

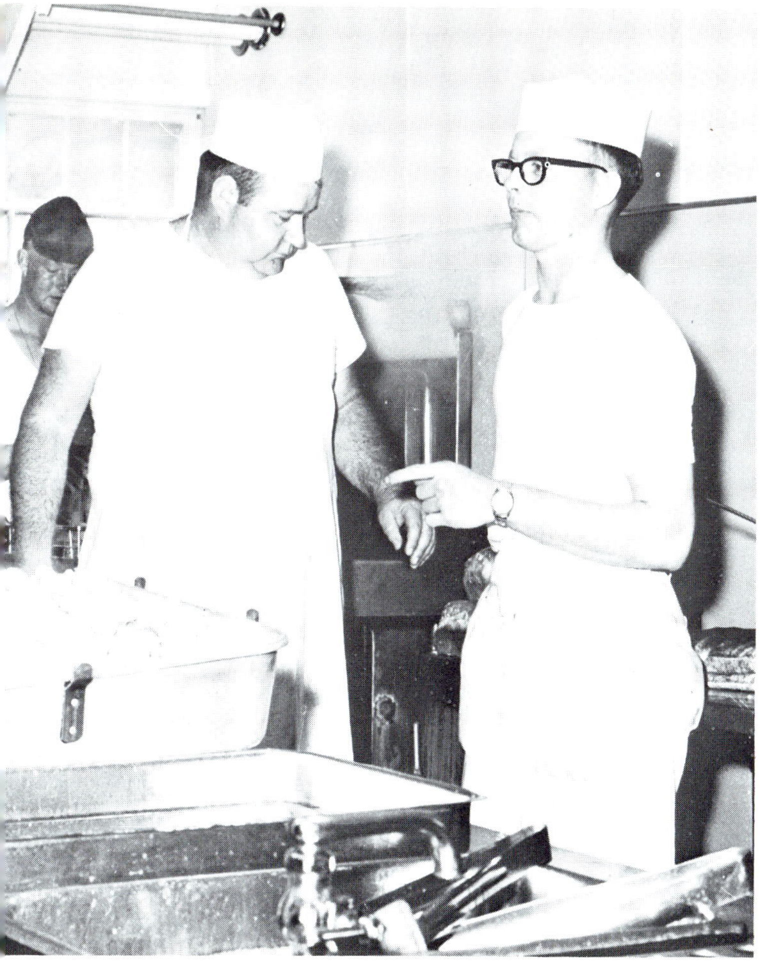

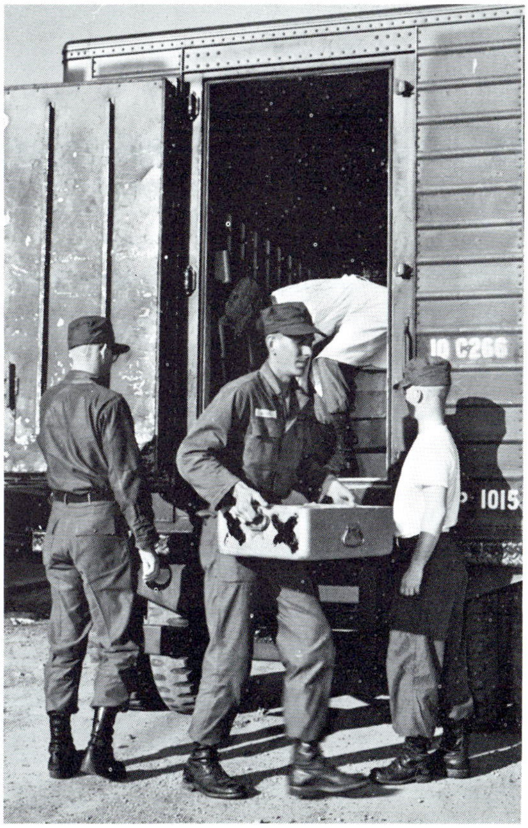
10 C266

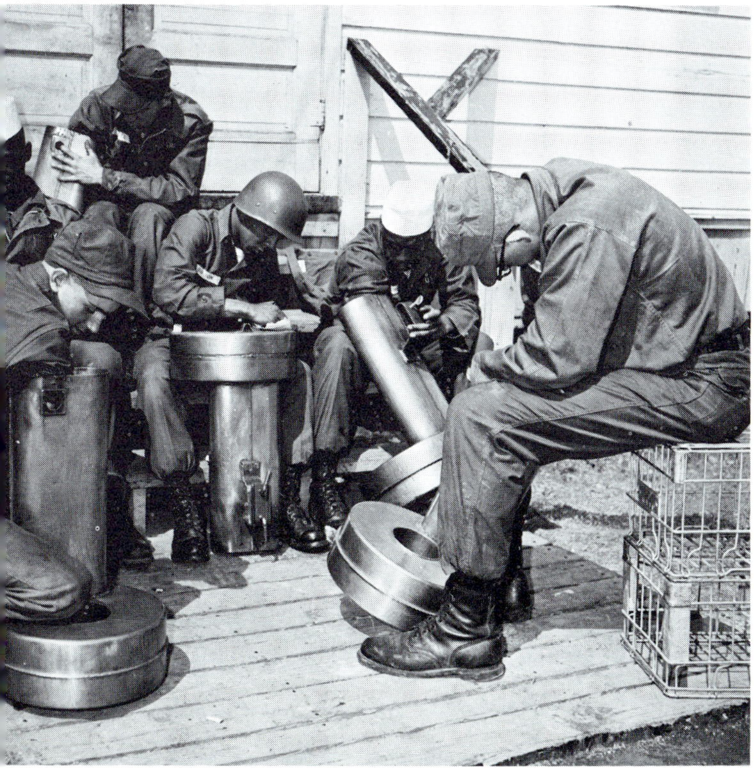

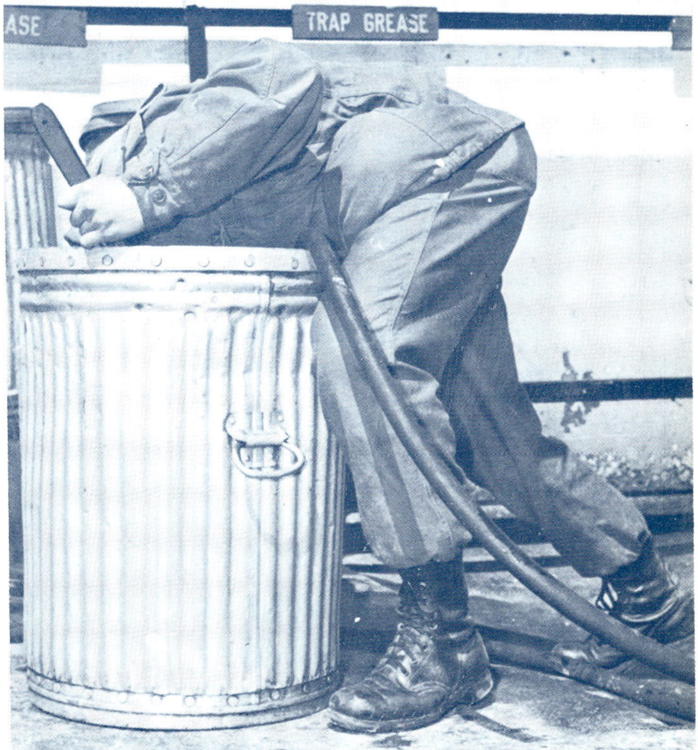
ASE
TRAP GREASE

Tent Pitching

Basic Marksmanship

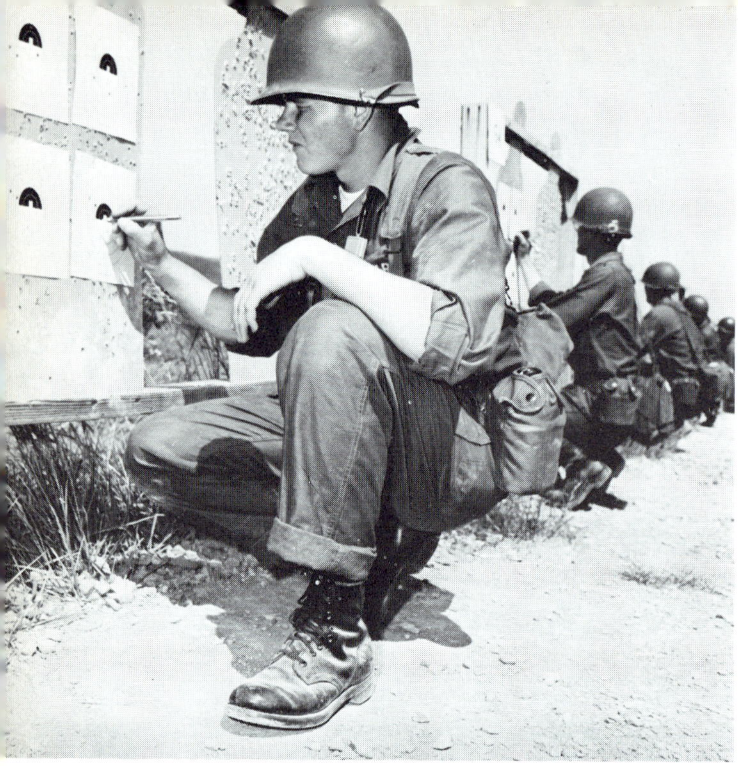

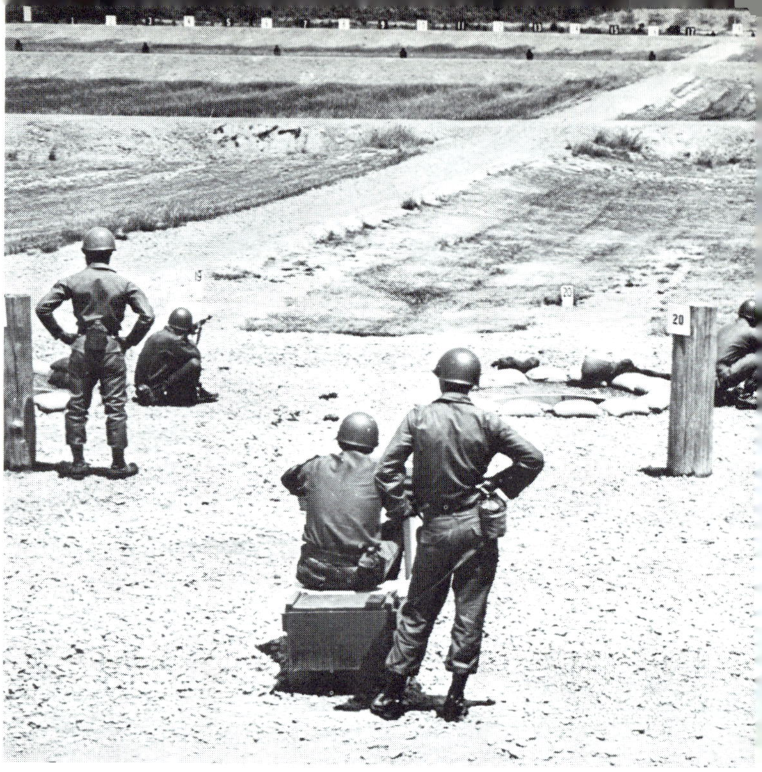
20

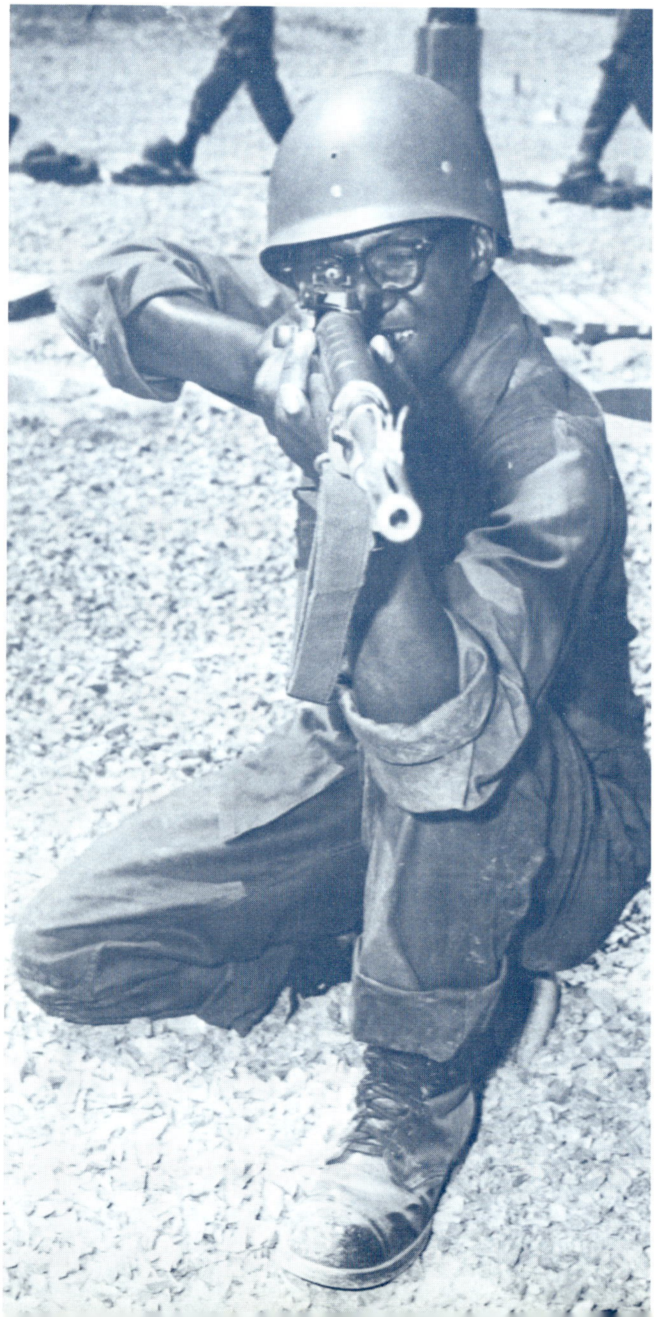

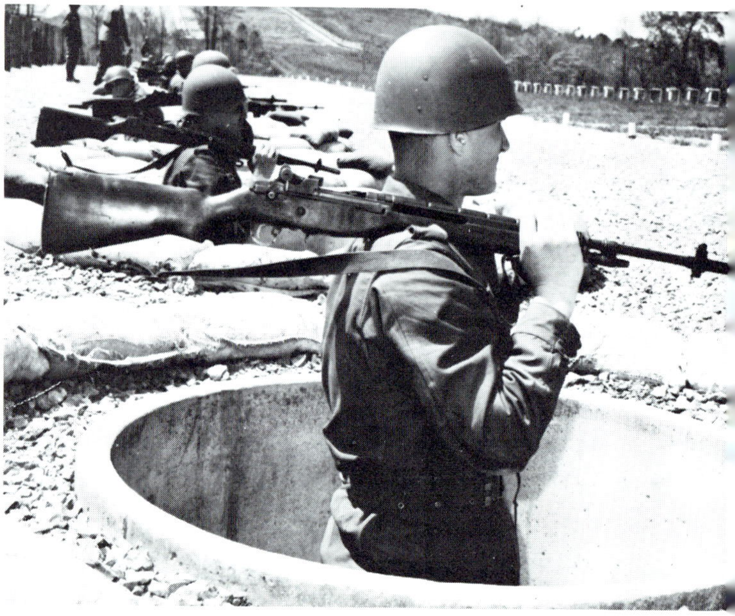

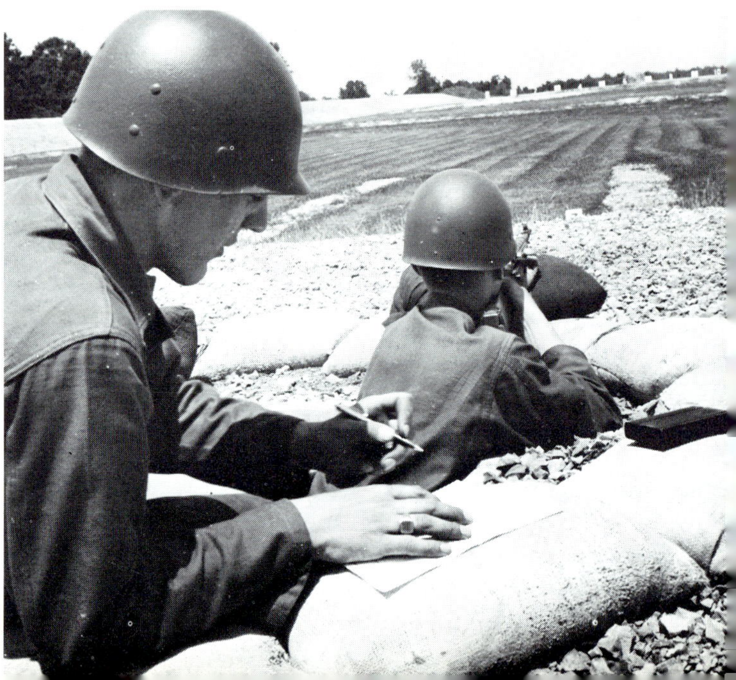

Zeroing In

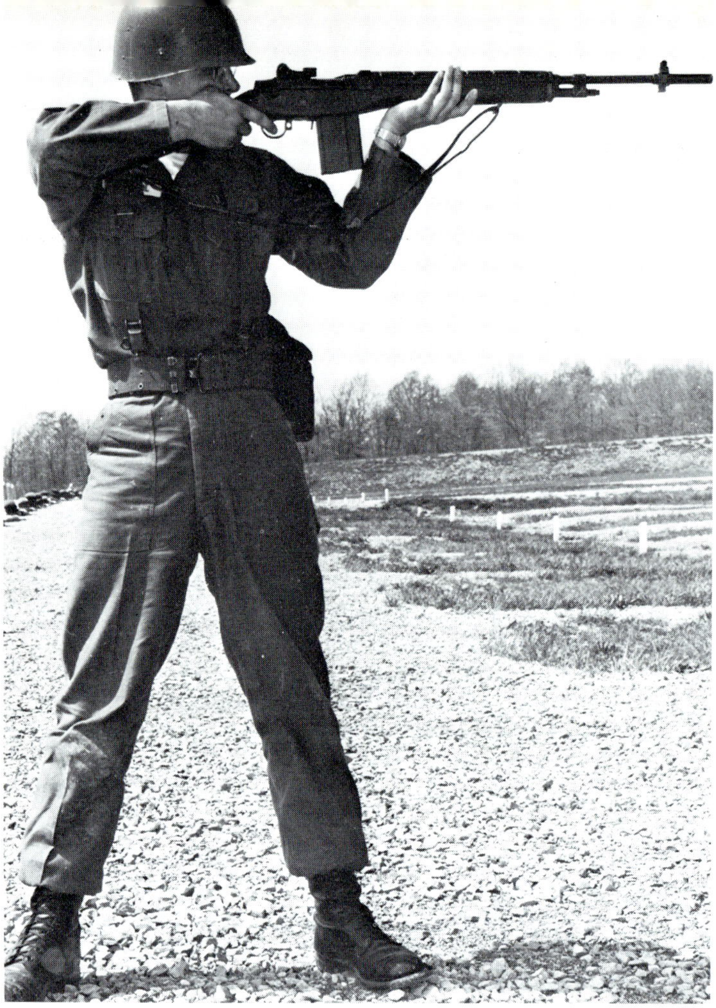

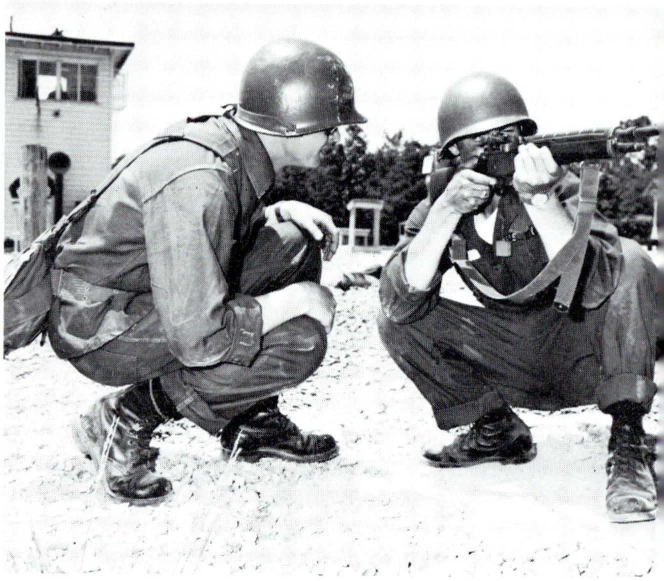

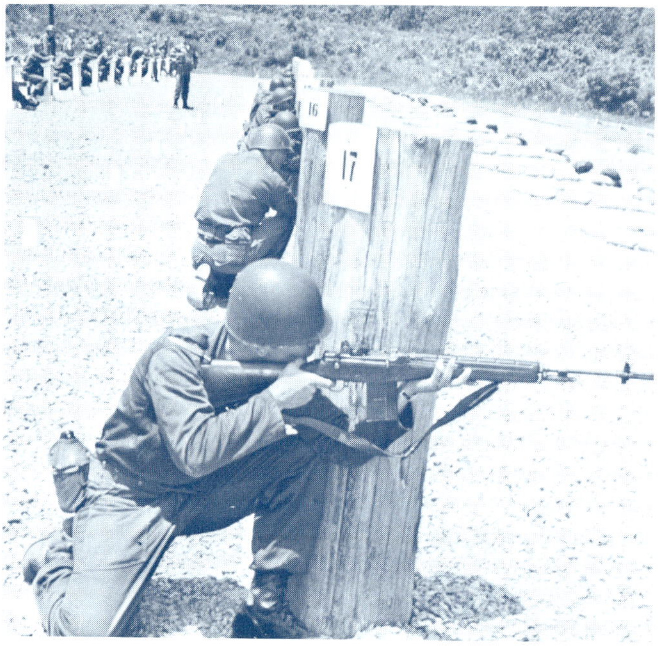
16
17

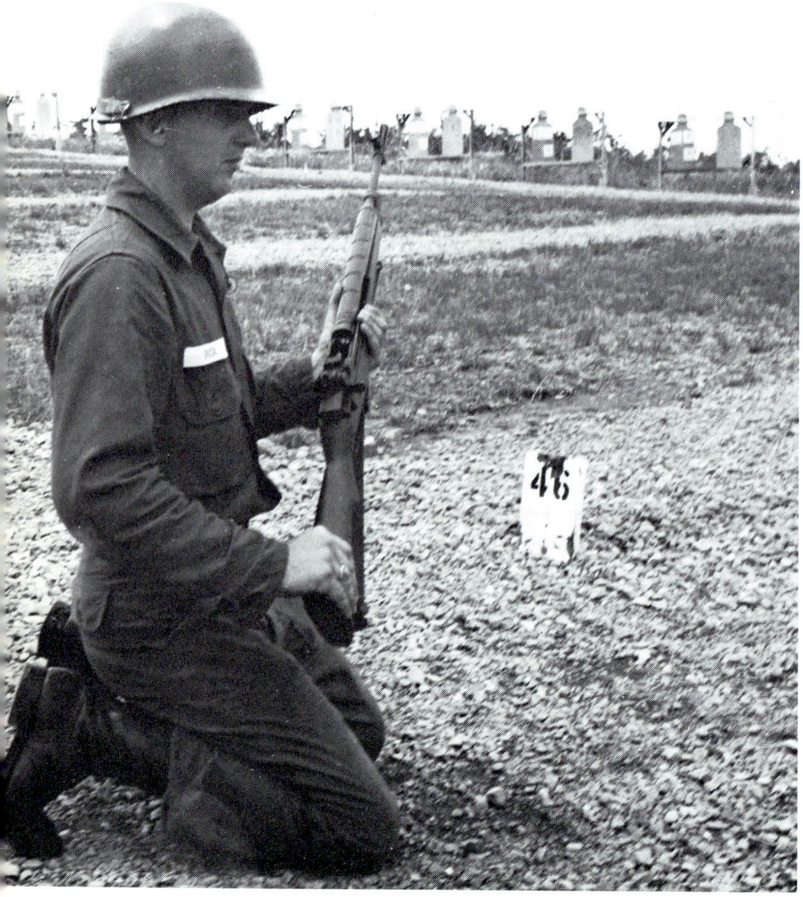
46

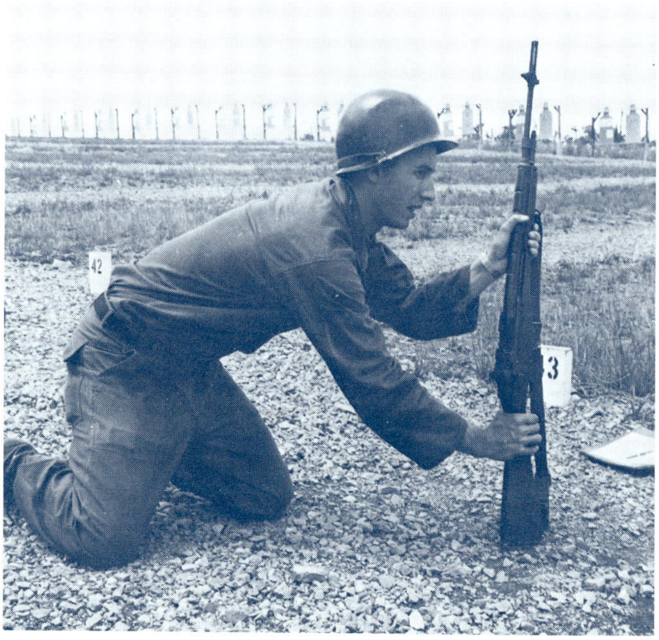
42

Field Firing

Record Firing

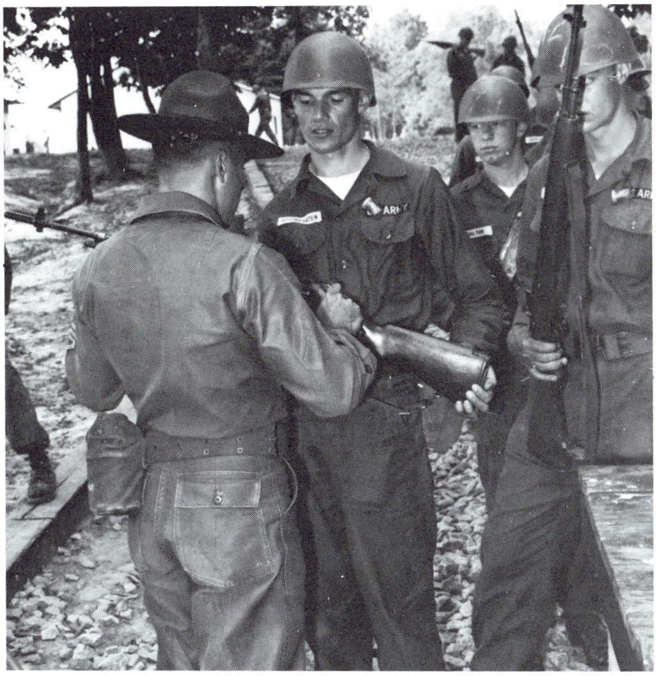
ARMY

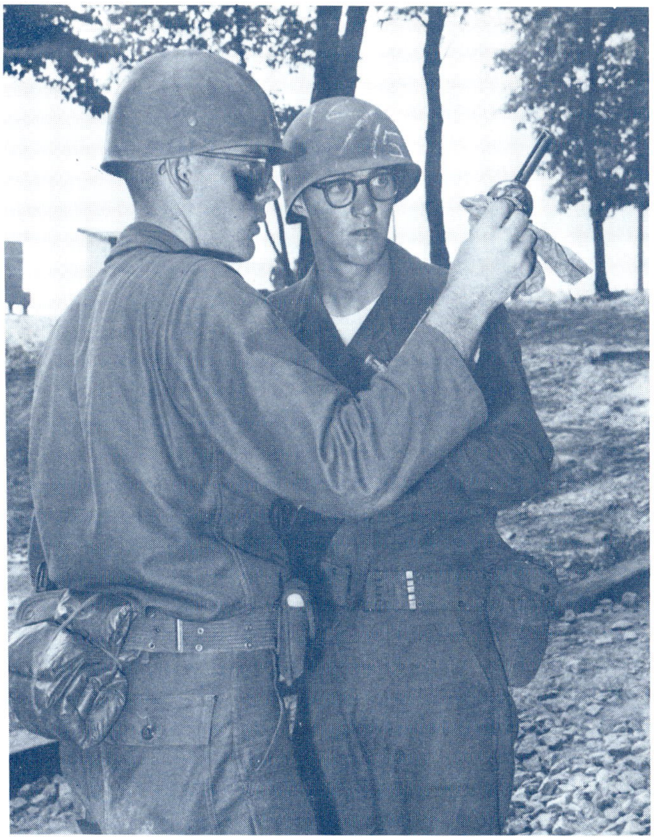

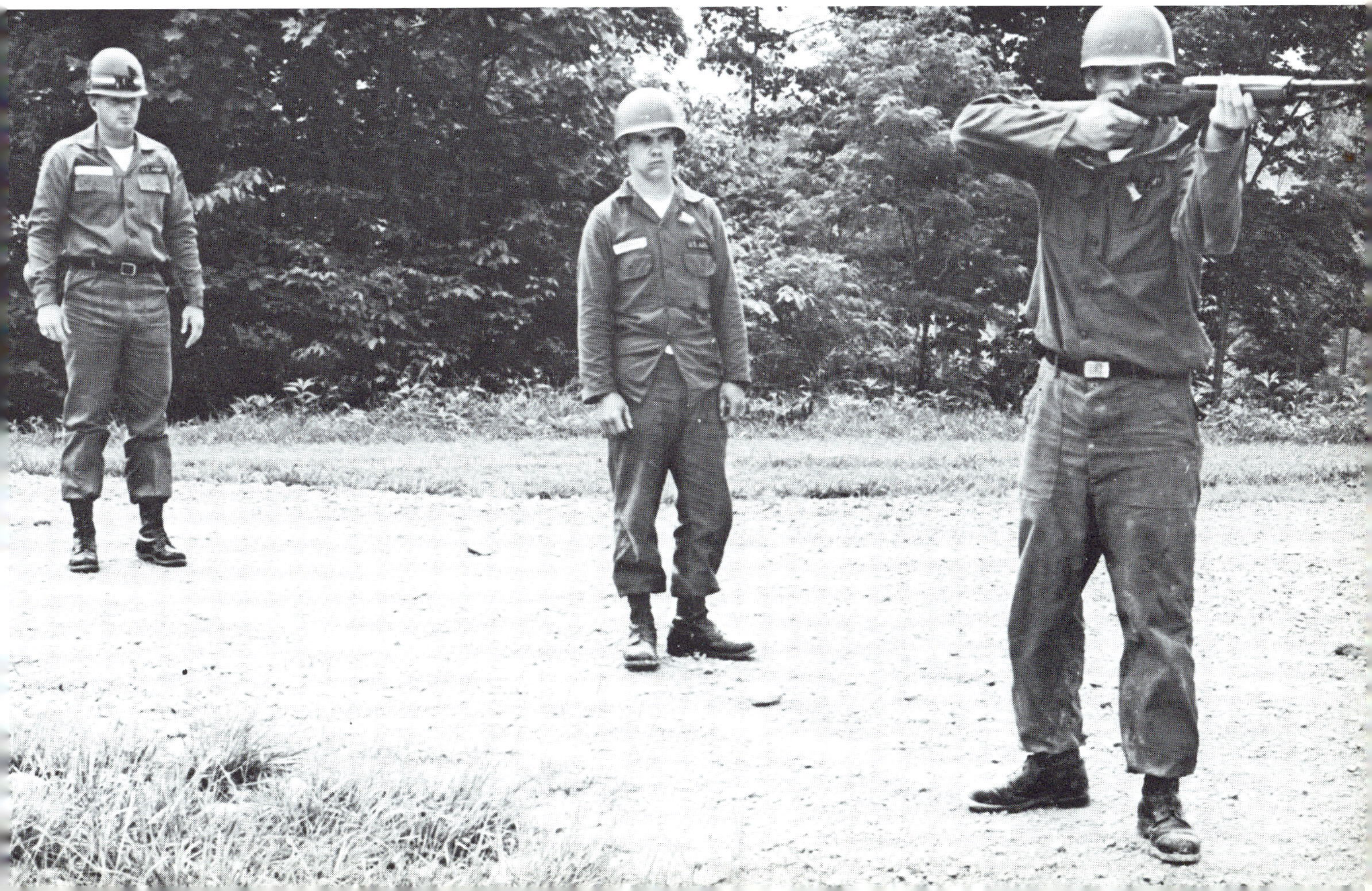

Target Detection

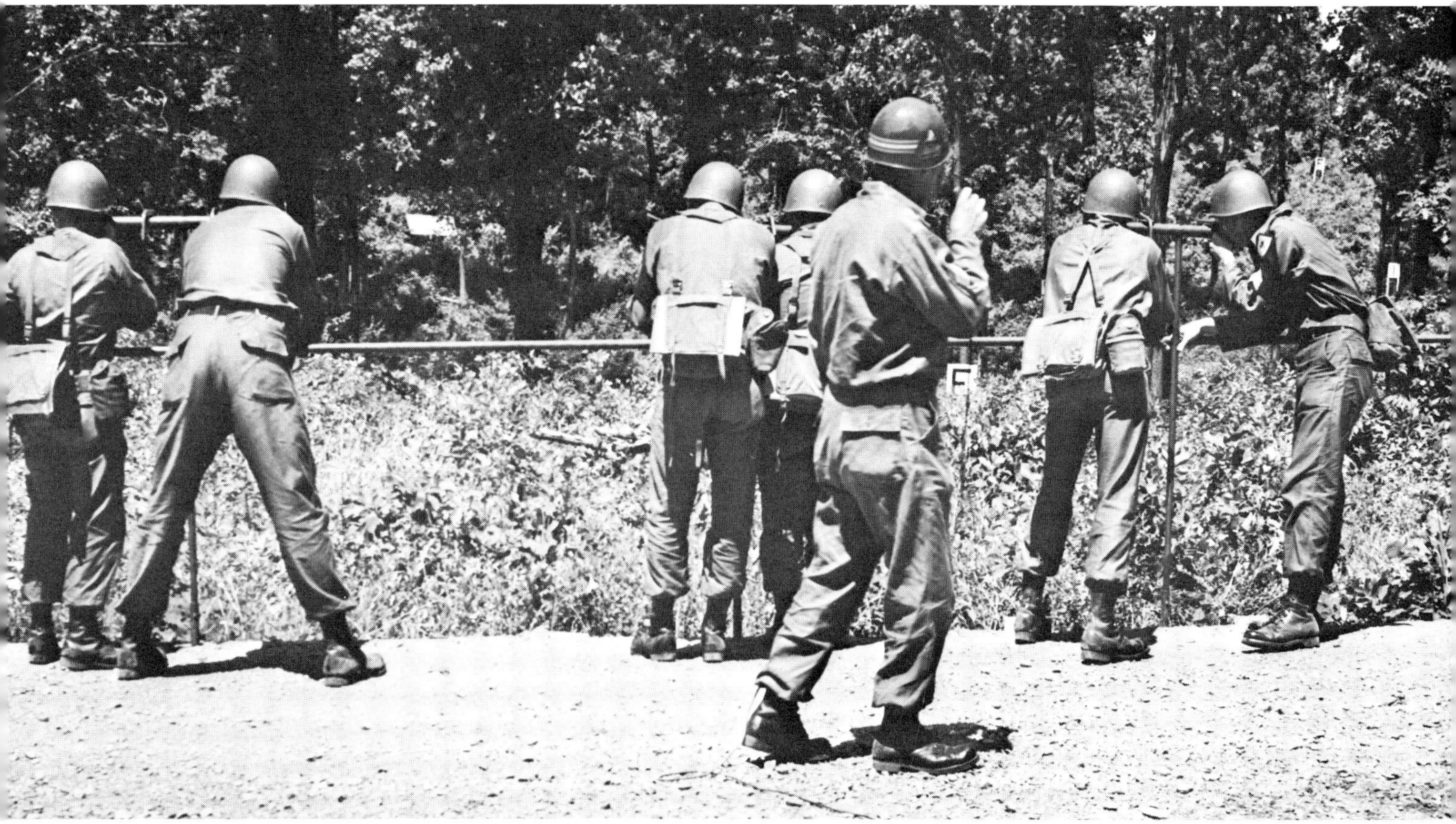

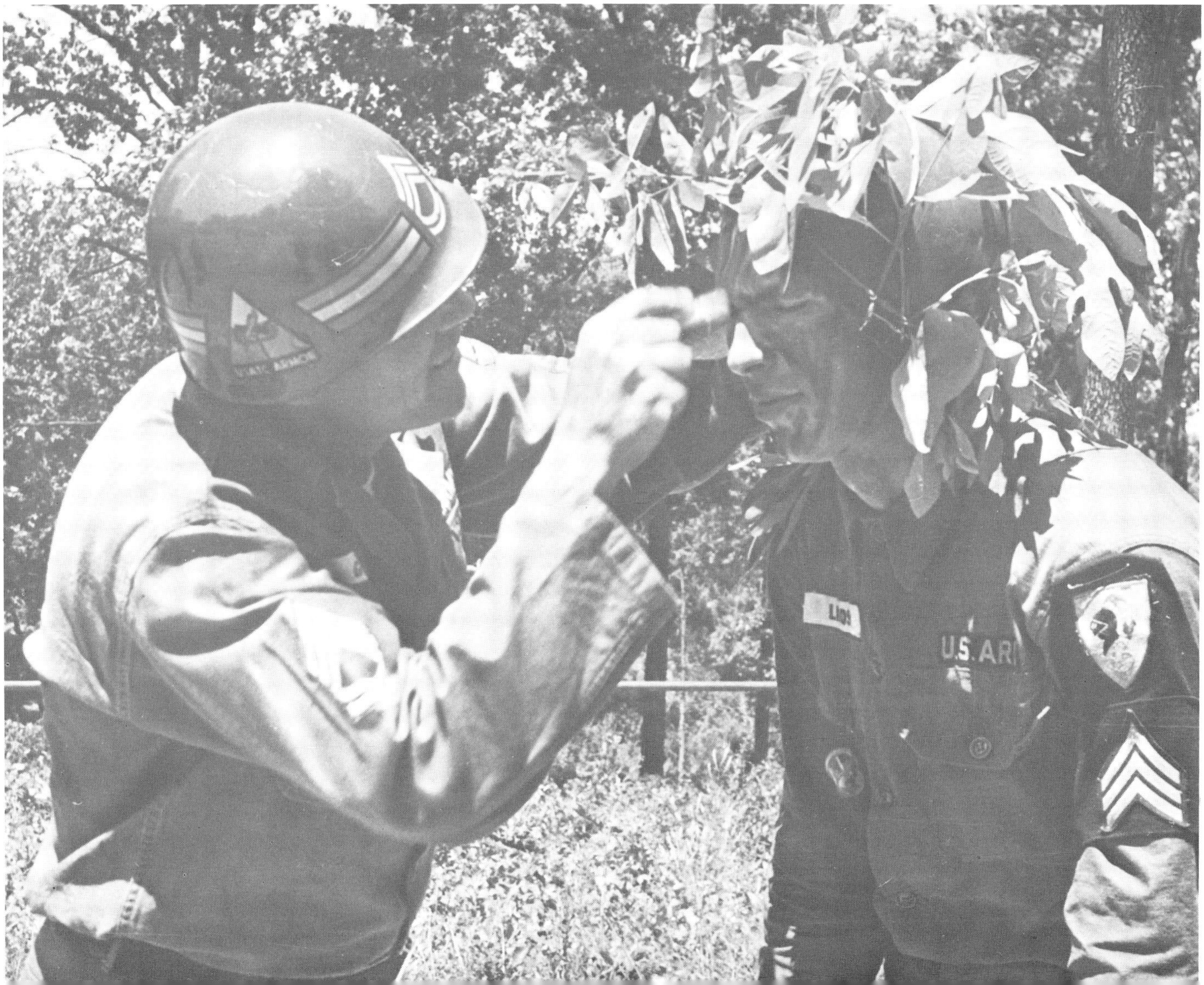

Bayonet

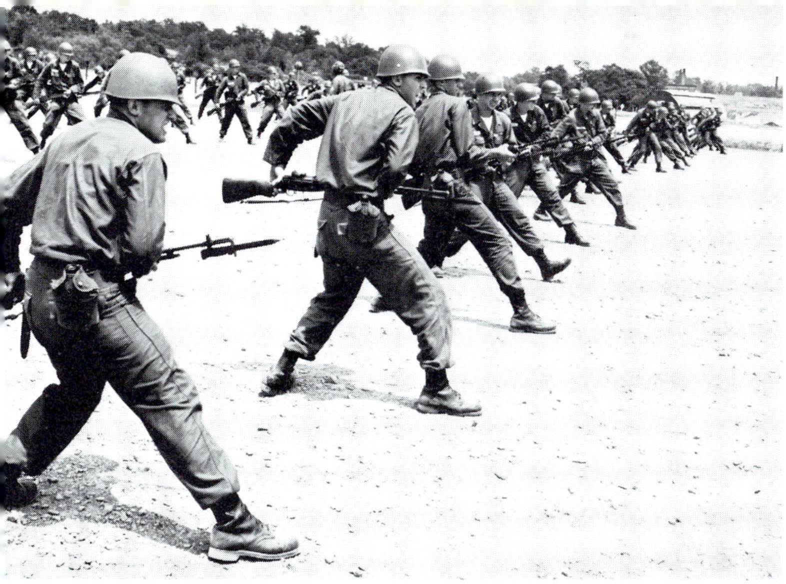
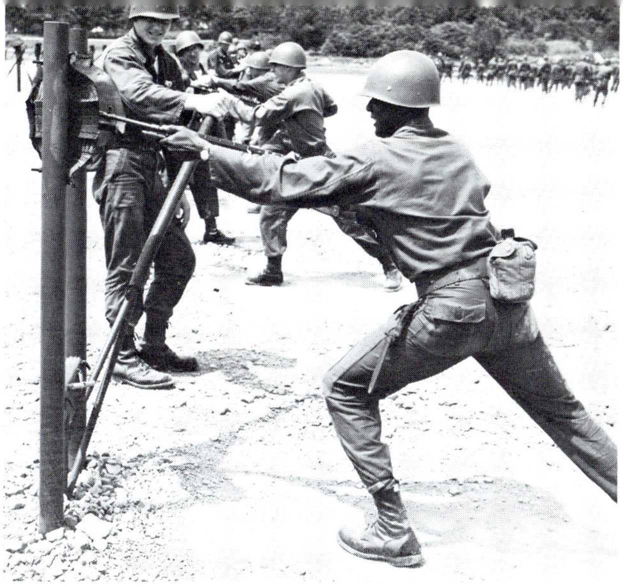
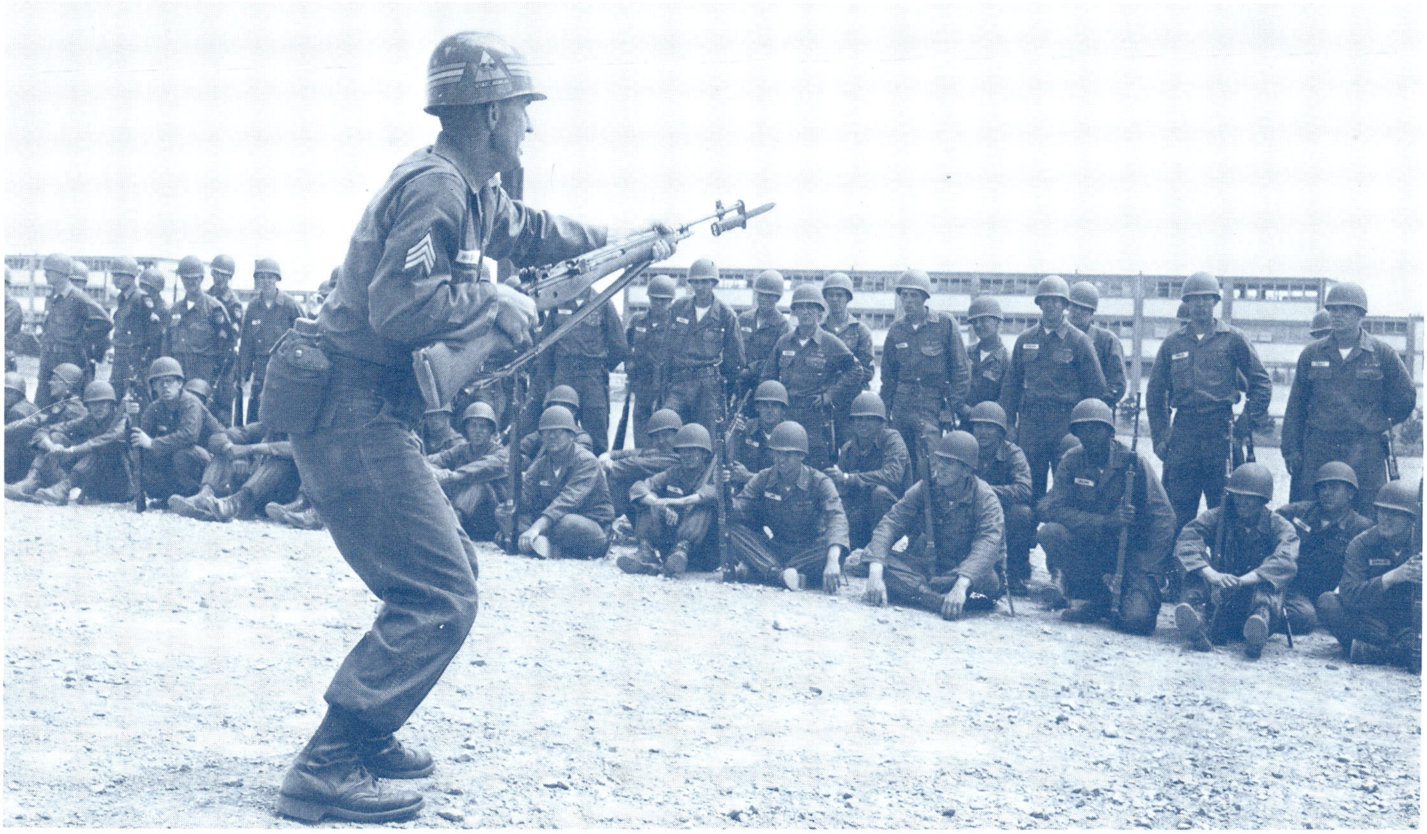
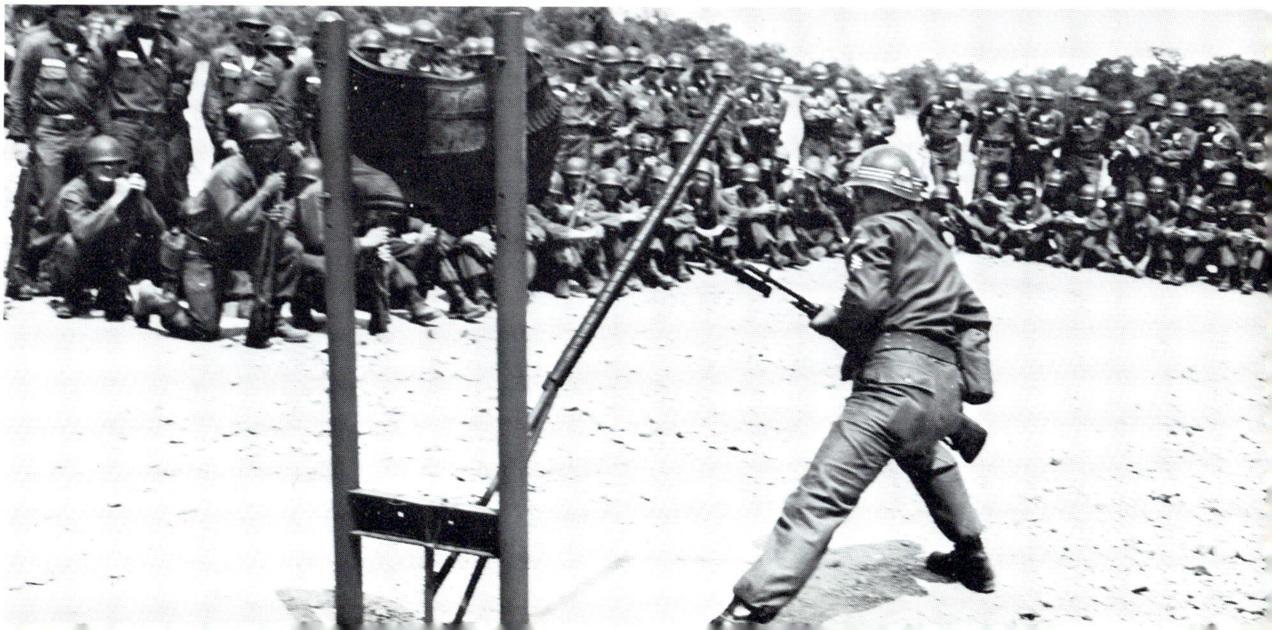

Hand To Hand Combat

Pugil Stick

Individual Tactical Training — Day

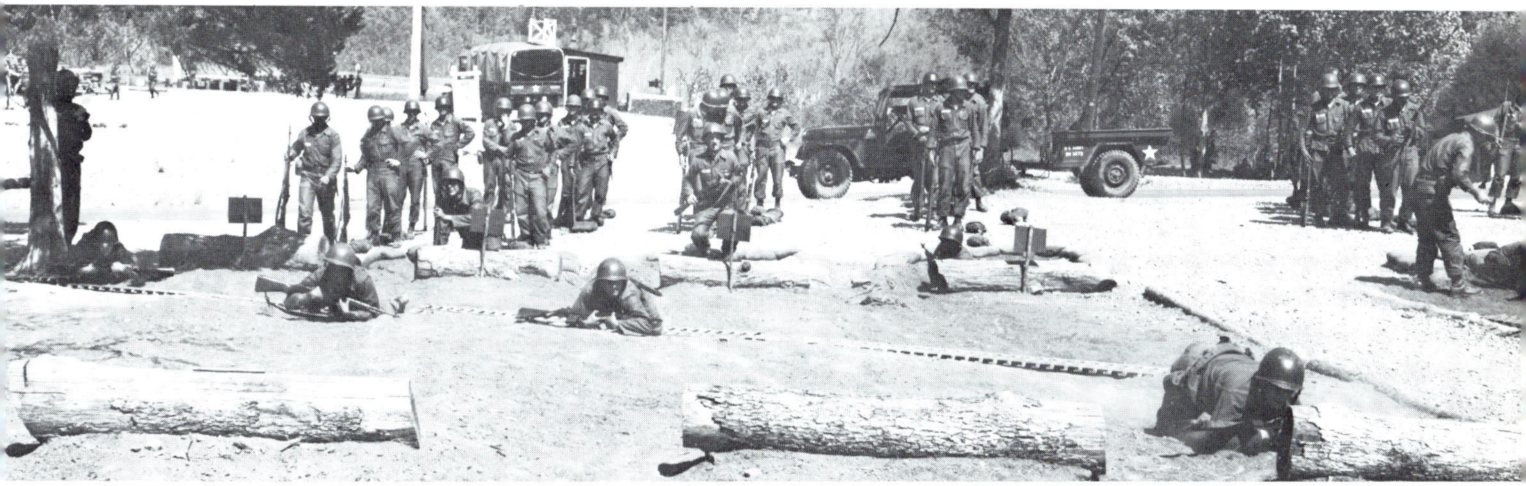

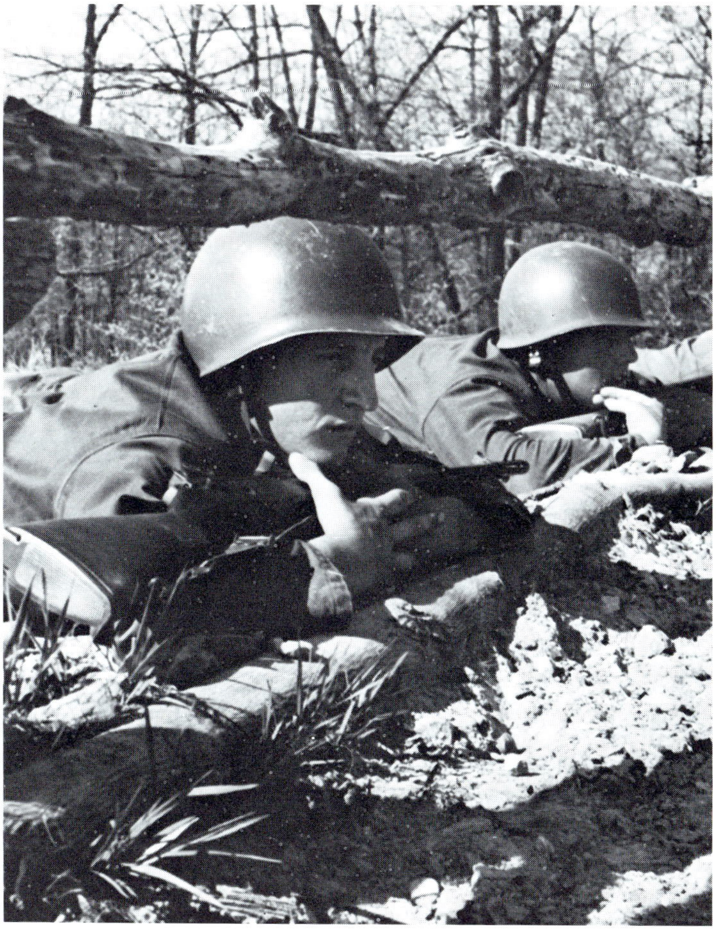

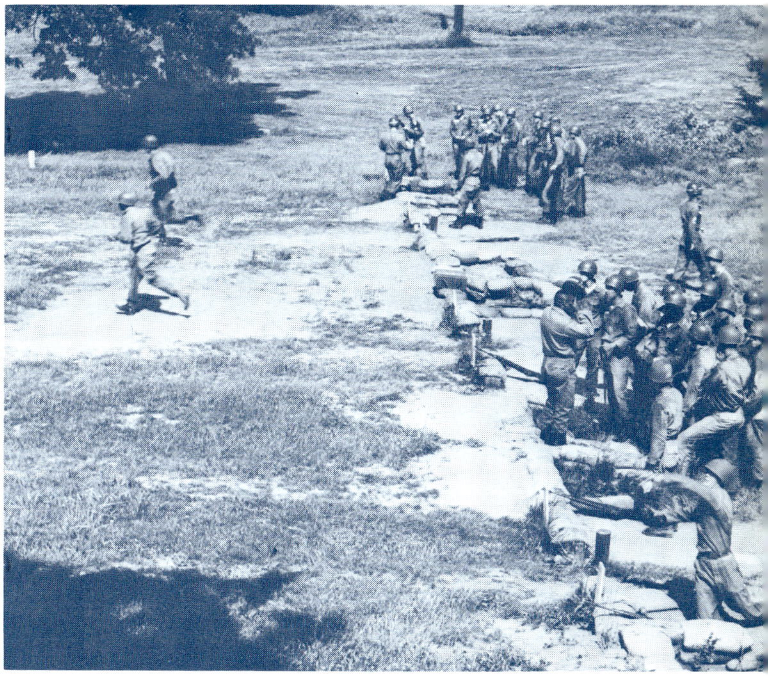

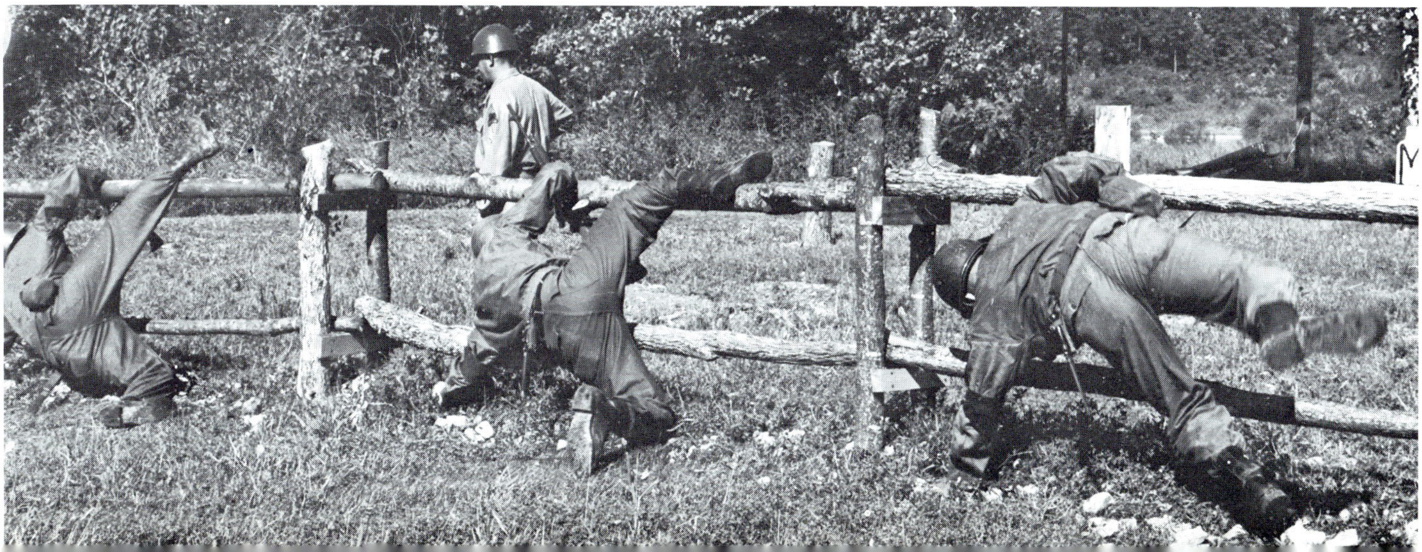

Individual Tactical Training — Night

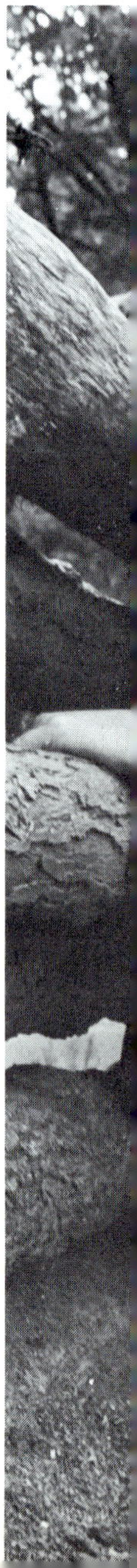

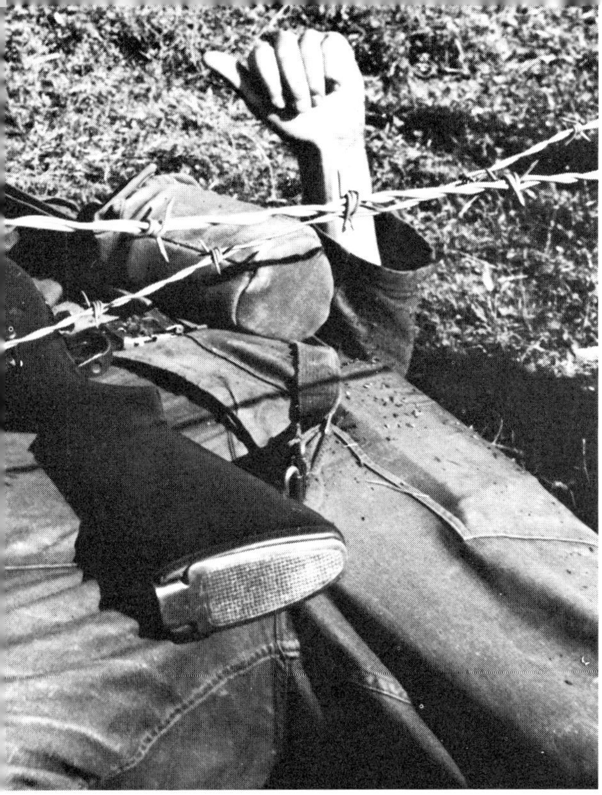
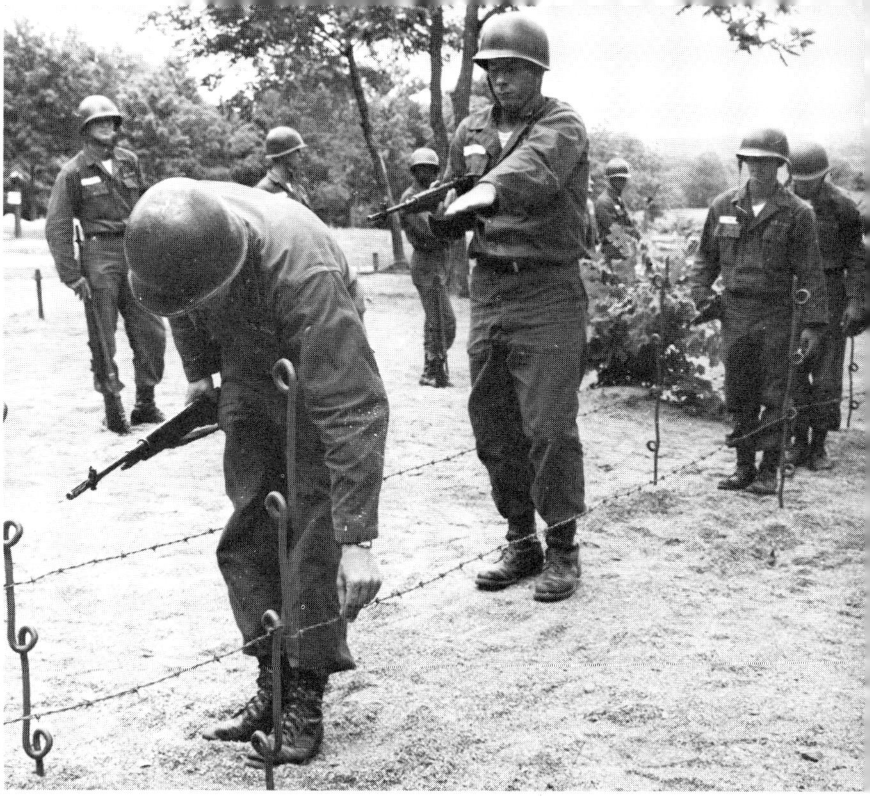
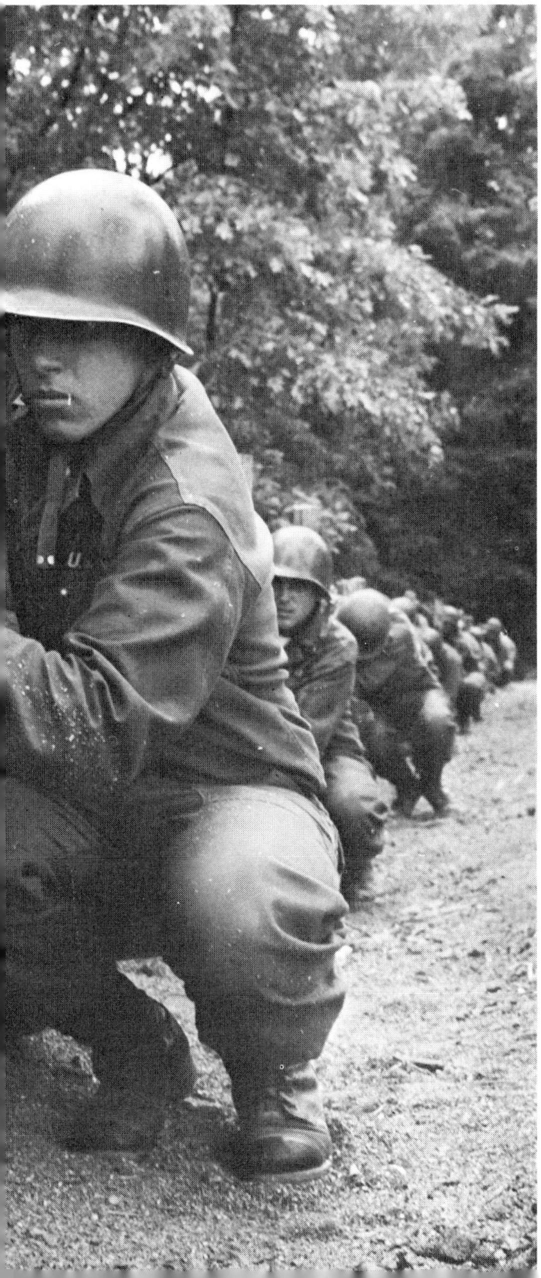
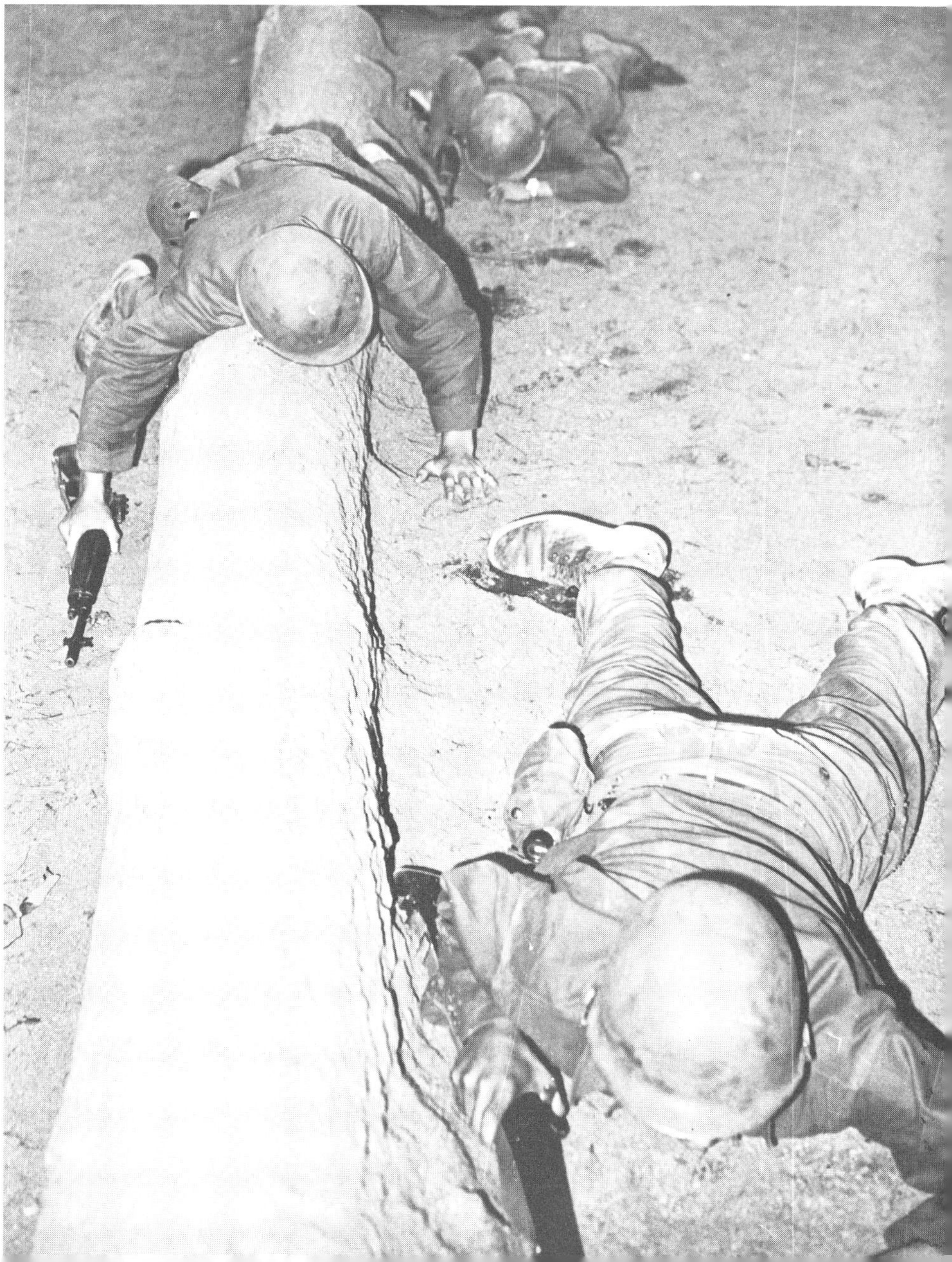

Physical Combat Proficiency Test

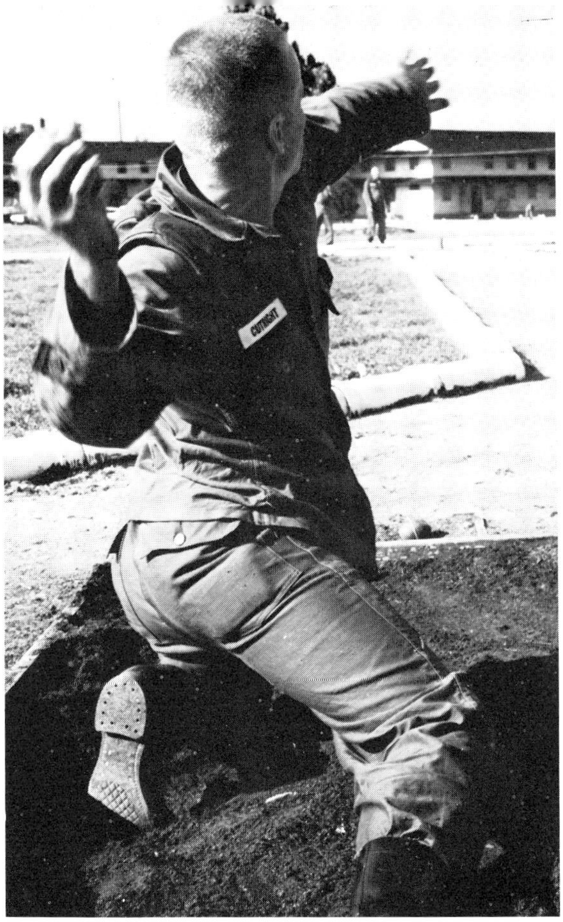

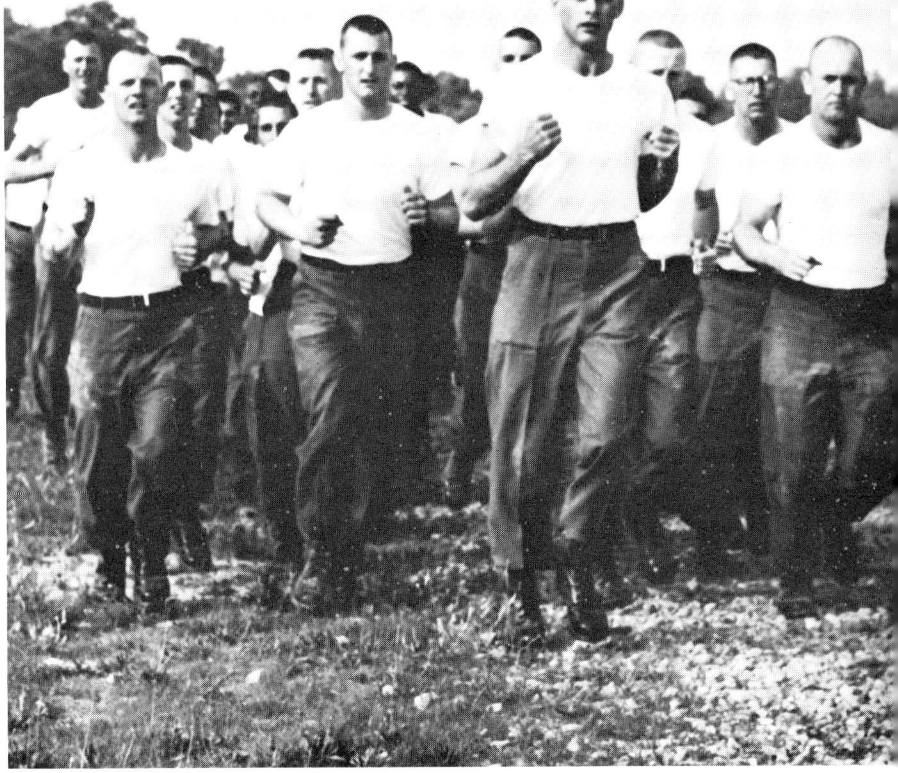

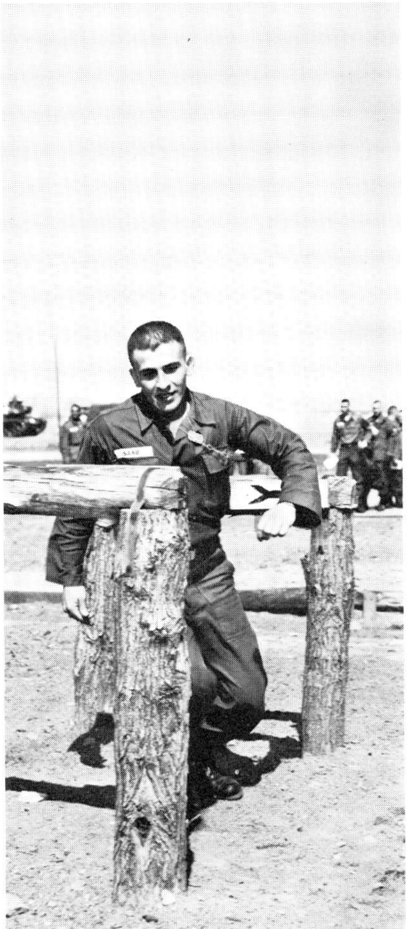

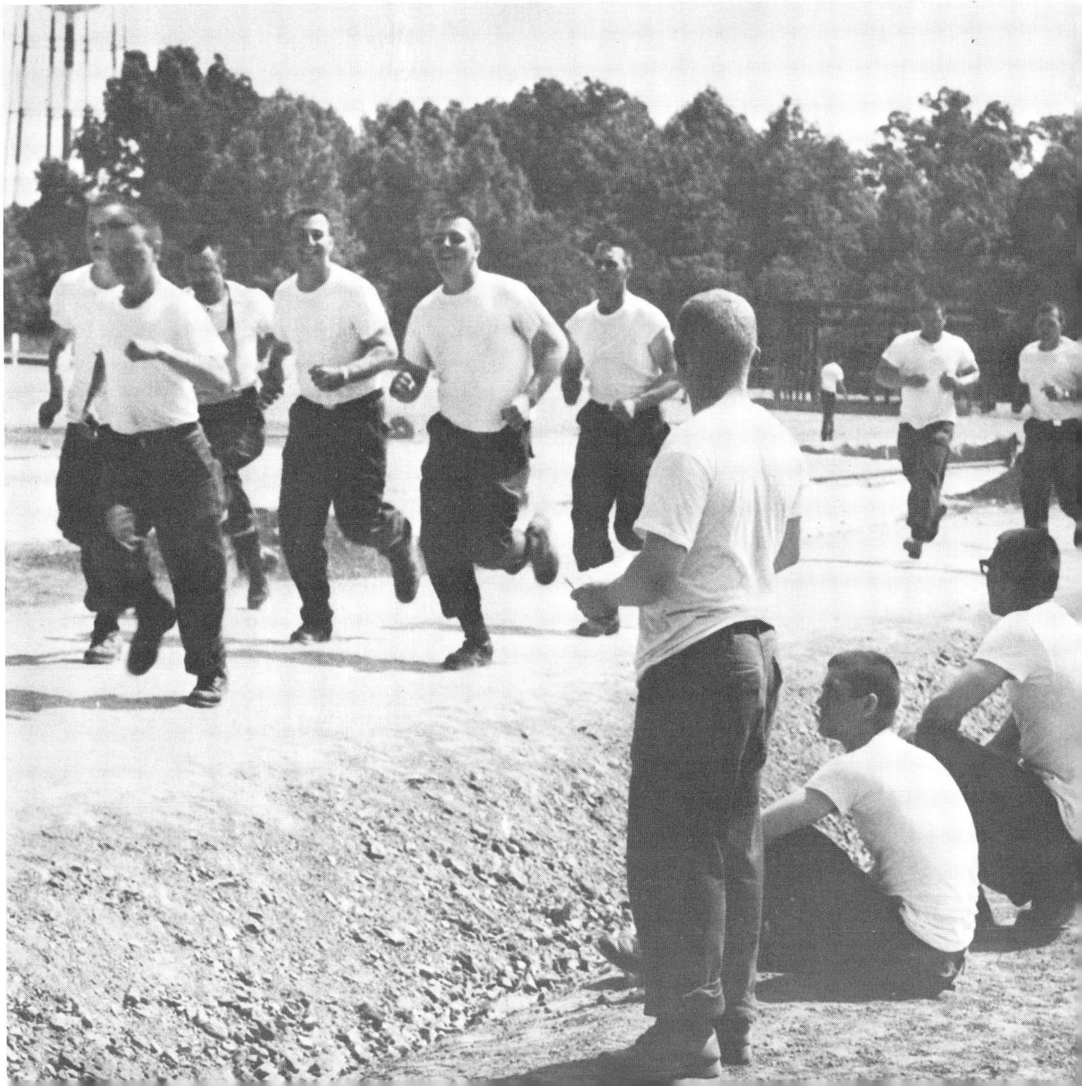

CBR

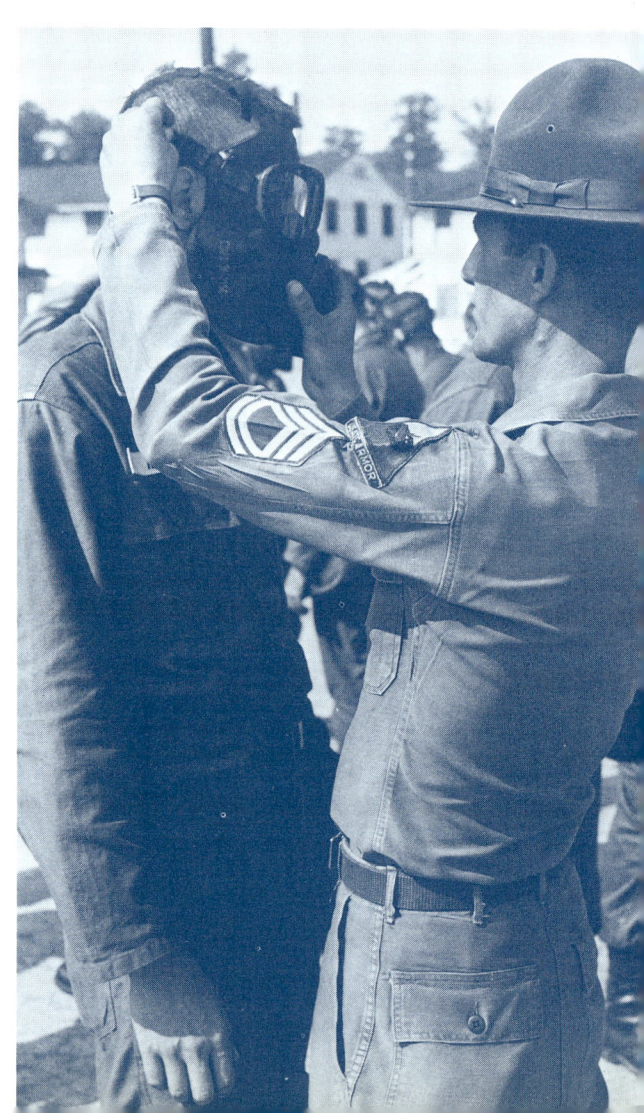

TEAR
GAS

USING UNIT WILL
← CN CL →
POLICE AREA
LATRINES
AND LOCK ALL DOORS
BEFORE LEAVING
NO ADMITTANCE

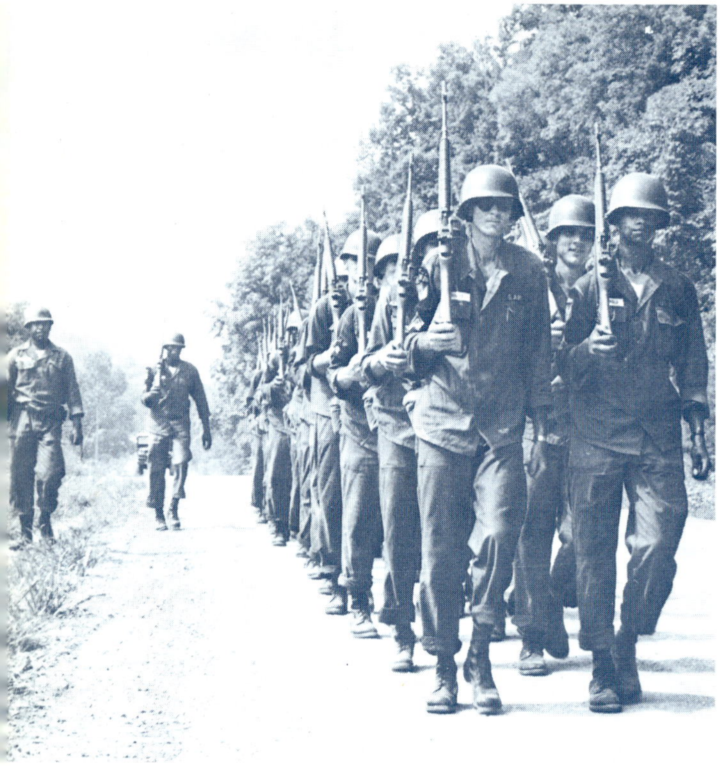

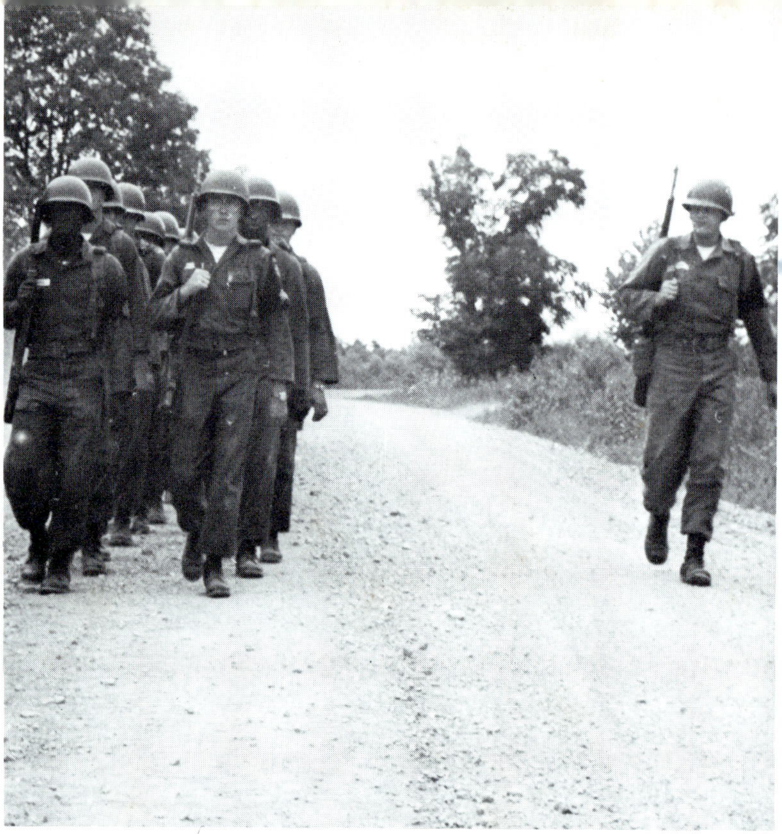

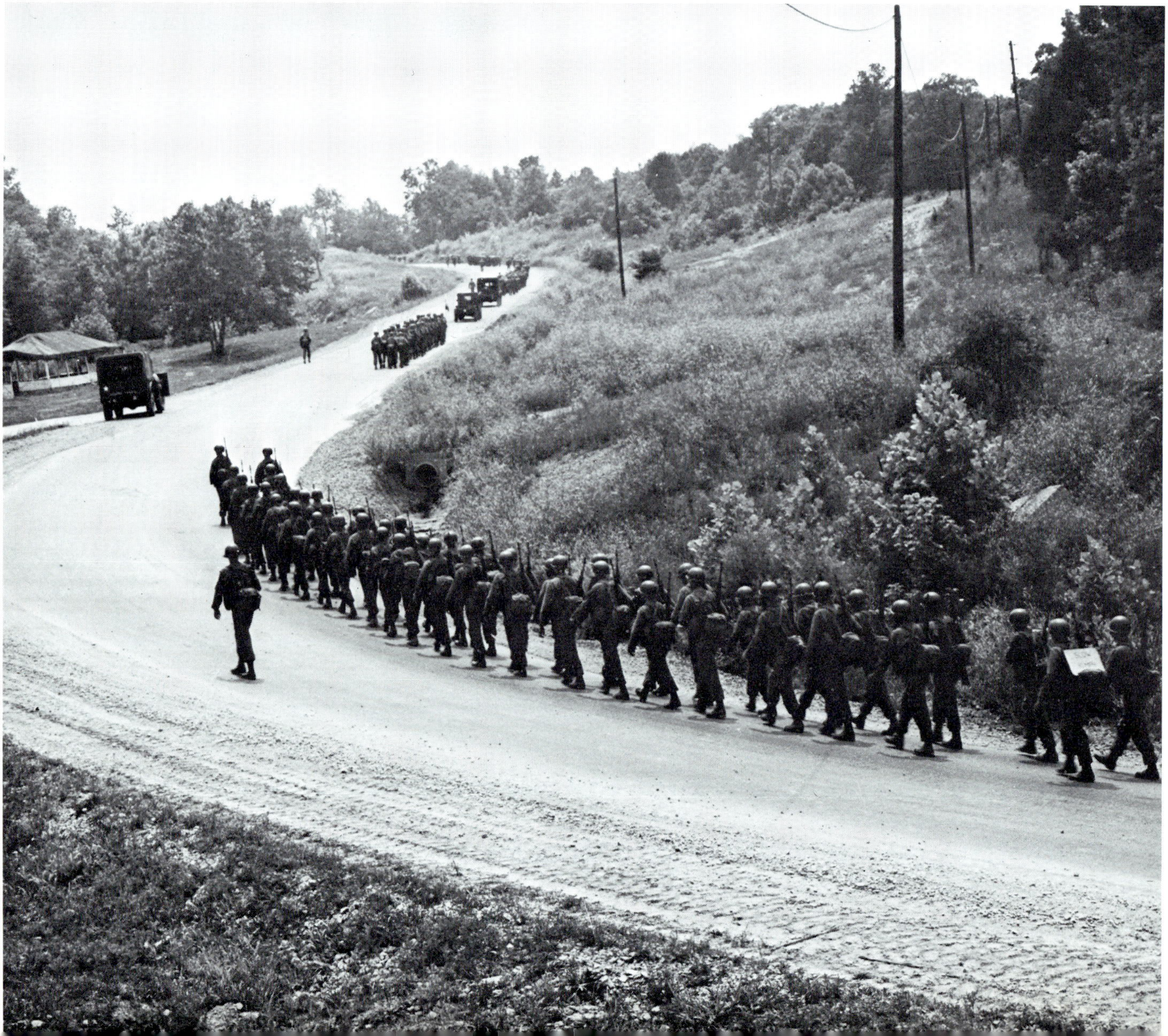

Marches

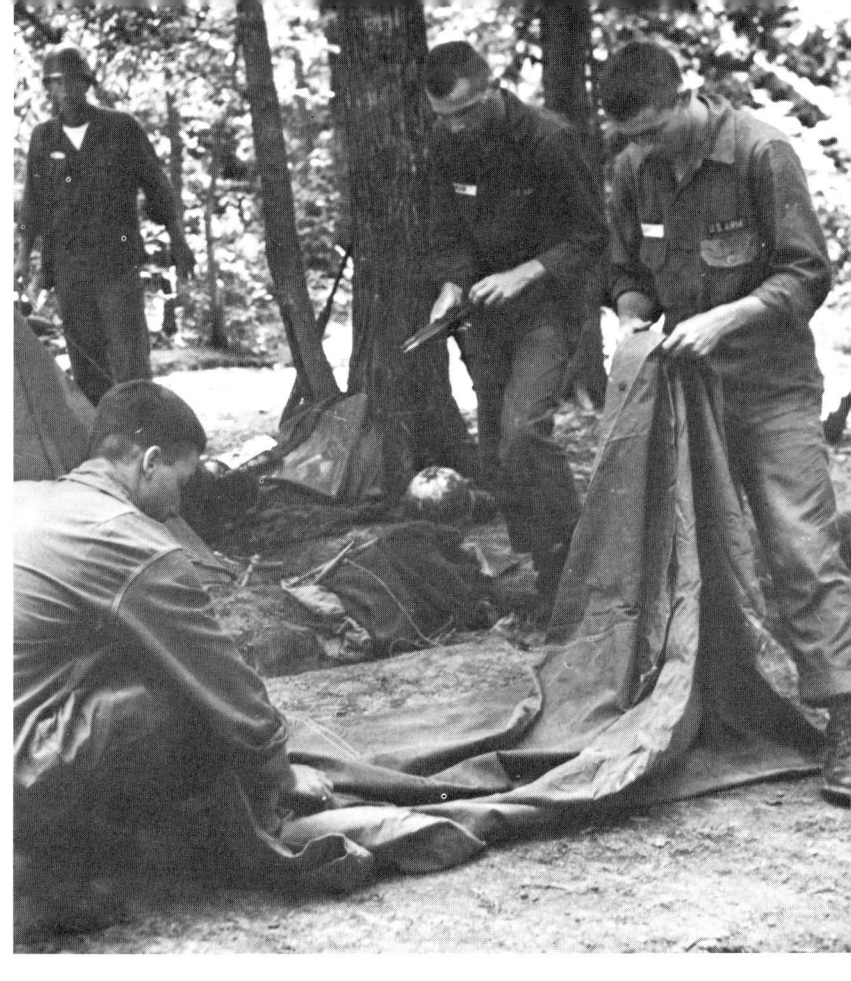

Bivouac

Chow In The Field

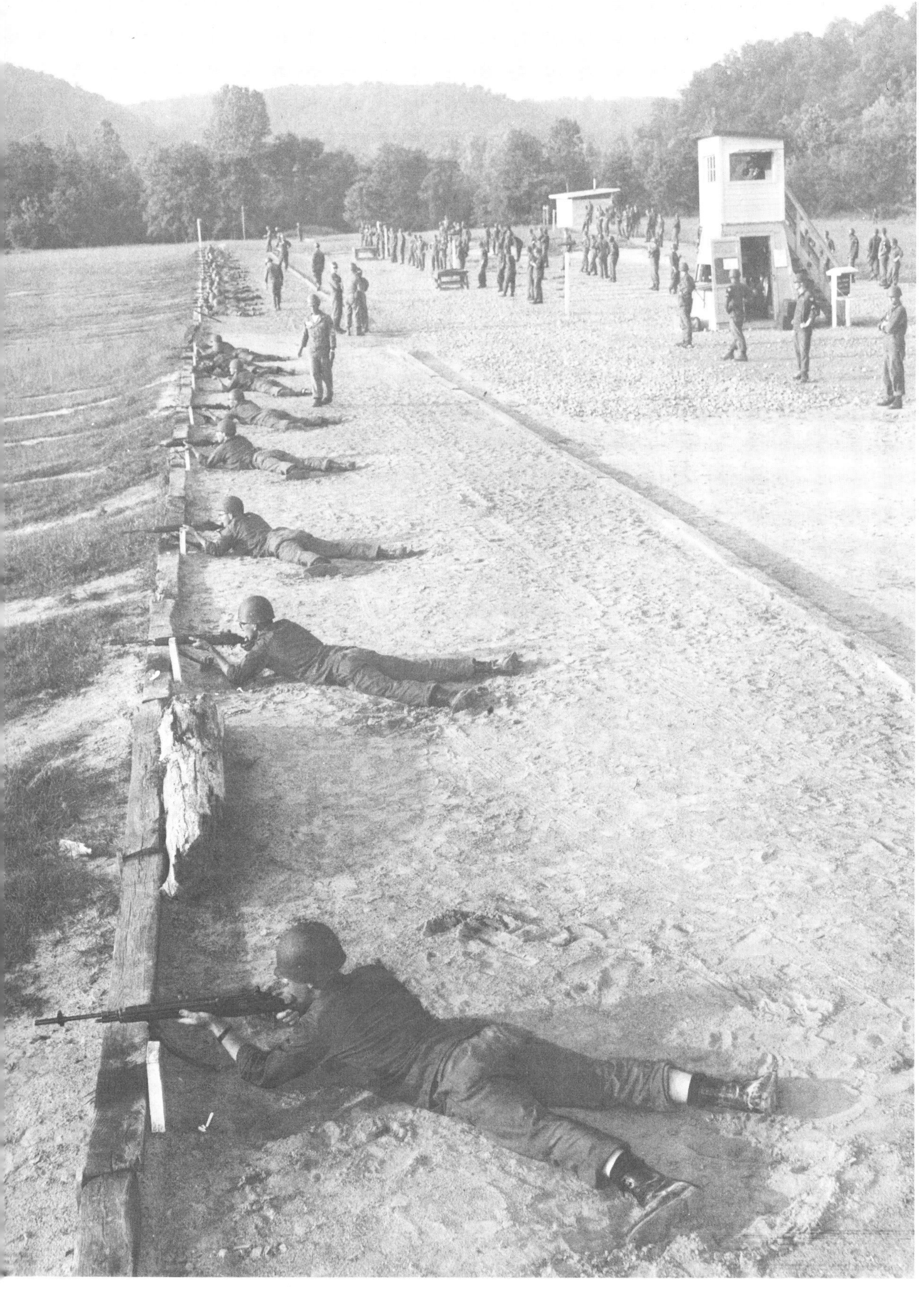
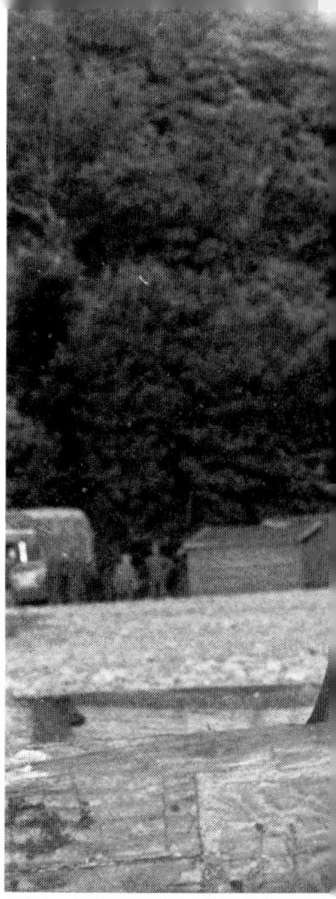
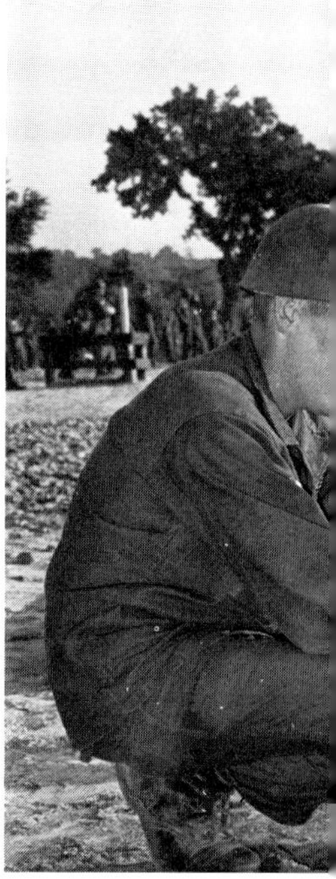
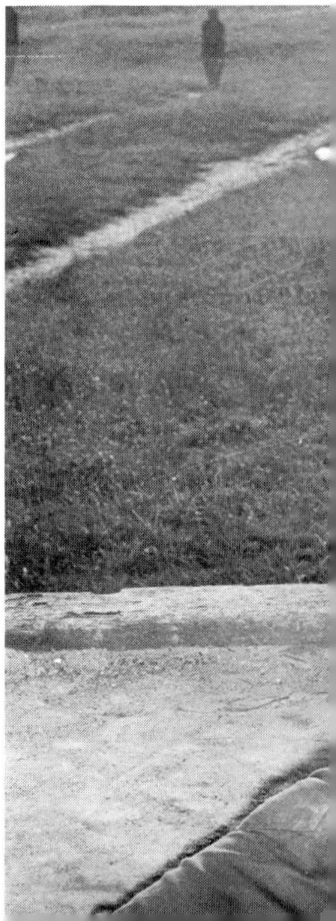

Night Vision and Night Firing

Field Inspection

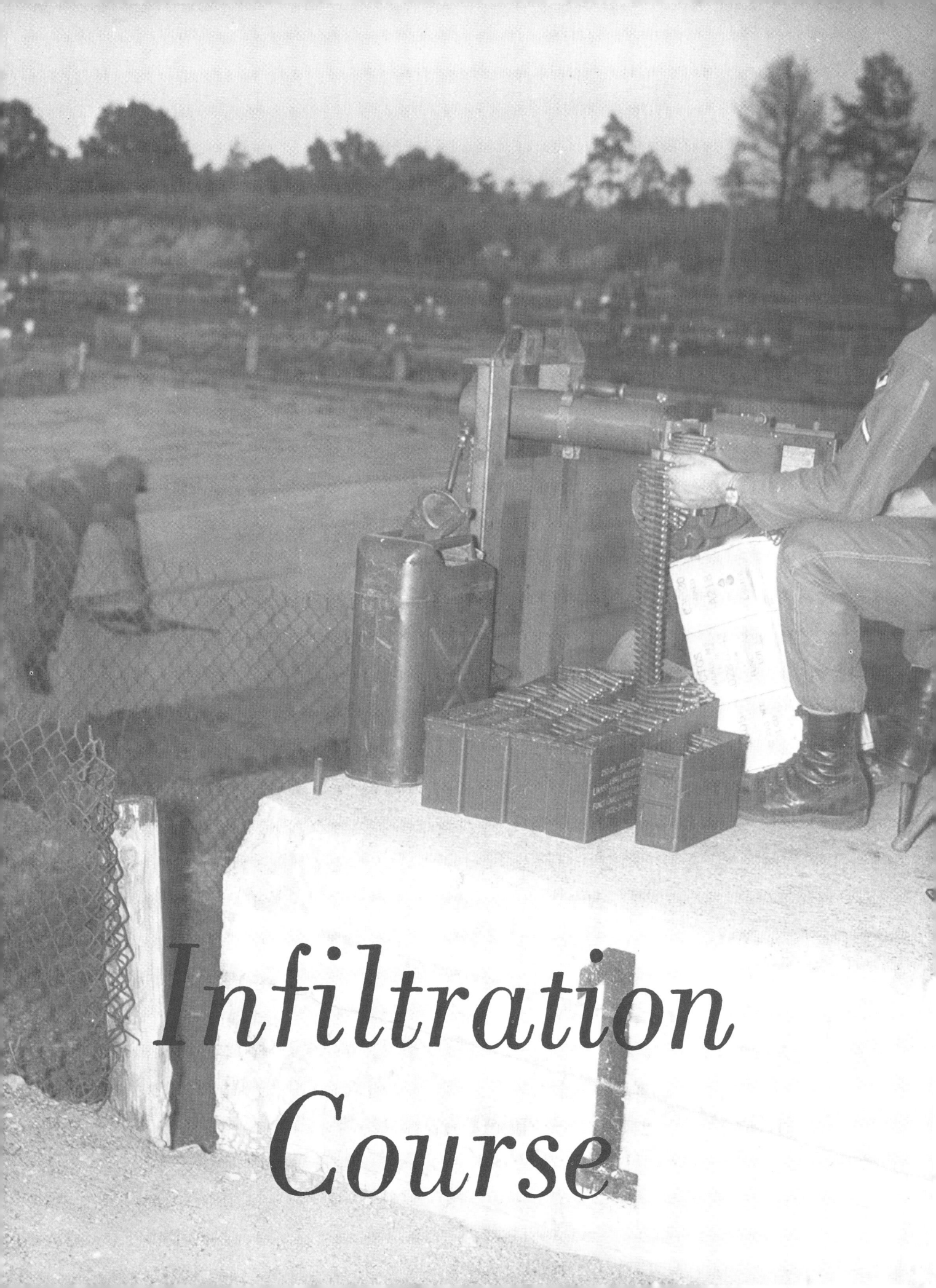

Infiltration Course

Infiltration Course

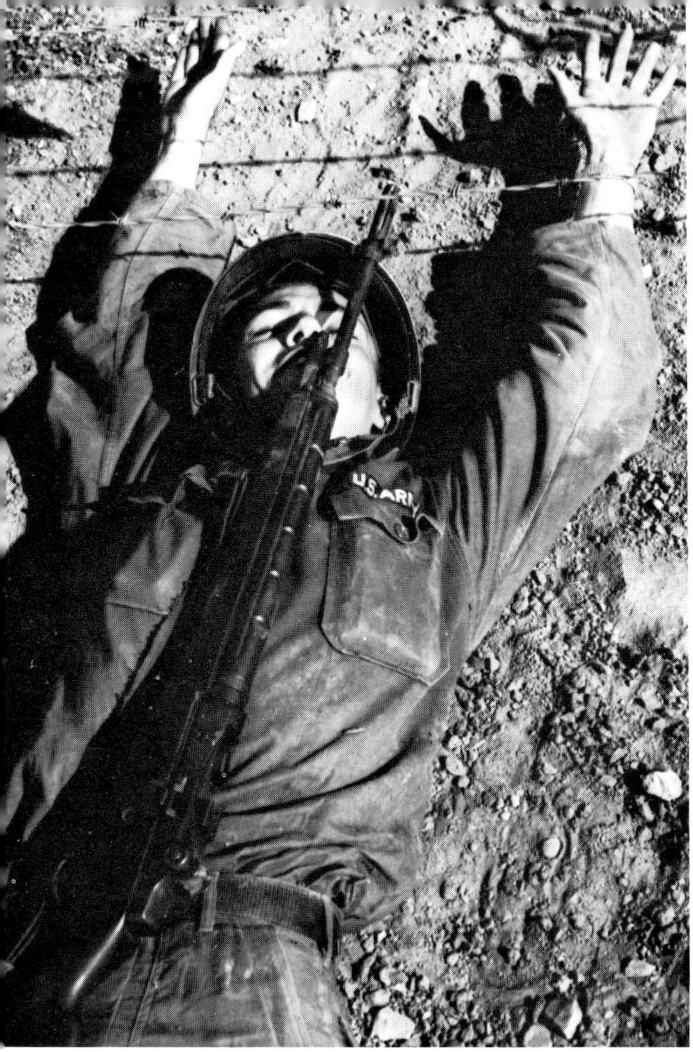

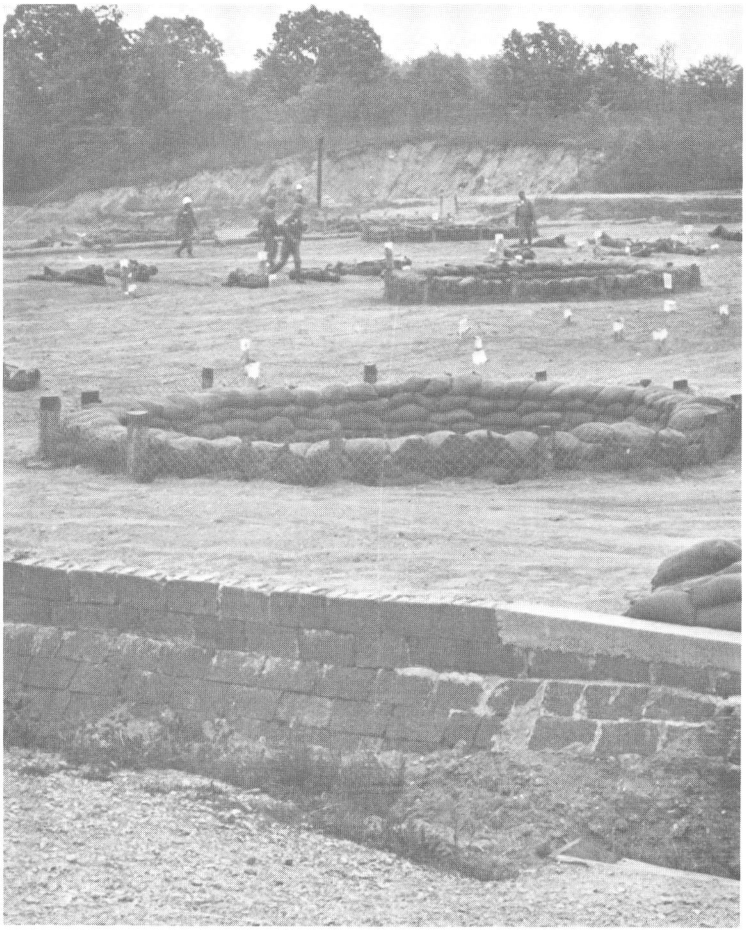

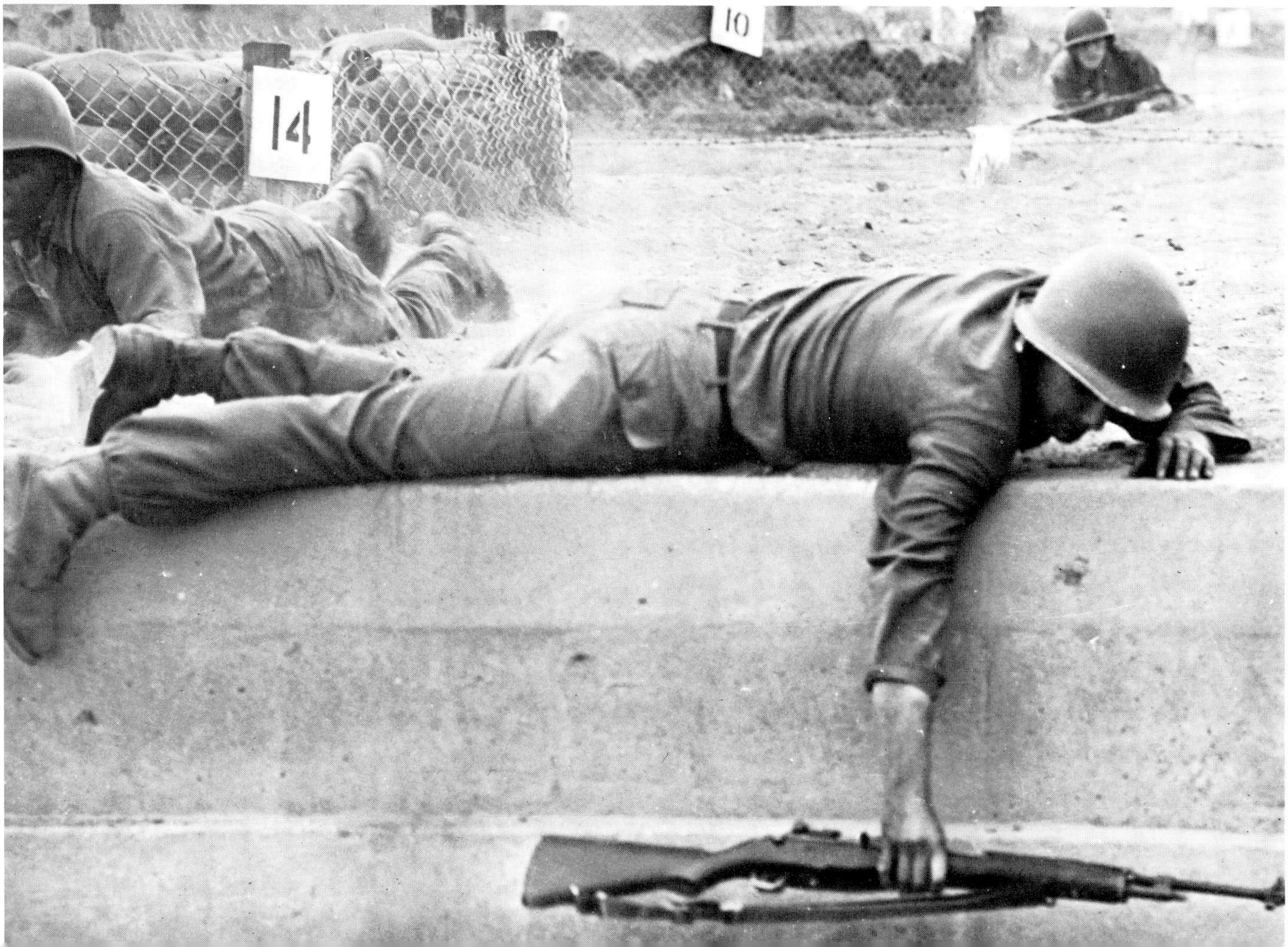
10
14

Hand Grenades

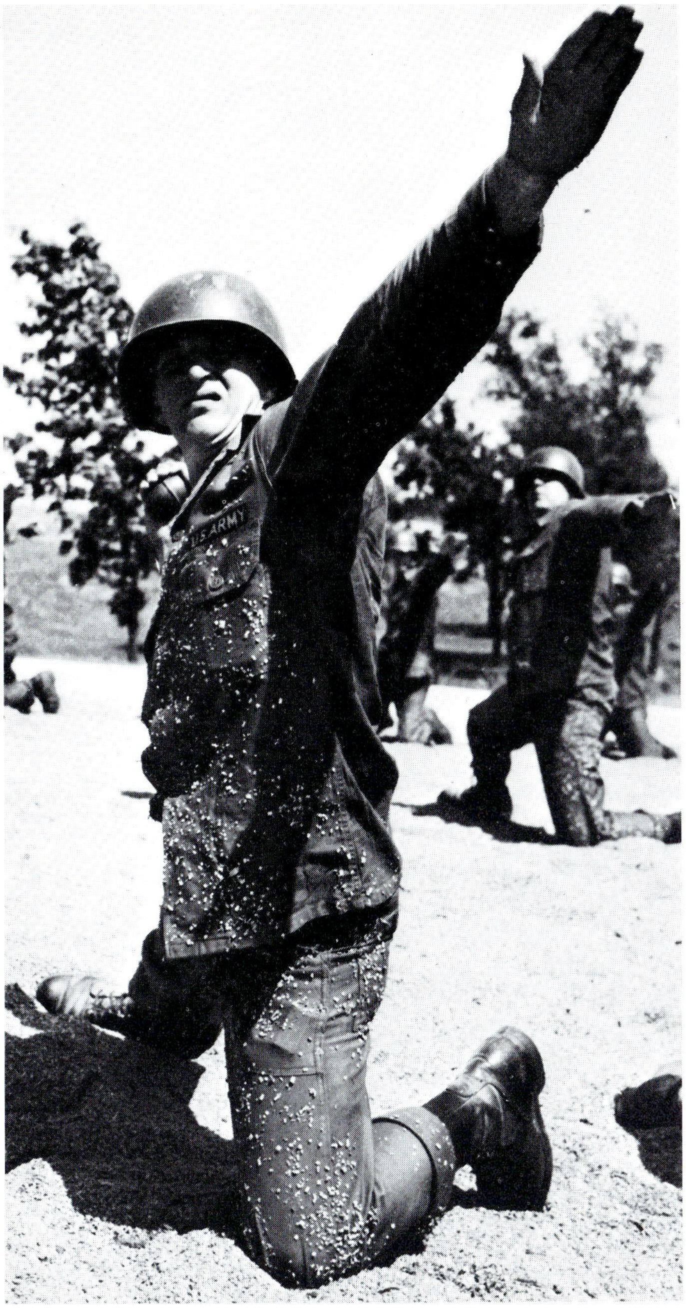
U.S.ARMY

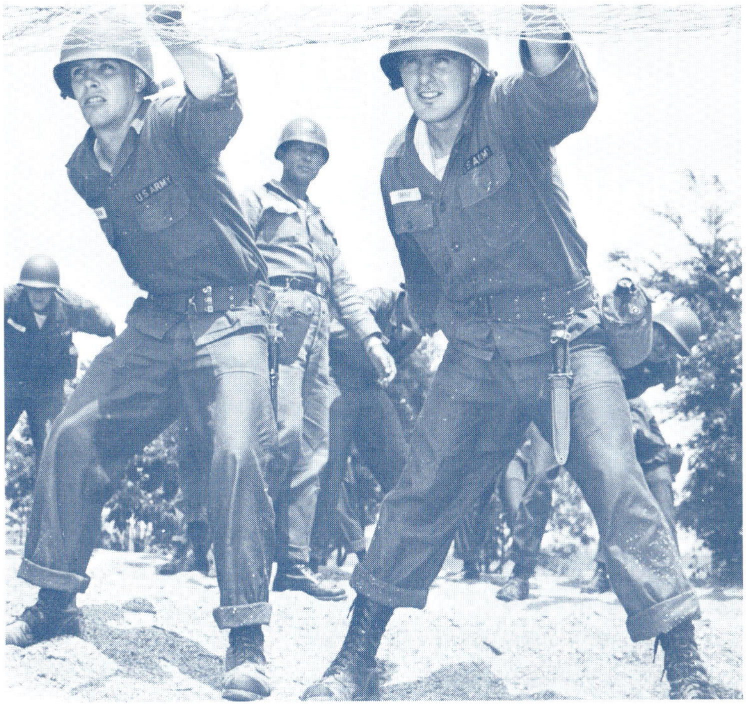
U.S. ARMY

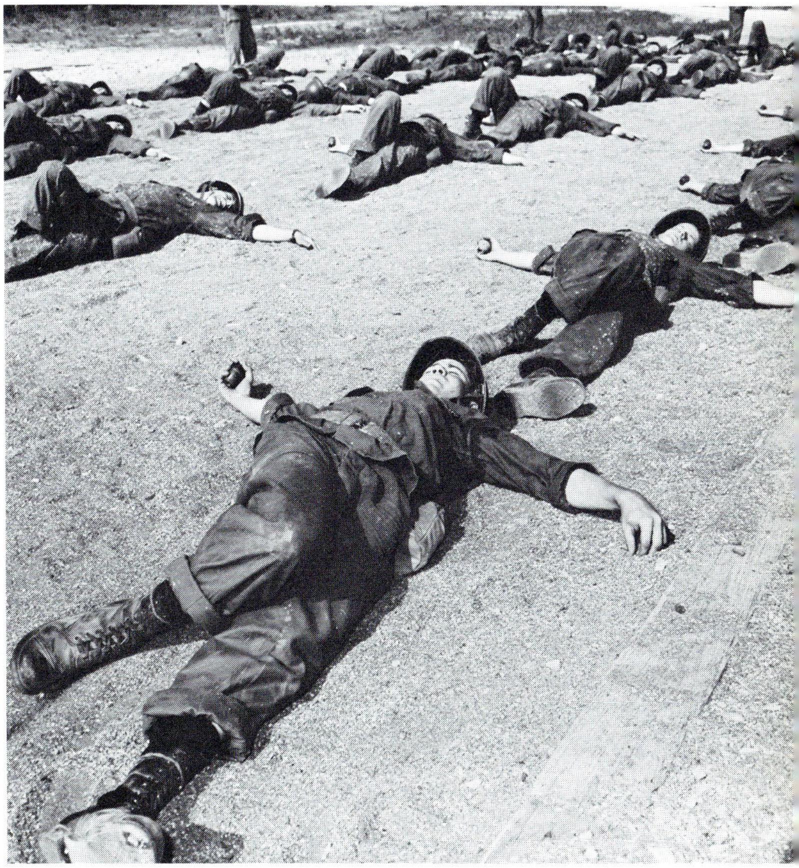

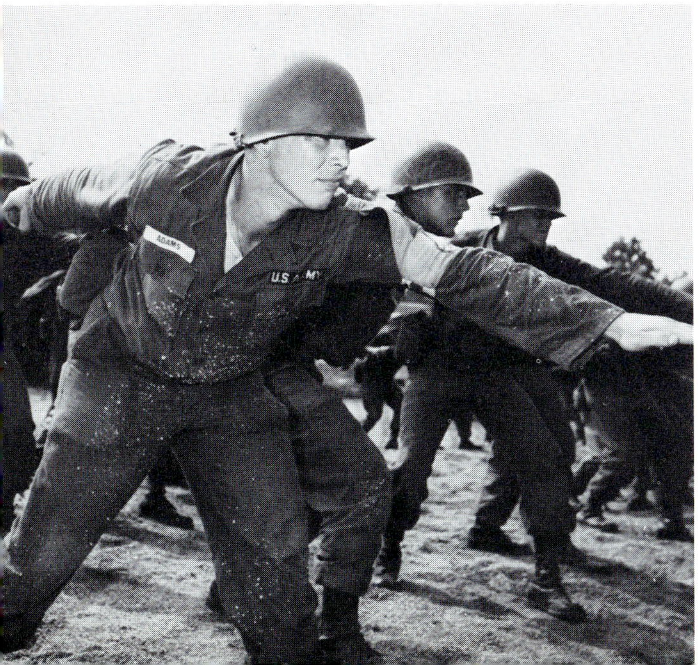
ADAMS

Close Combat Course

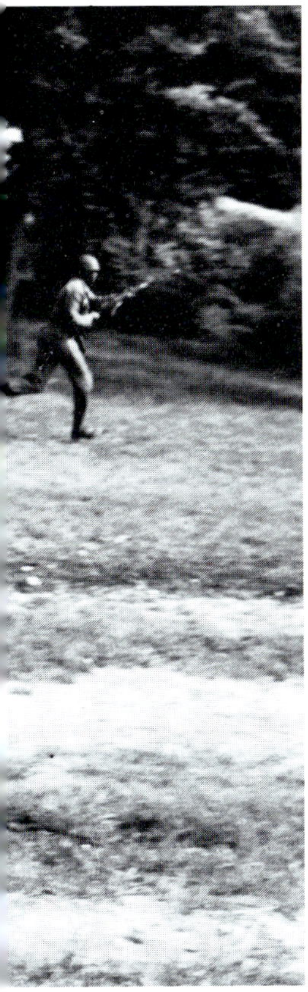

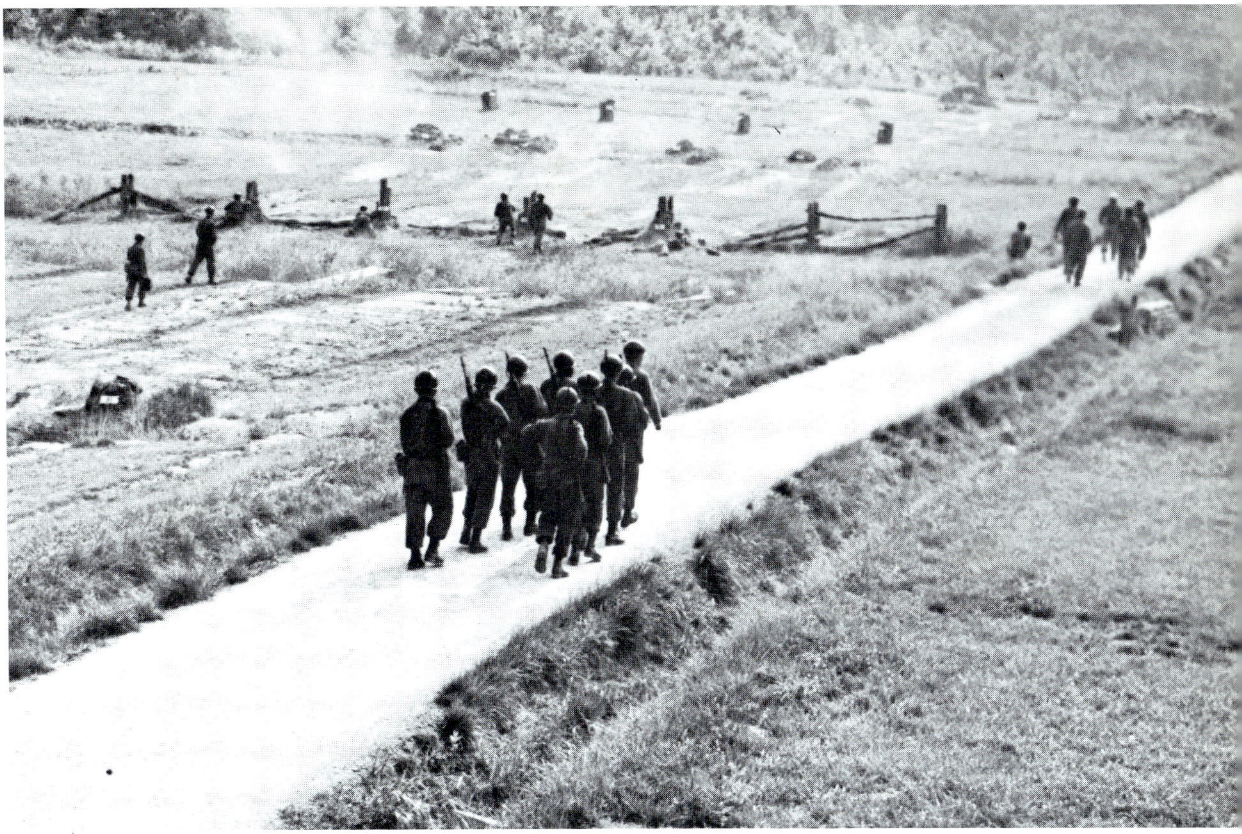

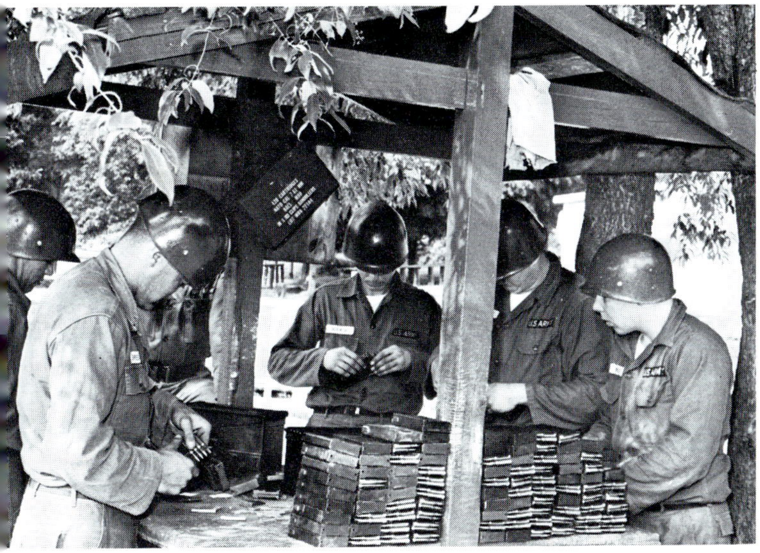

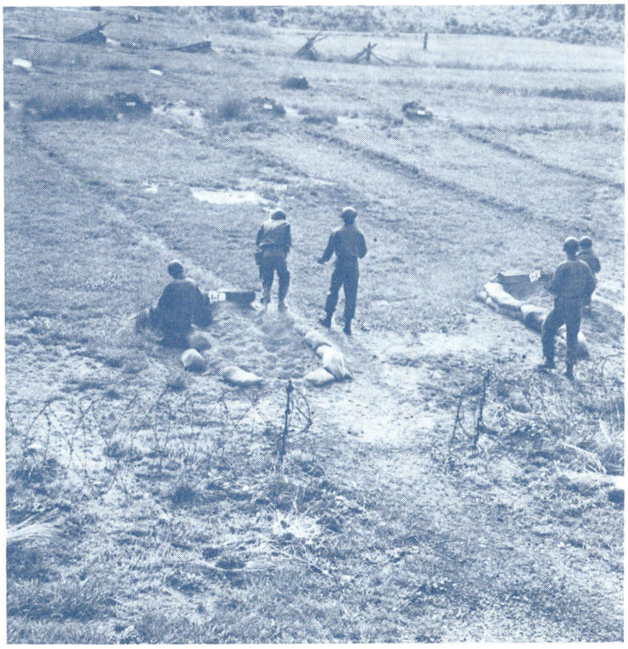

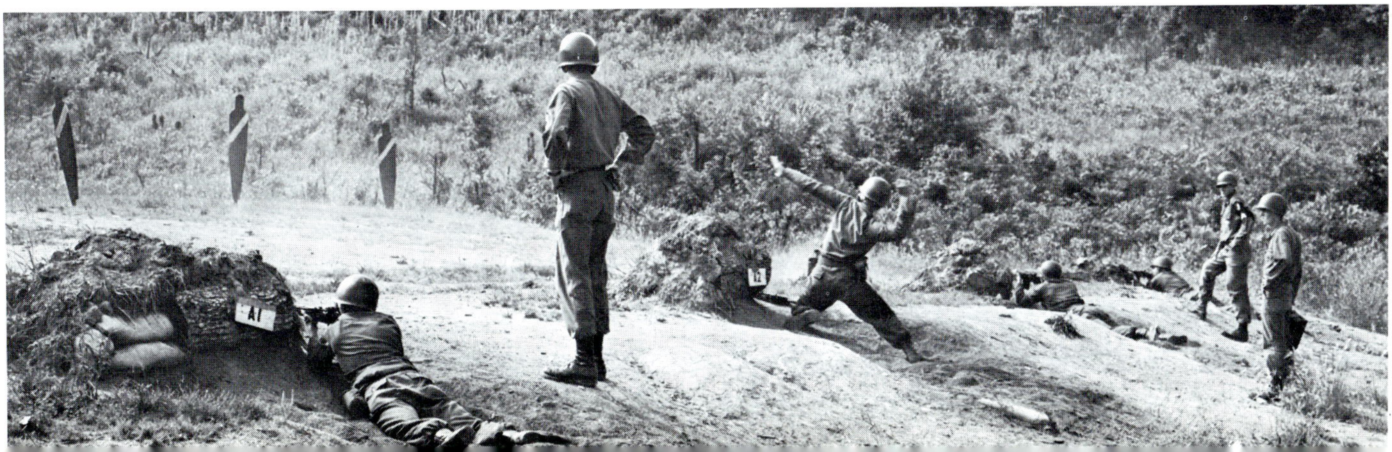
A1

Commanding Officer's Review

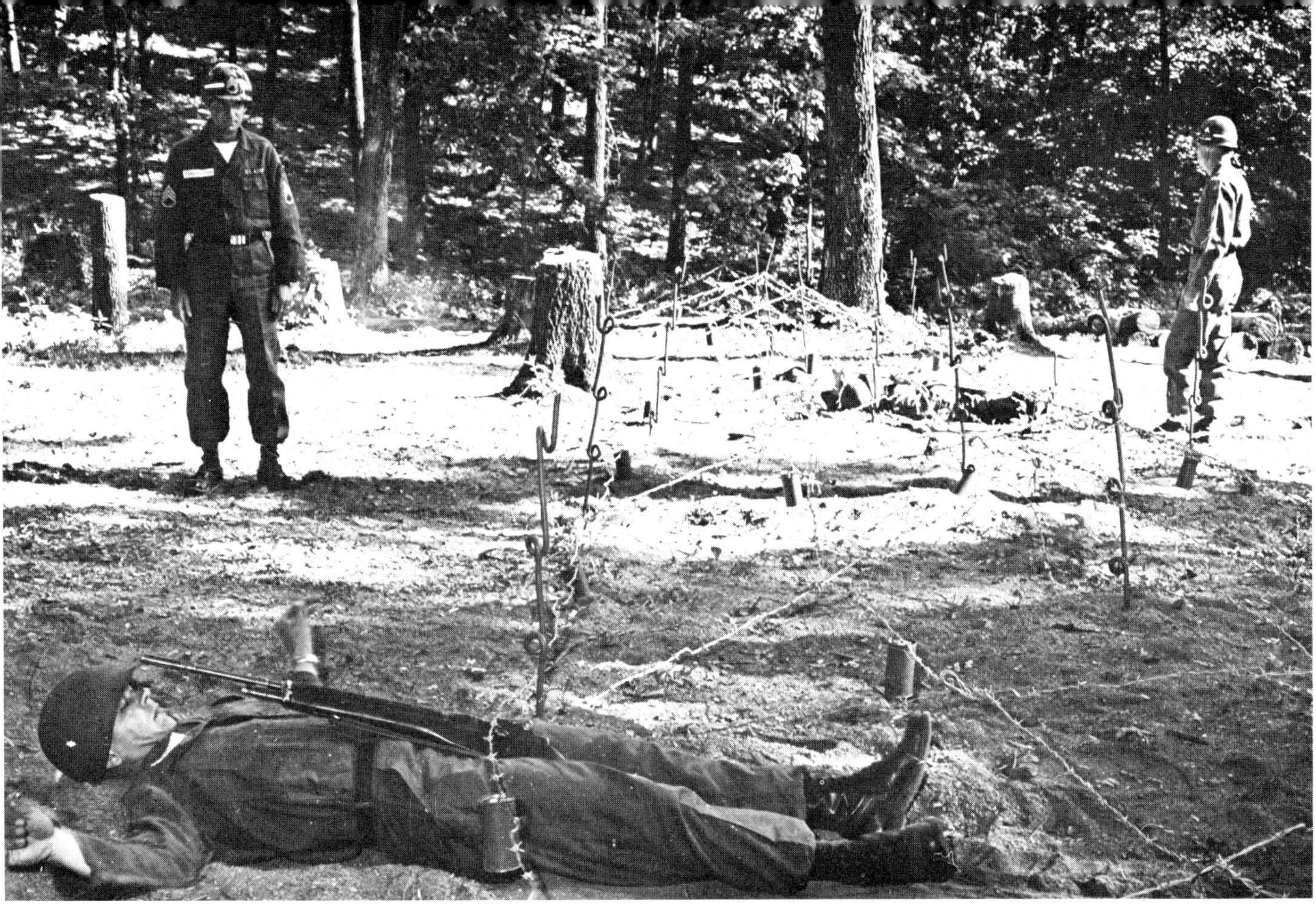

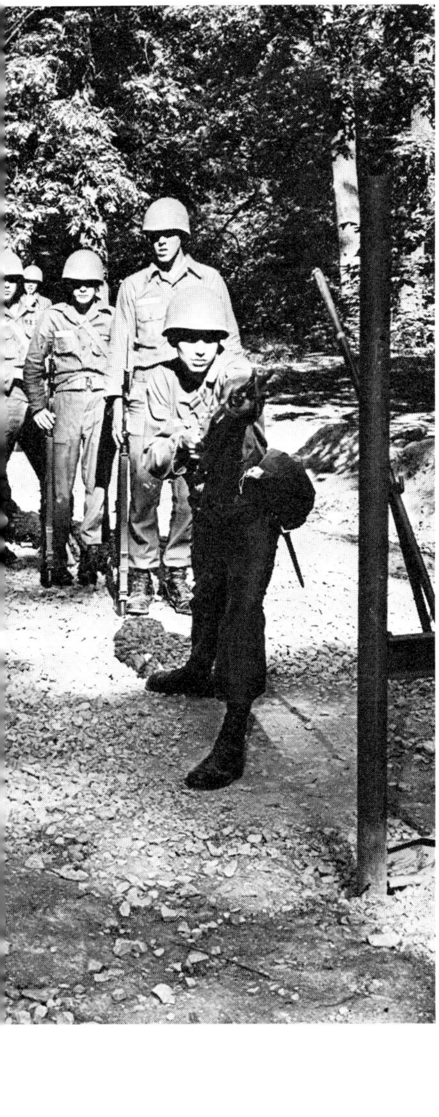

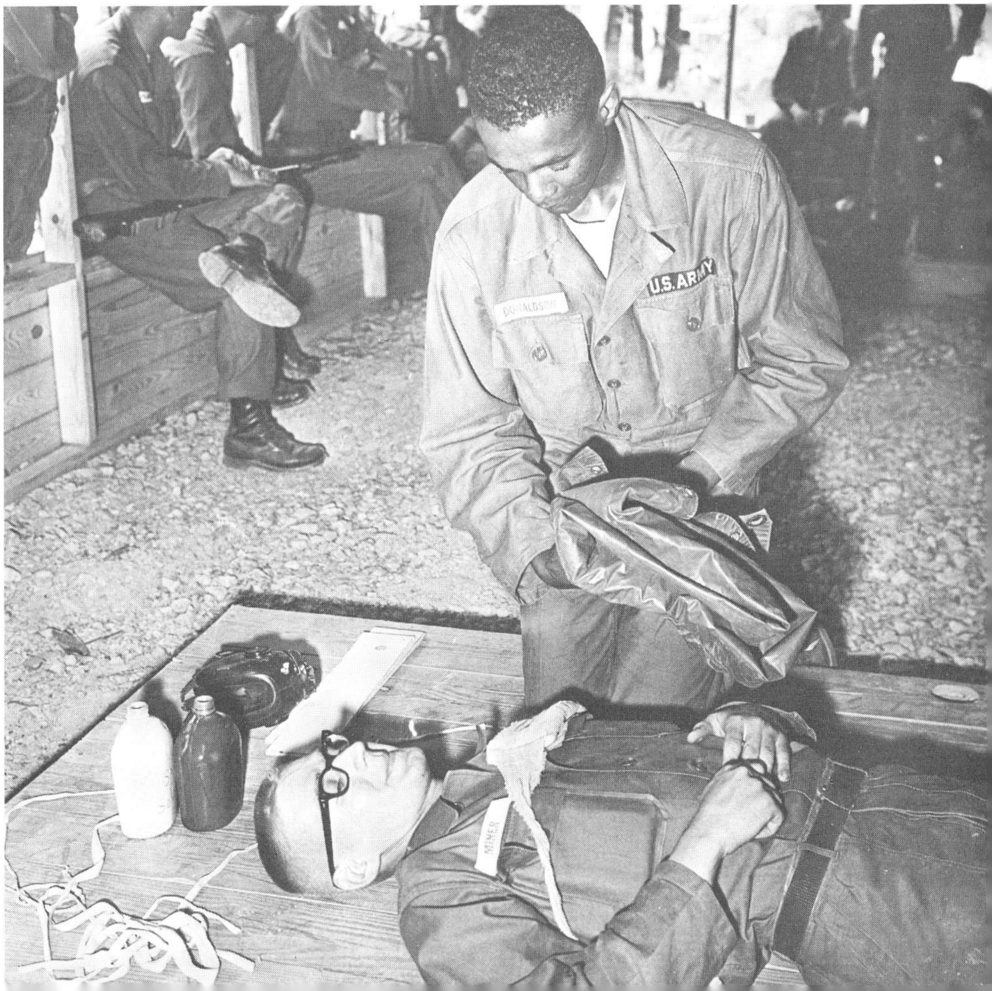
U.S.ARMY

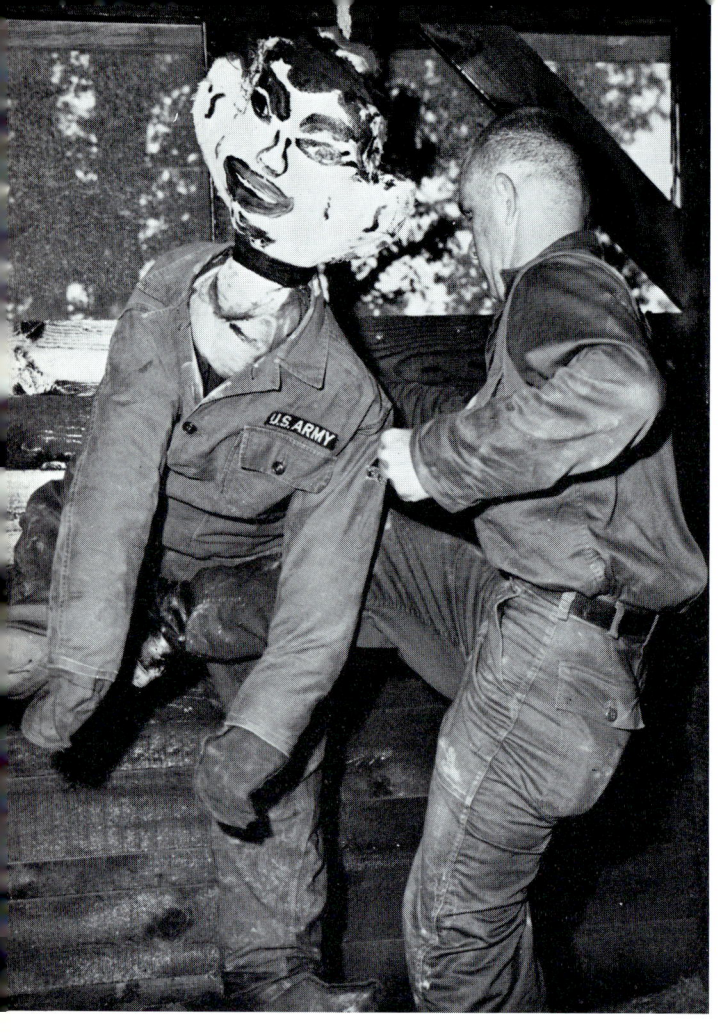

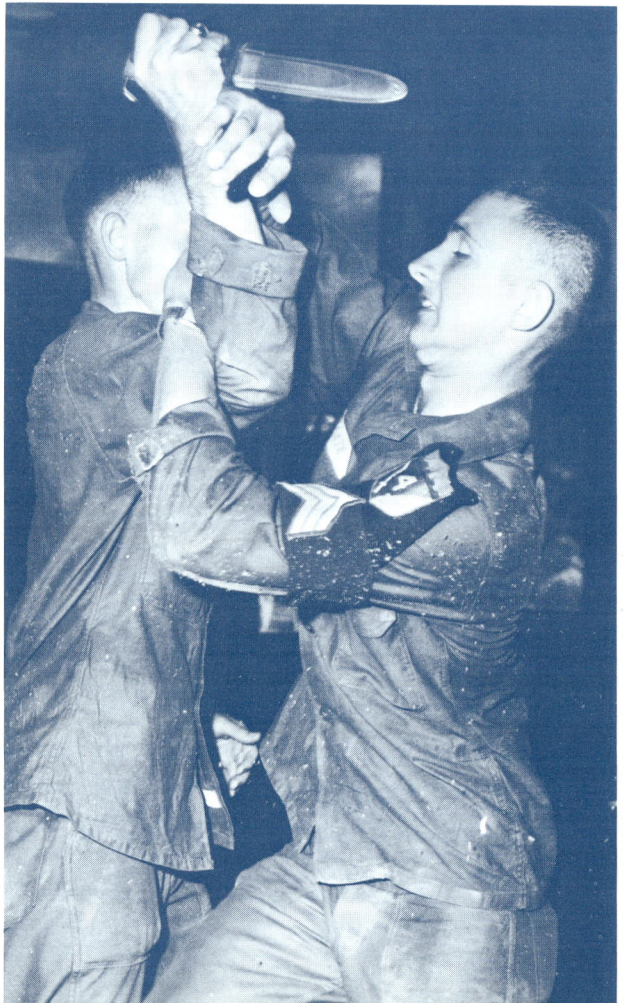

Proficiency Test

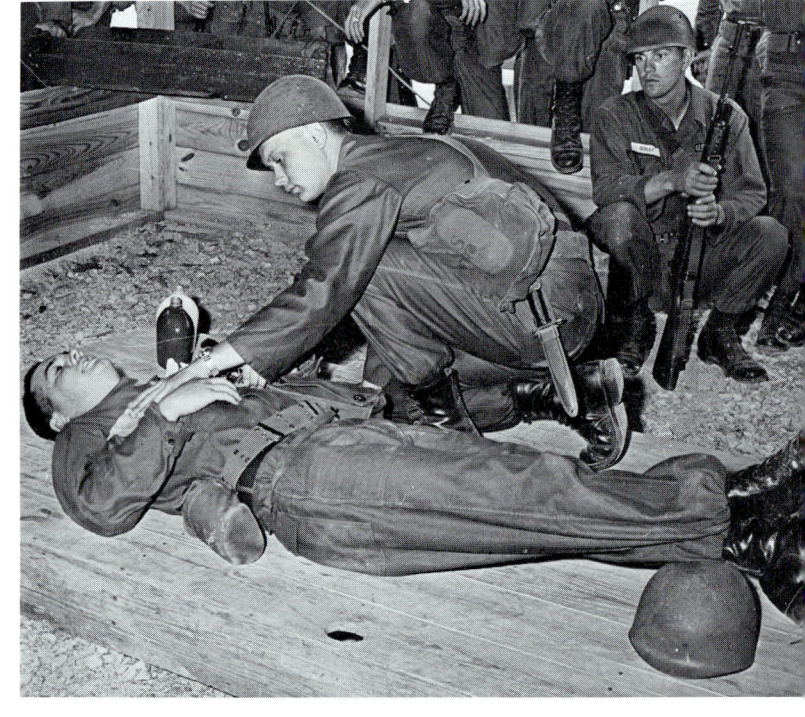

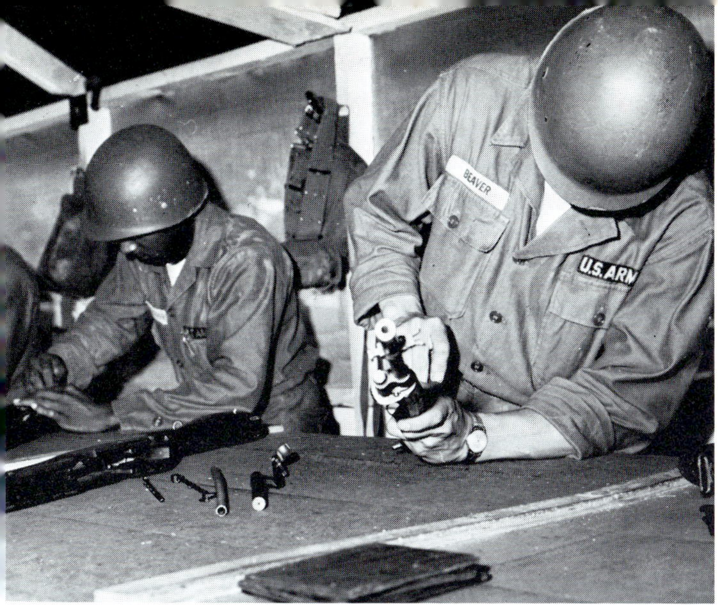
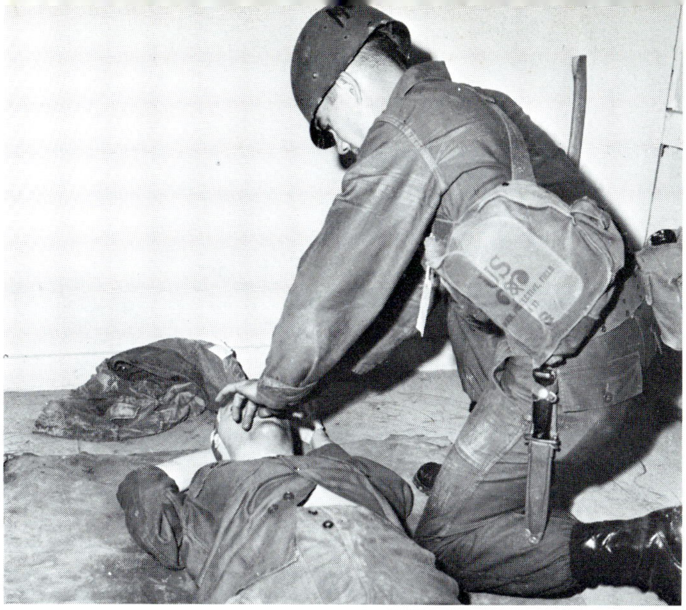
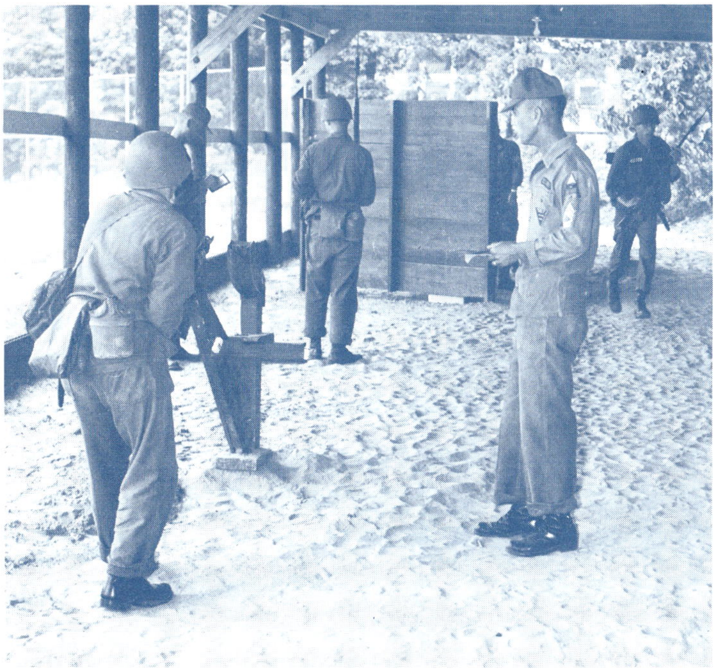
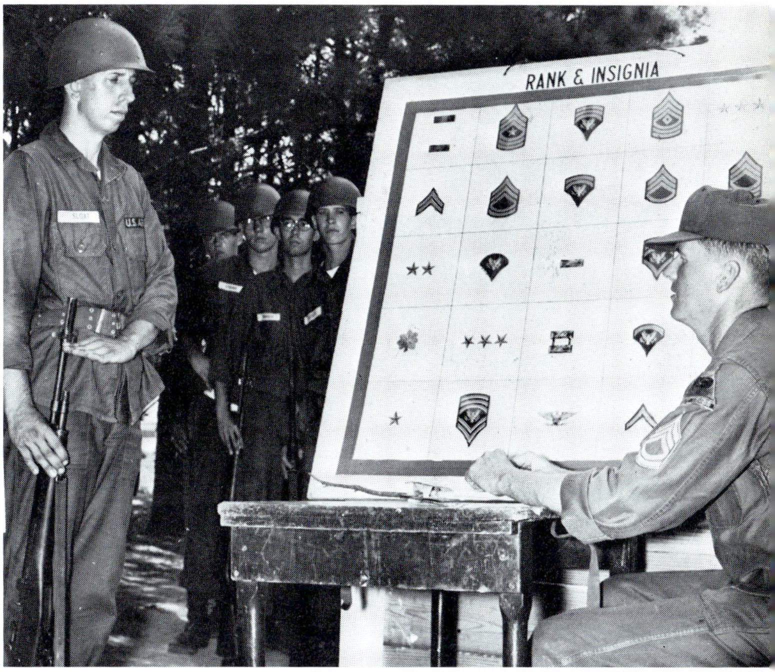
RANK & INSIGNIA
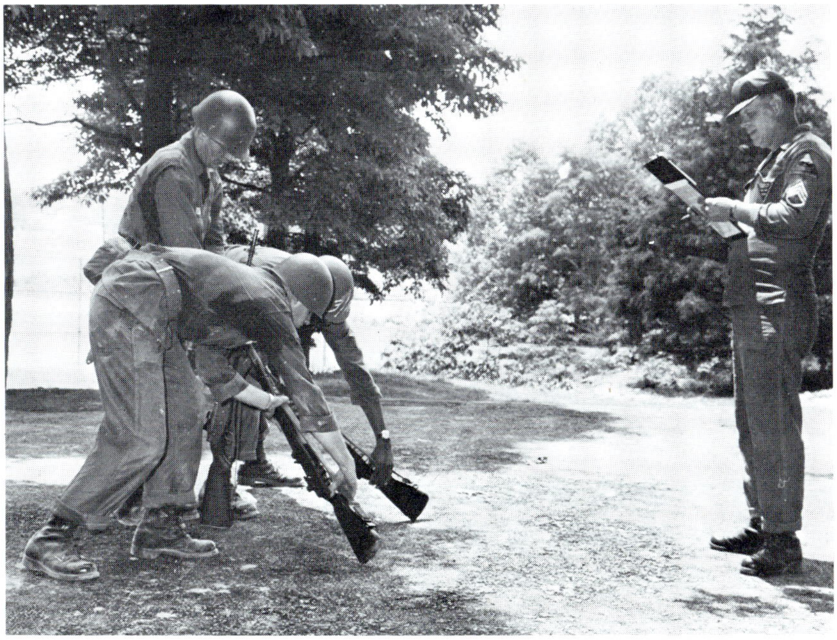
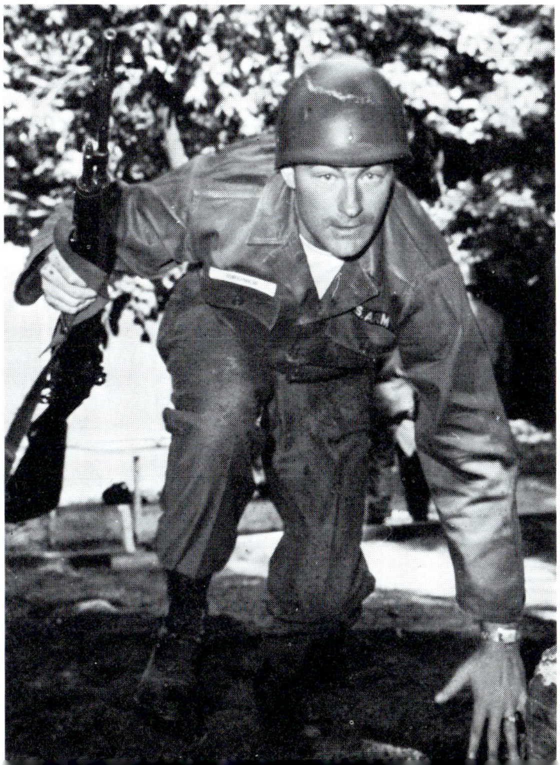

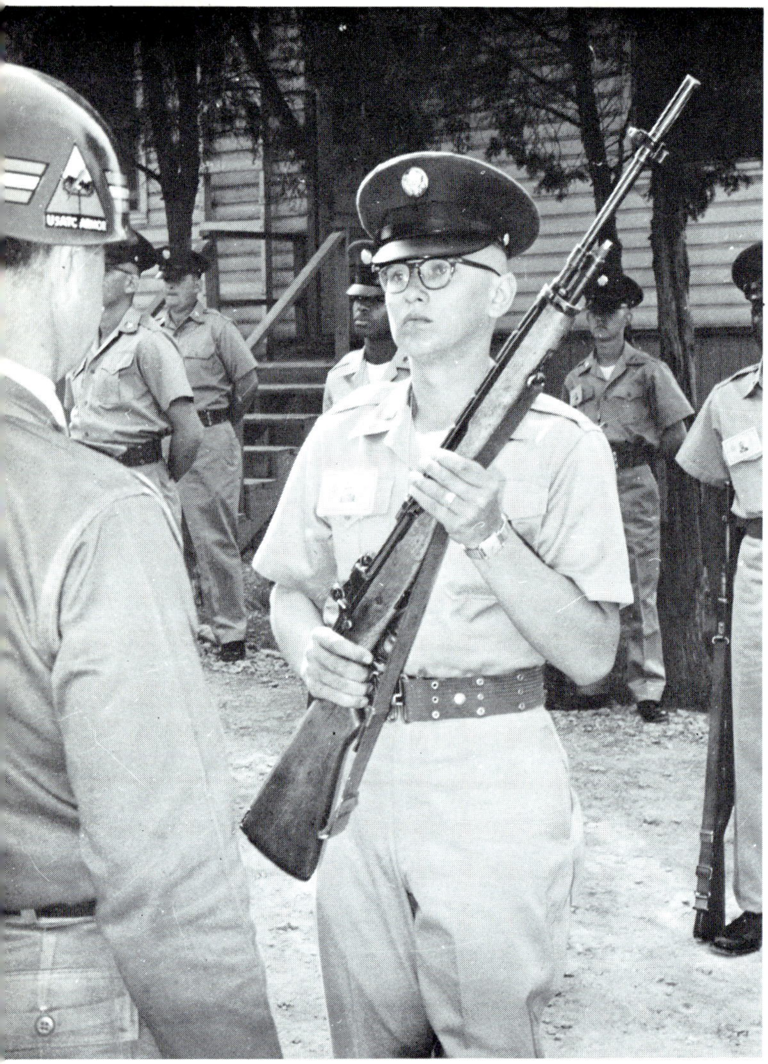
USATC ARMOR
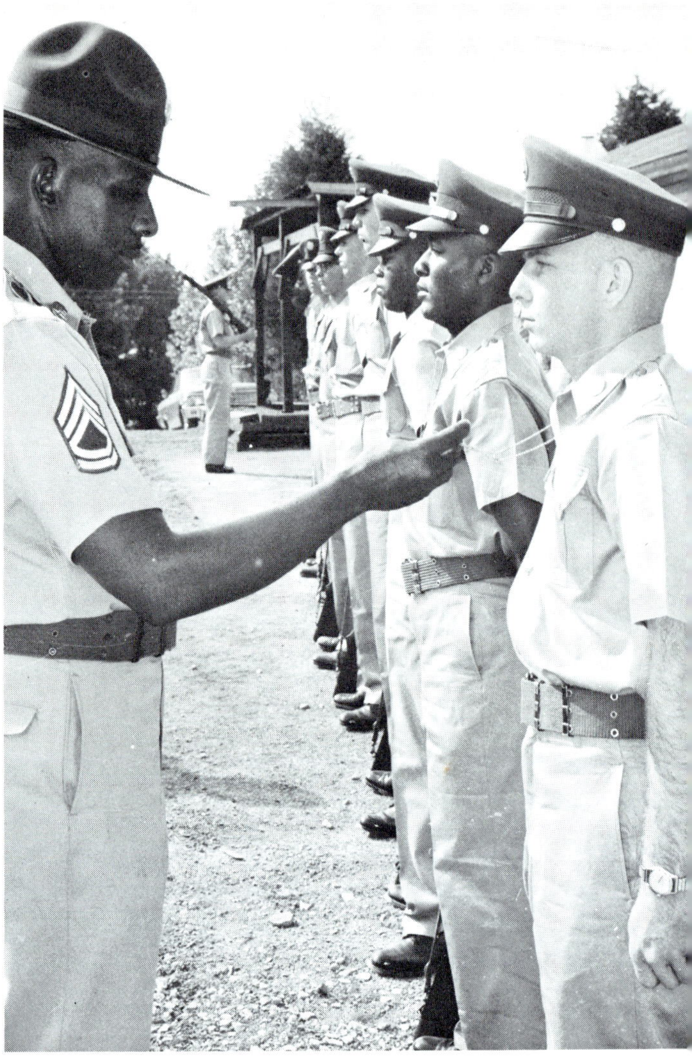
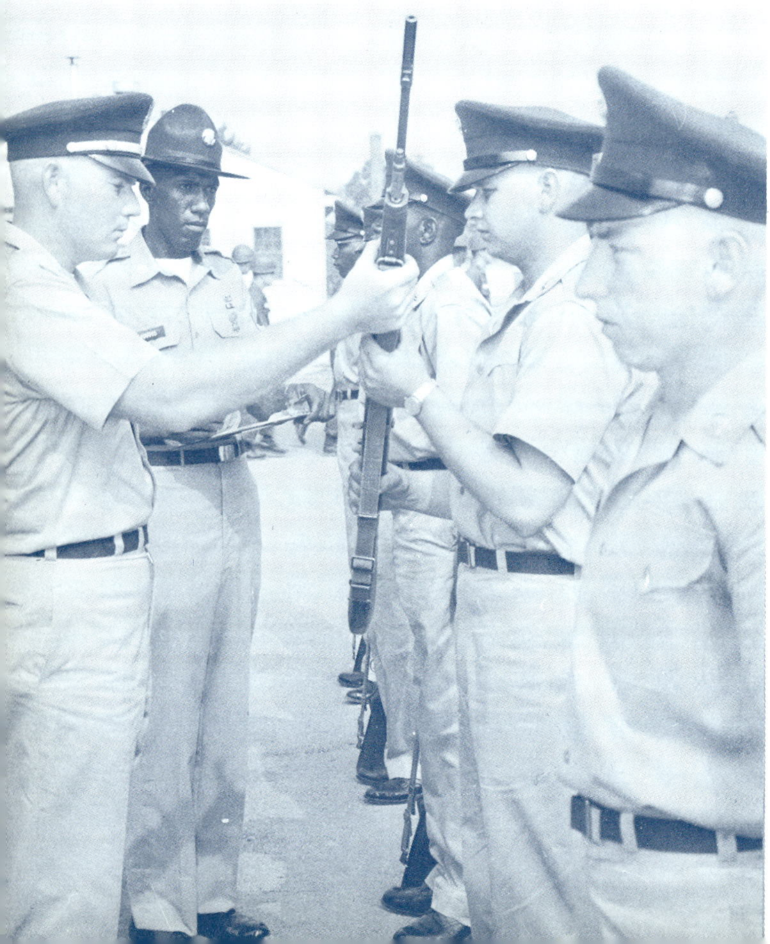
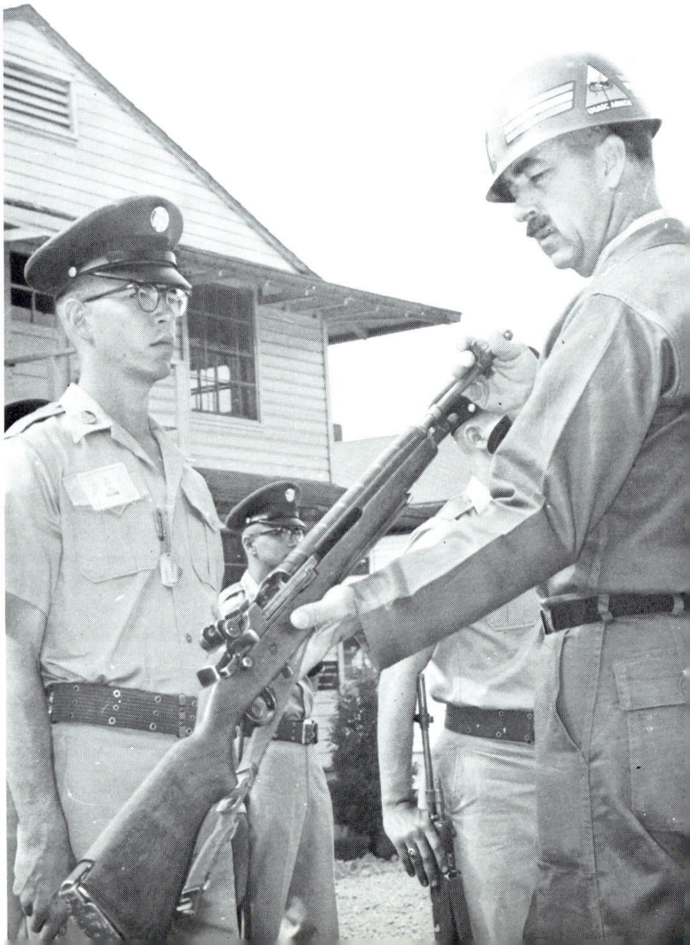

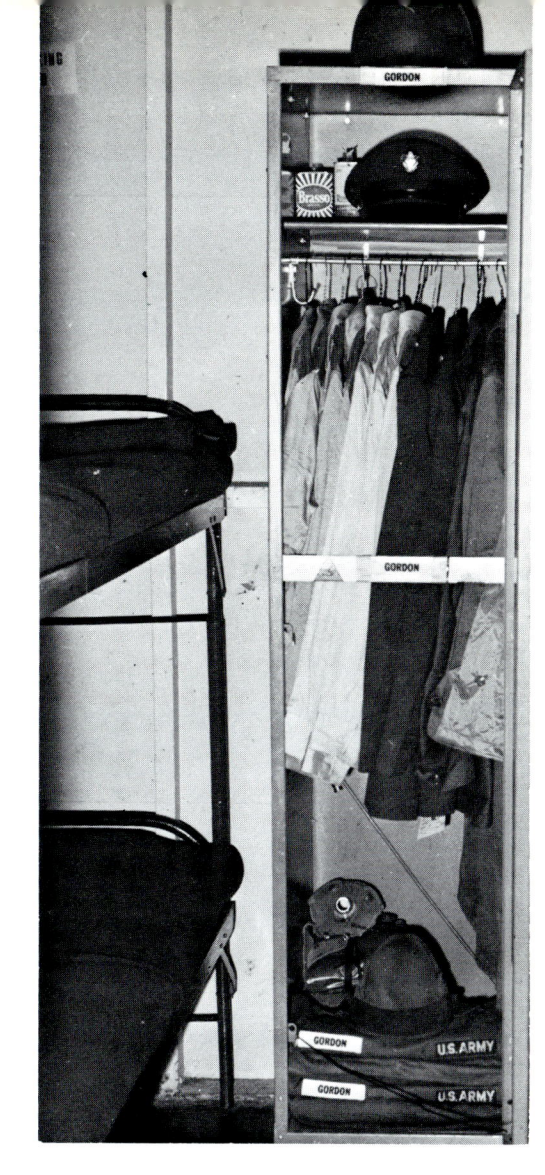

Inspections

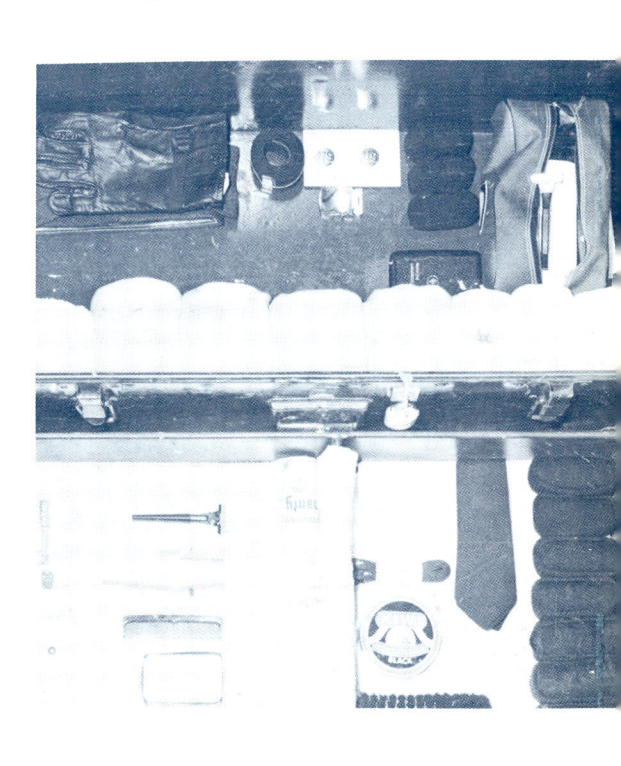

Free Time

Drill Team

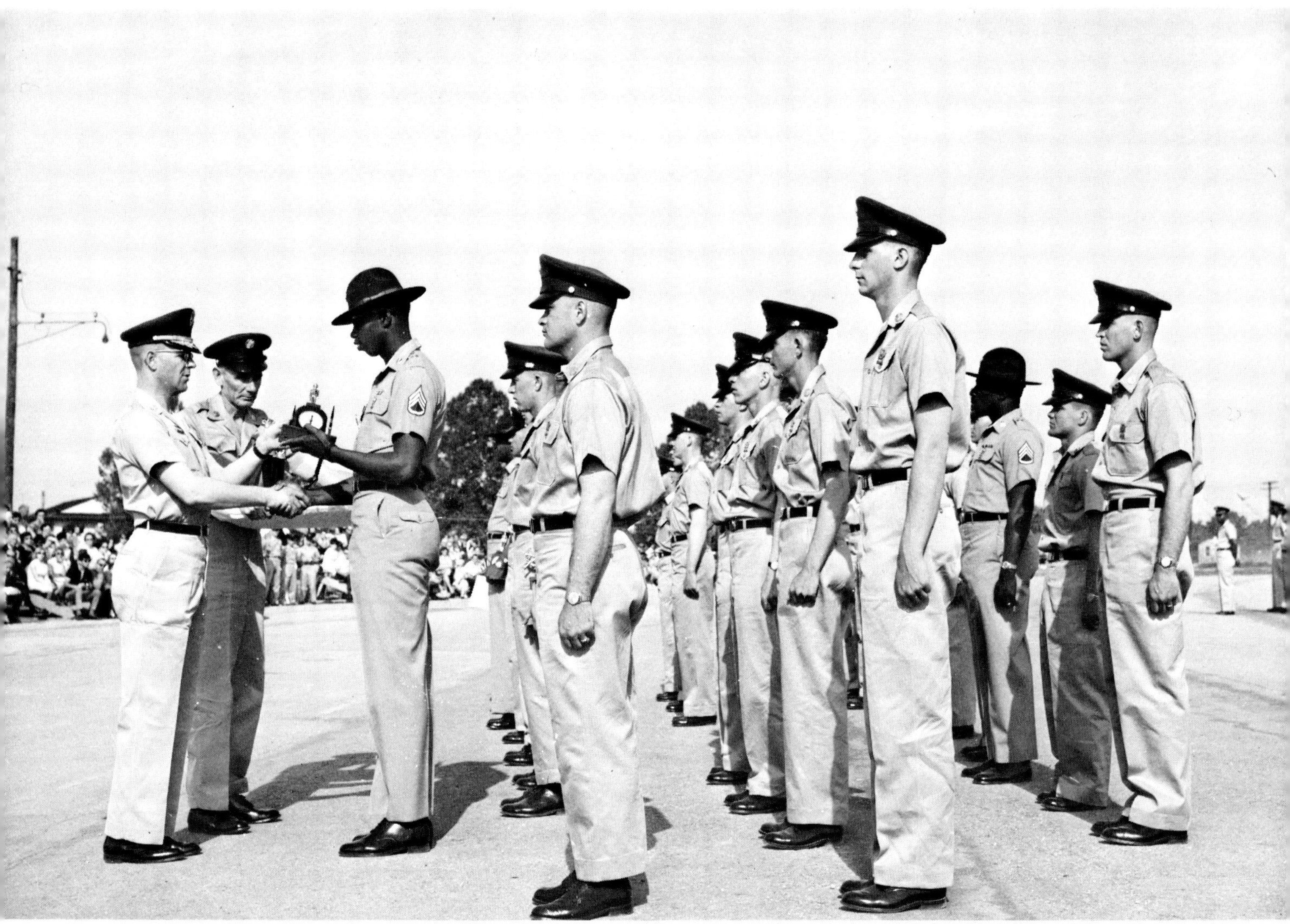

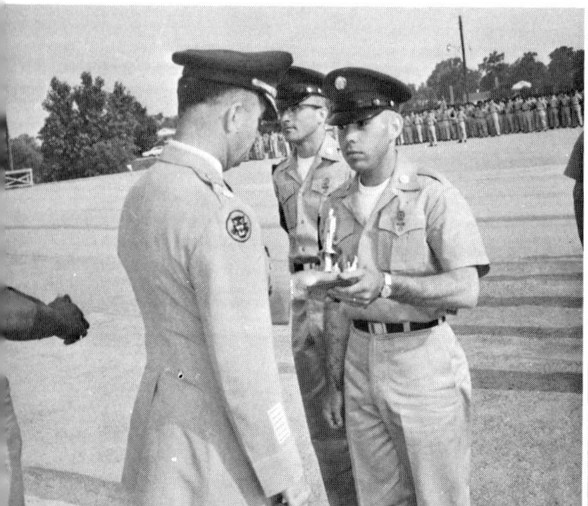

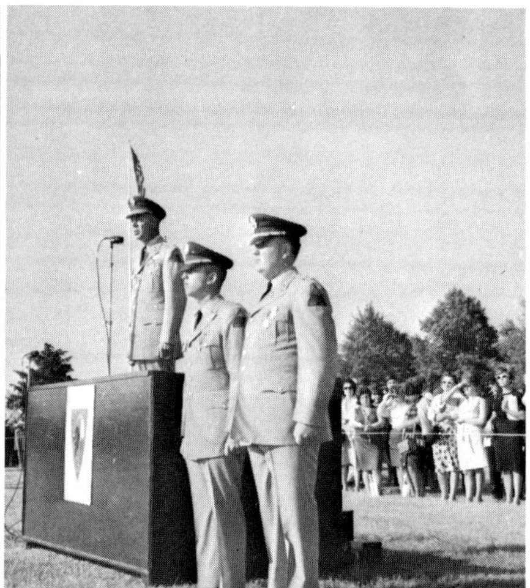

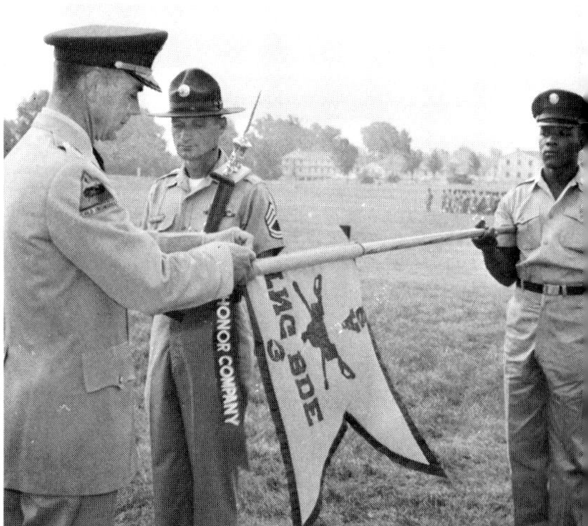
HONOR COMPANY

Graduation

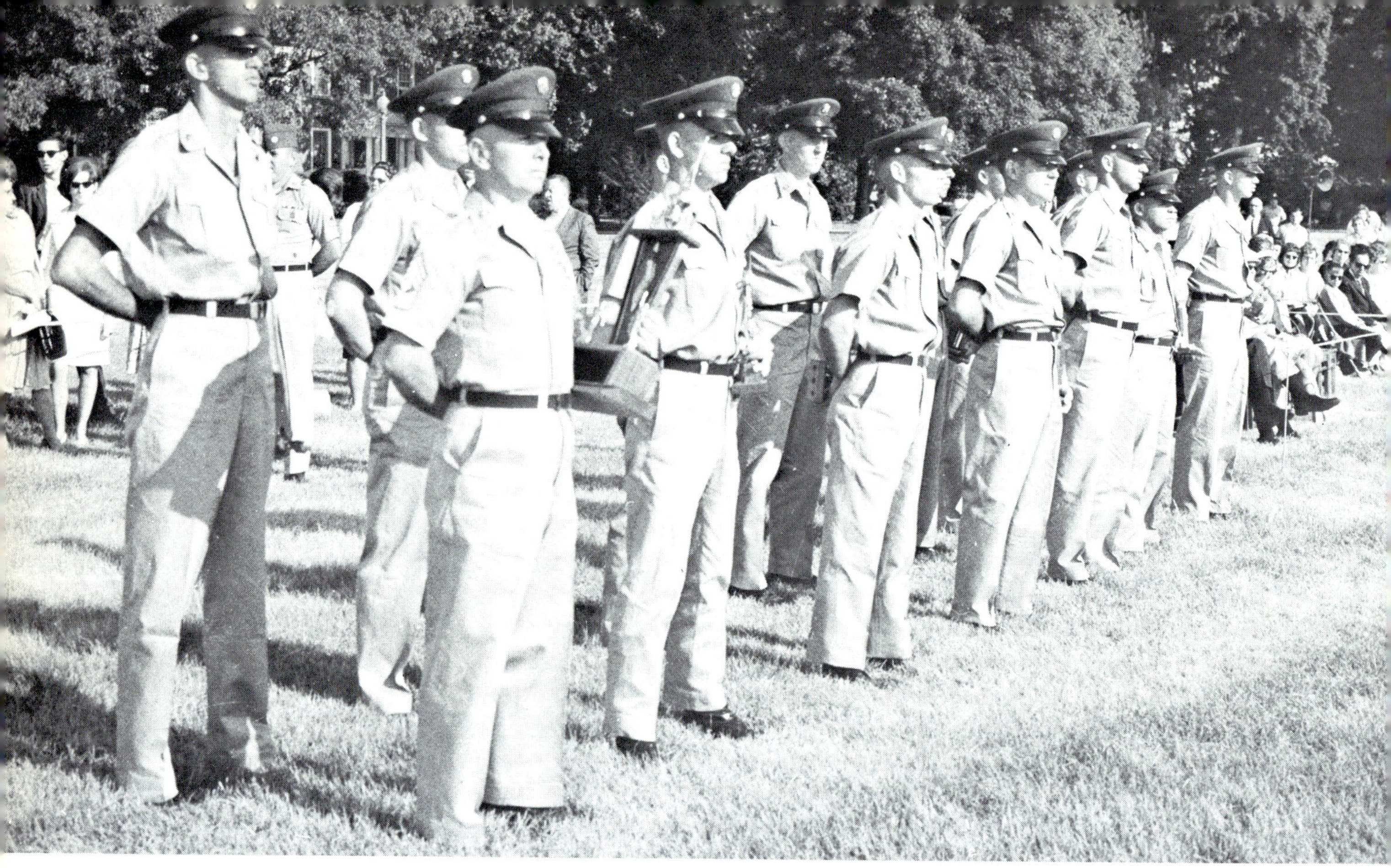

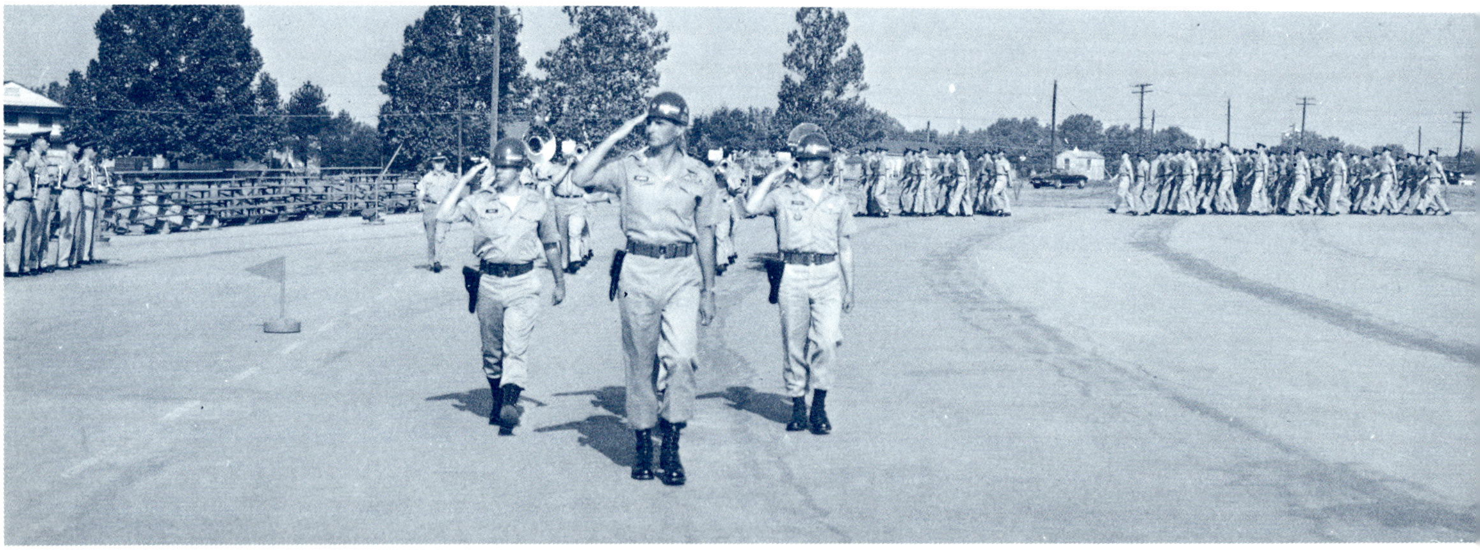

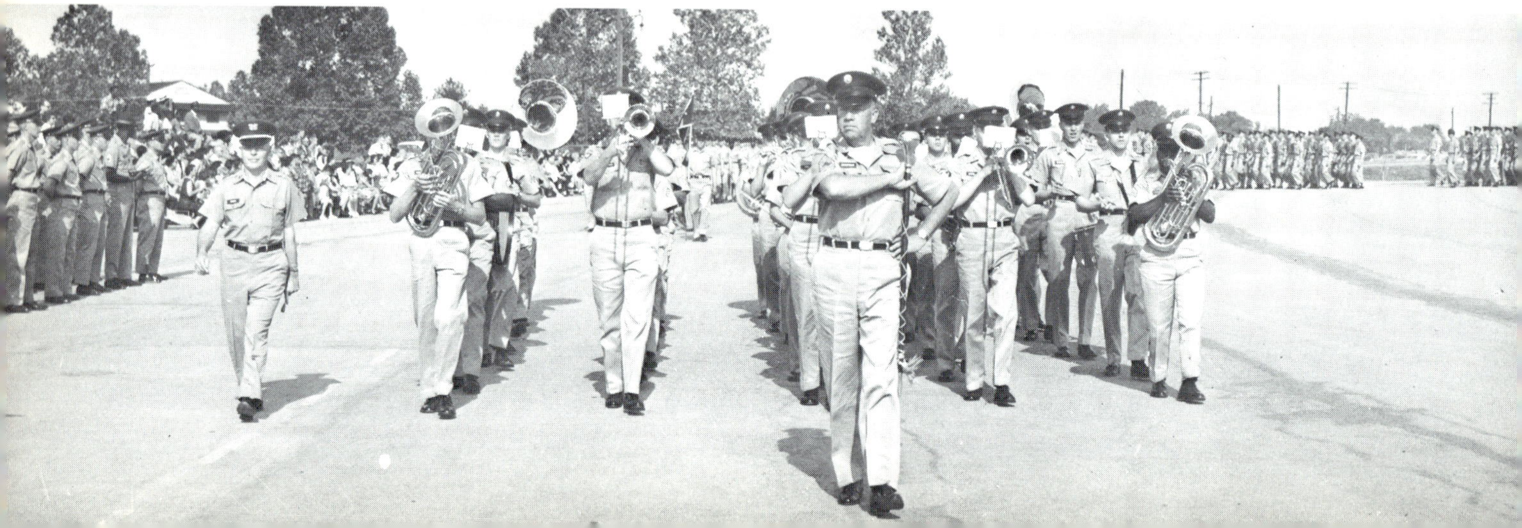

Out Processing

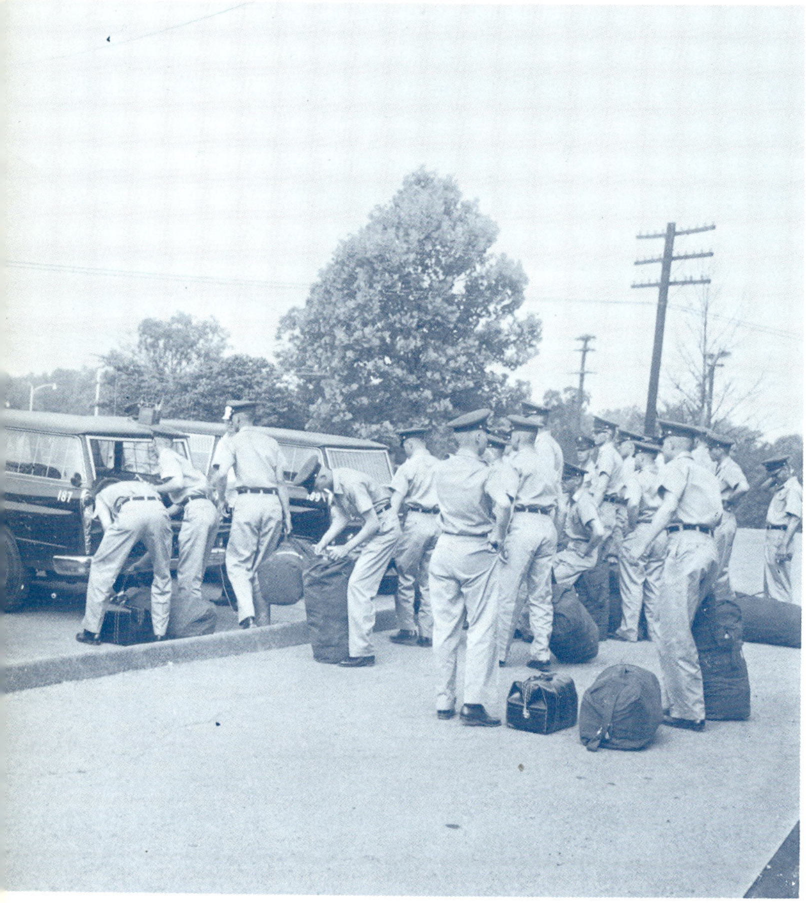

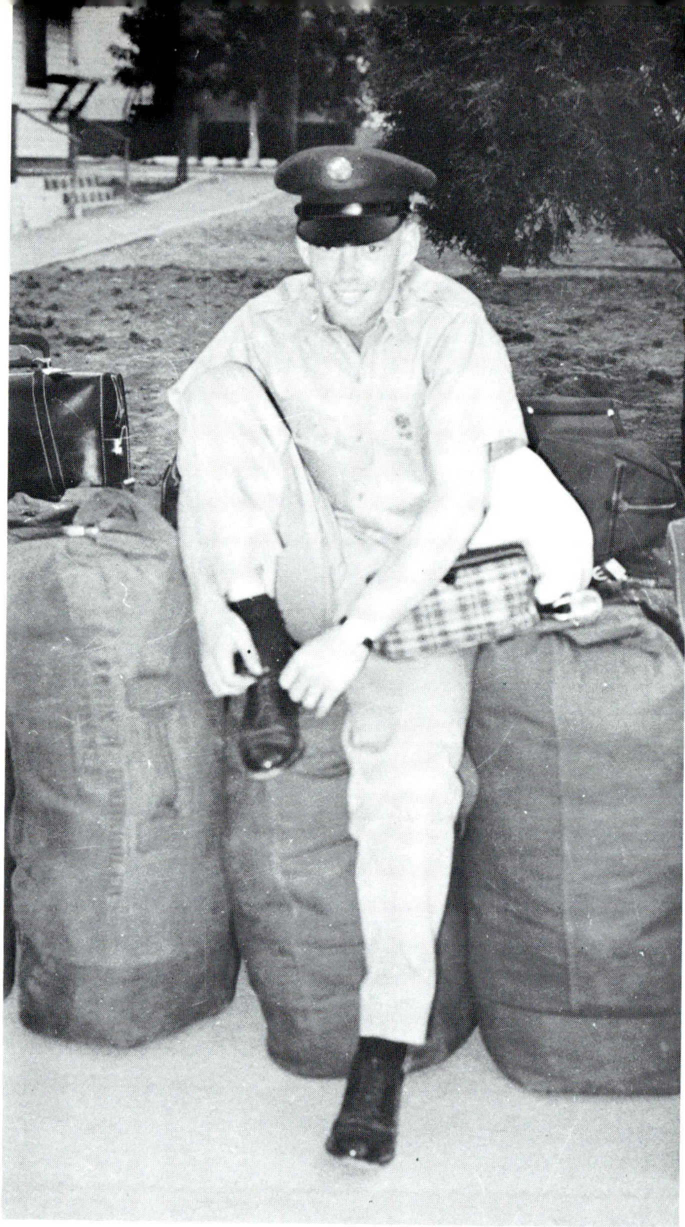

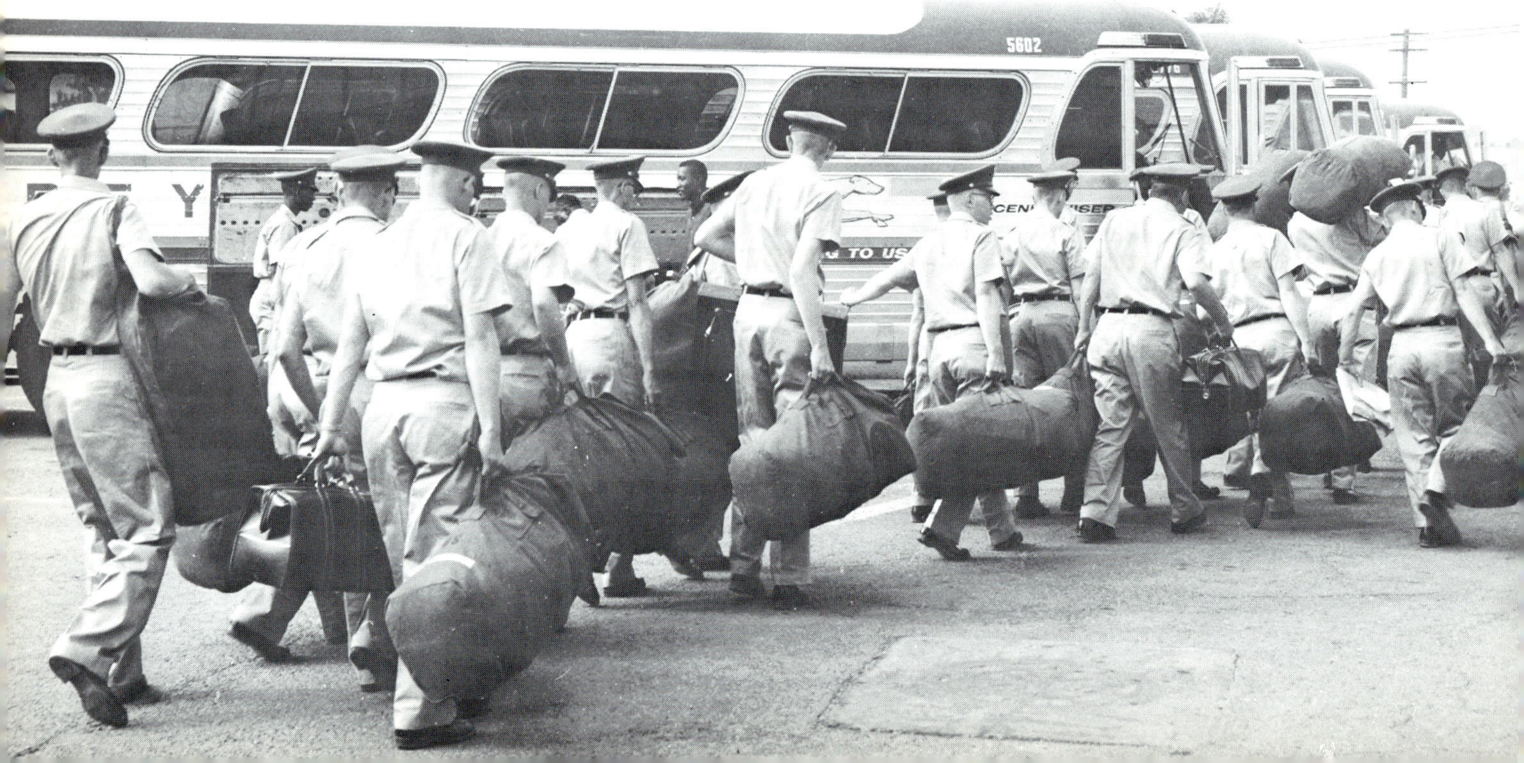
5602

Advanced Individual Training

Now that basic training is over, the soldier will remain in USATCA or go on to another post for Advanced Individual Training (AIT). If he is selected for advanced training in armor, reconnaissance or specialist fields, he will continue his stay in USATCA for 5 to 14 weeks.

Experienced instructors in the 1st Brigade will make the armor candidate a qualified tank gunner, driver or ammunition loader. The reconnaissance trainee will be assigned to a recon squadron to learn the principles of scouting and patrolling, and later will be assigned to one of the many armored cavalry units throughout the world.

Selected men will be trained in the Second Brigade as specialists—radio operators, cooks, clerk-typists, personnel specialists, wheeled vehicle mechanics and supply clerks.

If the trainee leaves USATCA, he may be headed for AIT in one of the following branches or specialties:

Infantry	Military Police
Engineers	Intelligence
Artillery	Finance
Signal Corps	Information
Transportation Corps	Air Defense
Quartermaster Corps	Aviation
Medical Service Corps	

Whatever his advanced training, the new soldier will earn a Military Occupational Specialty (MOS), a diploma which signifies that he is qualified to step into the job for which he has been trained.

How is it determined that a man will be trained as a radio operator and not an armor specialist? At the Reception Station during his first week in the Army, the trainee is administered the Army Battery of Aptitude Tests which help determine the type of work for which he is best suited. A form is filled out on each individual containing information about his civilian education, civilian occupation and the test scores. This information, in addition to the man's personal job preference, and USATCA's recommendation, is forwarded to the Department of the Army. USATCA is then notified of the specific advanced training the man is to receive.

Is training any different for Reserve Enlisted Personnel here under the short-term active duty program? No. These men undergo the same basic and advanced training as active Army trainees. Once the active army man has successfully completed his advanced training, he is sent to a regular Army unit overseas or in the United States, while the reserve trainee returns to his home town to remain a member of the reserve or national guard for $5\frac{1}{2}$ years.

ARMOR: The Combat Arm of Decision

Fire and steel spew from tanks on the firing line.

Advanced Individual Training, Armor

Before this eight week course is over, trainee "tankers" will be able to perform the duties of any one of the four tank crew members—that is the driver, loader, gunner and tank commander.

The more difficult and extensive armor subjects are taught by experienced specialists from the Instructor Group. These men, assisted by company cadre, lead trainees through tank gunnery, explaining how to fire and maintain the weapons of the M60 and M48A3 tanks. The trainee fires the 7.62 (light) and 50 caliber (heavy) machine guns along with the 90 and 105-millimeter main tank guns.

Armor training also includes classes on communications, driving and maintenance, combat skills (i.e. map reading), land mine warfare and general military subjects.

Waiting for the signal to commence firing.

Advanced Individual Training, Reconnaissance

An effective armor operation is a matter of teamwork, and a critical member of the team is the reconnaissance scout.

Trainees chosen to learn the skills of armor reconnaissance scouting will be assigned to one of two squadrons in the 1st Brigade for eight weeks of Advanced Individual Training, Reconnaissance.

During his eight weeks with a troop, the trainee becomes familiar with every aspect of the modern scout's horse—the jeep. He will learn how to take his jeep over all types of terrain under trying conditions. He will live with it in the field, learn how to keep it in top shape at all times. At the end of the training cycle, eight weeks of classroom theory and field practice will be put to the test when the trainee takes his "iron horse" through a rugged course designed to measure the scout's reactions to various combat situations.

Most of the training is devoted to scouting and patrolling. The trainee learns the principles of mounted and dismounted combat and reconnaissance patrols, the establishment of observation and listening posts, map reading and ways of making route, area and zone reconnaissance. At least five days are spent in the field, giving the trainee the opportunity to put theory into practice.

Tank communications is taught on this mock-up of a tank interior.

A tank, just back from the field, gets a cleaning.

Instruction also is given in firing and caring for weapons—the light and heavy machine guns, the M-14 rifle, and the .45 caliber pistol. The trainee also will study the latest radar surveillance equipment and CBR warning devices, bridge classification, artillery adjustment, message writing, and intelligence reporting.

Upon successful completion of training, men are awarded the MOS of scout and assigned to an armored cavalry unit. They may patrol the Iron Curtain, the Demilitarized Zone in Korea, or be assigned to one of the divisions in the United States.

The modern recon man's horse is his jeep.

LASER Device

The LASER, an experimental device, is tested in the 1st Brigade as a possible substitute for the conventional machine gun in non-fire training exercises and as a substitute for sub-caliber firing on Tables I, II, and III. LASER works by amplifying and controlling light as no other device can. (A LASER beam can be focused to 50 millionths of an inch, can dissolve any known substance.) "LASER" is the acronym and easier way of saying "Light Amplification through Stimulated Emmission of Radiation."

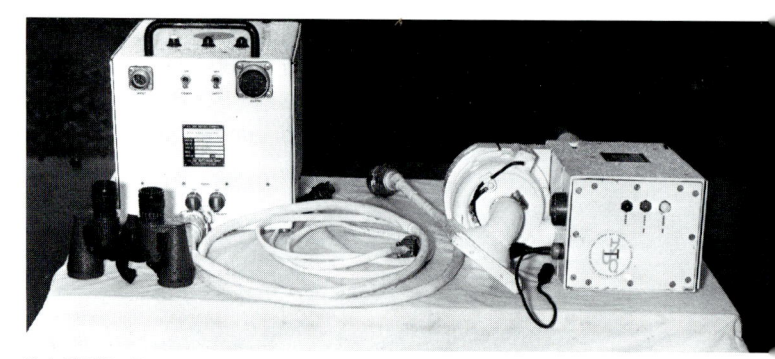

LASER Device

Gunnery Practice

Combat Support Training

Just as one branch of the service depends on another for support on the battlefield, as infantrymen rely on artillerymen, so do all the services depend on "specialists" to do hundreds of vital jobs. Specialists—radio operators, auto mechanics, cooks and clerks—are common to all branches of the Army, thus the term Common Specialist Training.

The 2d Brigade conducts all Common Specialist Training in USATCA, with the exception of bandsman training. Selection for this training is dependent upon a candidate's aptitudes, abilities and individual desire. The battery of tests he takes at the Reception Station upon his arrival at Fort Knox are heavily weighed.

Should a man be selected for specialist training—Radio School, for instance—he reports to a specific company, in this case Company A, 6th Battalion. The company will train him and provide housing, mess facilities, supply of equipment and administration. Radio instructors are also assigned to this company. These specialist courses are as follow:

Radio Operators Course

A vigorous ten-week course qualifying the student as a Radio Operator (MOS 05B.20). Graduates are capable of sending and receiving International Morse Code at 15 words per minute. The trainee also received instruction in radio procedures, field radio sets, operation of tactical radio nets and vehicle driving. Selected Active Army students who distinguish themselves early in the 10-week course by transmitting and receiving 10 words per minute of International Morse Code, and who have maintained an 80 per cent examination average, may be selected to attend the 11-week Radio Teletype Operator's Course (MOS 056.20) at Fort Gordon, Georgia, upon completion of seven weeks training in MOS 05B at Fort Knox.

Clerical School.

Clerical Course

An eight-week course devoted to instruction in basic Army administration. The 352-hour course includes the theory and procedures of typing, filing, preparation of military correspondence and reports, and special administrative procedures. Graduates of the school are awarded MOS 71A10 (General Clerk) or 71B20 (Clerk-Typist), depending upon their typing skill.

Trainees learn how a radio works.

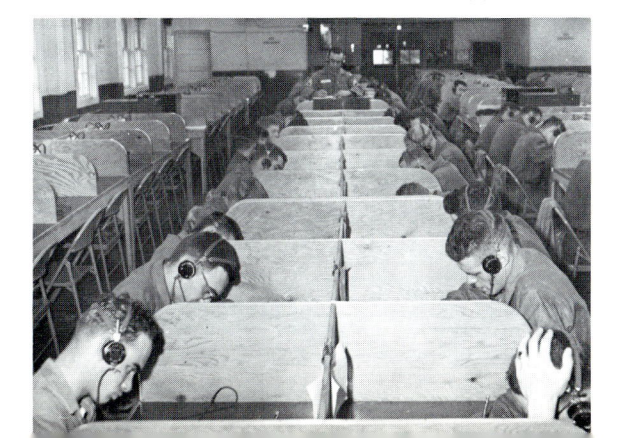

Personnel Administration Course

Offers 352 hours over an eight week period. Intensive training is conducted in typing, military correspondence, duty rosters, personnel actions, and the operation of modern office machines. Graduates of this course are designated Personnel Administration Specialists (MOS 71H20).

General Supply Course

Provides a concentrated six-week course of 264 hours. The supply course encompasses office machine operation, supply records and publications, administrative procedures, packaging and preservation, and storage procedures. This training results in qualification as a General Supply Clerk (MOS 76A10).

Automotive preventive maintenance training.

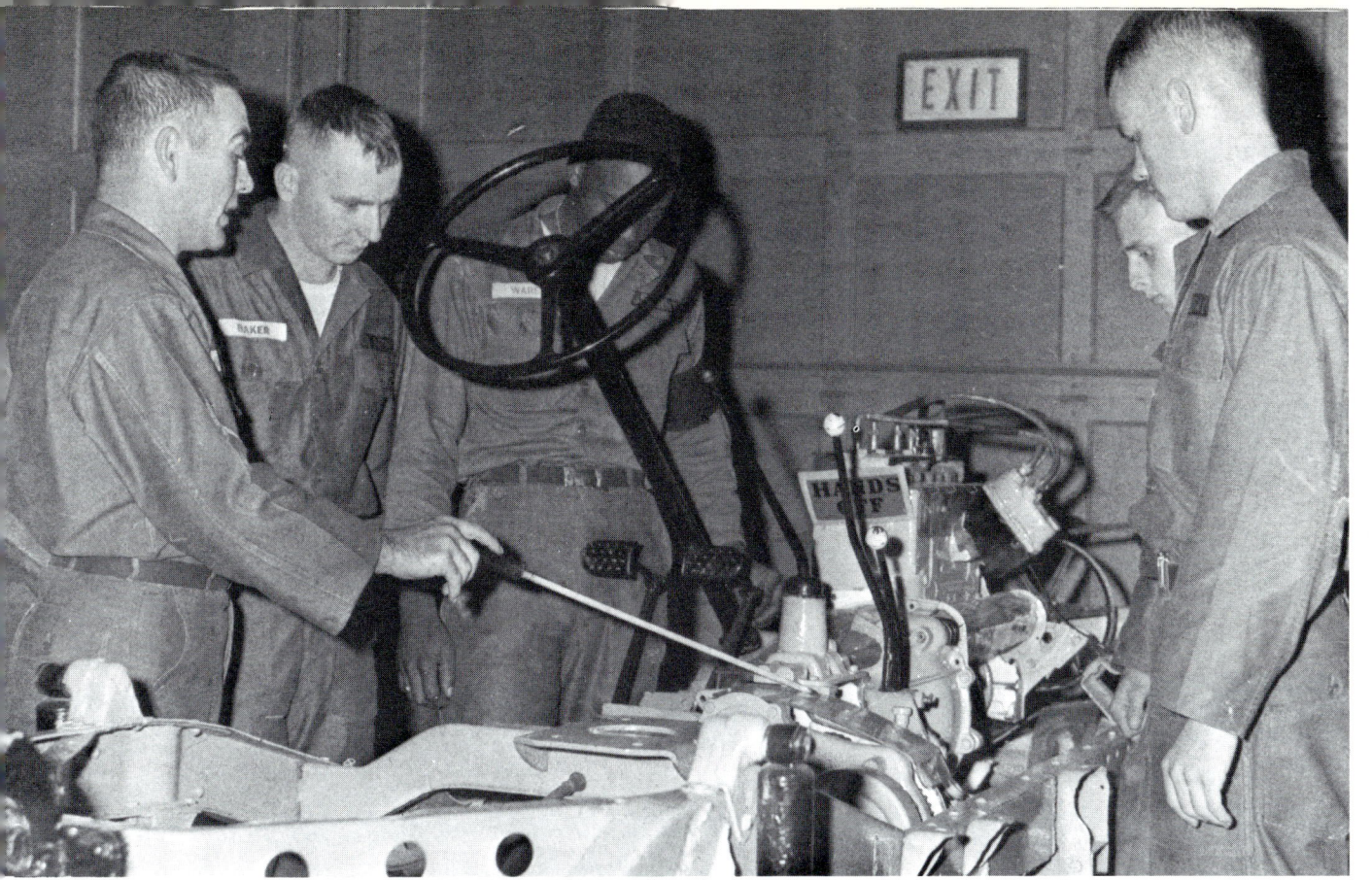

Maintenance is an important part of automotive training.

Automotive Mechanic's Course

Seven weeks of comprehensive training in automotive maintenance leads to qualification as an Automotive Mechanic (MOS 63B20). Approximately 68 per cent of the 308 hours are devoted to practical work on wheeled vehicles. The course includes such diverse topics as internal combustion engines, transmissions, brakes, axle assembly, vehicle trouble shooting, preventive maintenance and vehicle recovery operations.

Food Service Course

Six weeks of theory and practical exercises are devoted to the intricacies of food preparation within the military. Of the six week course, two weeks are devoted to on the job training. The 352 hours include meat cutting, pastry baking, small quantity cooking and garrison and field mess operations. According to an individual's ability and prior experience, he is awarded MOS 94B20.

Roast Beef—2d Brigade Style

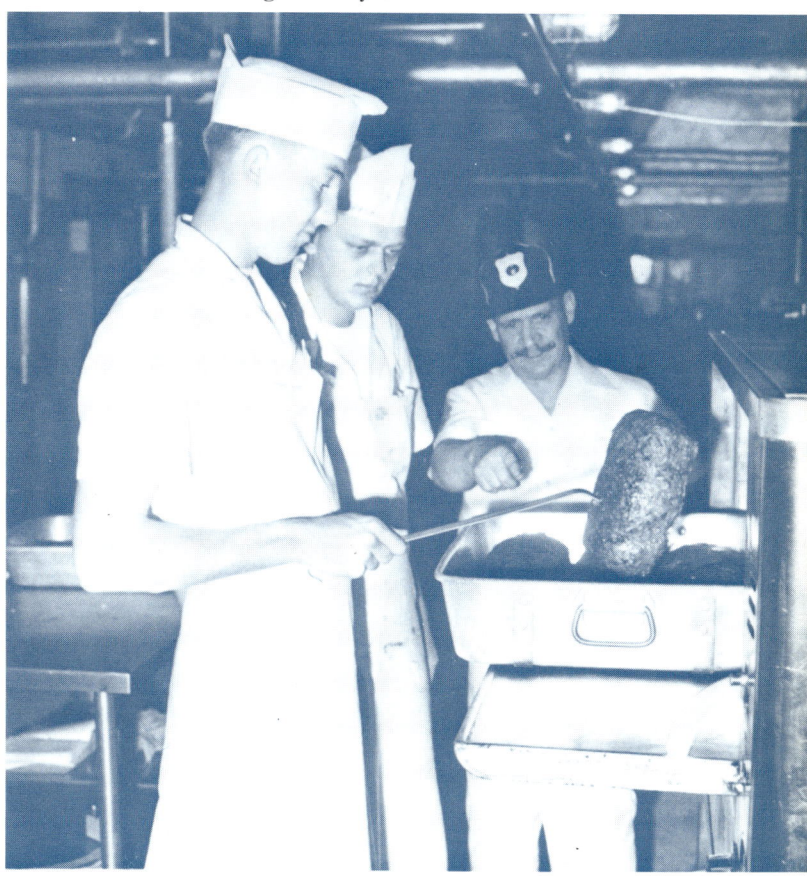

Armor Leaders Preparation Course

"Leadership" trainees receive instruction in the .50 caliber machine gun.

The First Army Noncommissioned Officers Academy offers this two-week course to basic training graduates who have demonstrated leadership ability. Final selection is based upon aptitude and intelligence level scores (on tests administered at the Reception Station), coupled with trainee "peer" ratings and the company commander's recommendation.

Trainees report for the course immediately following basic training and subsequently are assigned to USATCA's 1st Brigade for advanced armor or reconnaissance training. In the course they are taught leadership principles and duties as well as armor and reconnaissance subjects, and they are given positions as platoon guides and squad leaders in their advanced training companies.

THIRD TRAINING BRIGADE
ELEVENTH BATTALION

COL Robert E. Hayes
Brigade Commander

LTC Neil O. McCray
Battalion Commander

Commenced Training:
12 December 1966

COMPANY D

Completed Training:
17 February 1967

CPT James P. Ross
Company Commander

2LT Alden W. Whitmore, Jr.
Company Executive Officer

2LT Michael P. Gardner Training Officer	1SG Guy E. Emanuel First Sergeant	SFC Paul F. Jones Field Training NCO
SSG Burley J. Tipton Field Training NCO	PSG Frank J. Moultrie, Jr. First Platoon Sergeant	SSG Kenneth Anderson Asst. First Platoon Sergeant
PSG William E. Day Second Platoon Sergeant	SSG Richard V. Williams Third Platoon Sergeant	CPL Robert S. Hahn Asst. Third Platoon Sergeant

SSG Hubert C. Hicks
Fourth Platoon Sergeant

CPL Dennis G. Fleck
Asst. Fourth Platoon Sergeant

SSG Joe N. Ellis
Fifth Platoon Sergeant

CPL Larry A. Carby
Asst. Fifth Platoon Sergeant

SSG Charles E. Hall
Supply Sergeant

SSG Ralph E. Litman
Mess Steward

PFC John G. Silwa
Company Clerk

John L. Adams	Garey J. Ahler	Thomas J. Aldrich	Stanley H. Alger	Richard Amidon
Foy L. Amsden	Francis G. Andre	Calvin W. Austin	Richard C. Azzarella	David C. Bagley
Stephen P. Baich	Jeffrey Bain	Dennis A. Baker	Albert S. Bangs	C. A. Bartkowski, Jr.
Edward J. Beauchaine	Robert W. Becroft	Wayne E. Berry	Mak L. Blair	Jimmy V. Bombard

Michael Bond	James H. Bouldin, Jr.	Billy Boyd	Robert S. Bradbury, Jr.	William M. Brennan
Warren G. Brown	James A. Bryant	Harold Buchner	Joseph Bunacci	Alan W. Burnett
Neil L. Butler	John A. Butts	Ralph L. Calabrese	Albert Campione	William C. Carlson
James E. Carney, Jr.	Joseph L. Carr	Robert L. Carroccetto	Michael A. Caschera	Alfred A. Casella

Donald Cass	Gary J. Cassiol	Donald L. Chase	Richard J. Chornopyski	Charles A. Cline
Gary J. Compton	Mickle A. Comstock	William Conopka	John G. Conover	H. E. Constatine
Thomas E. Cornell	Michael T. Crotty	Michael L. Coyle	Joseph F. De Soreo	David J. DeWallace
Paul Defreest	Paul Degener	Thomas P. Delany	Daniel R. Dillenburg	Paul Dodge

Daniel J. Donahue	James J. Donato	Parris Duff	Albert A. Dumont	Roosevelt Dunn, Jr.
Steven F. Durgin	Forest Durkee	Robert P. Ego	Harvey S. Elowitch	Donald C. Faureau
Walter Fitz	Joseph C. Formichelli	Robert C. Forquette	Thomas Fatcheric	Howard E. Fowler
Steven A. Gaykan, Jr.	Norman H. Gebo	Robert L. Gehling	David Goldman	Charles L. Goldstein

Stanley H. Gottlieb	Walter L. Green	Michael Halas	James Hall	Kenneth J. Hanning
Rober B. Hansen	Harlan F. Haven	Theodore B. Henderson	Kenneth J. Herr	Robert Horne
James S. Horvath	Daniel R. Hourahan	Gustu J. Hufland, Jr.	Ronald Hutton	Wally C. Jandoli
James R. Jimenez	James B. Jones	Wilford G. Kaenzig	David L. Kaus	Douglas S. Kennedy

Christian Klaiber	Lawrence Korczykowski	Adam Kreuter, III	David W. Lagram	Gerald Lefson
Andrew Lehtomem	Francis Leonard	Frank Lombino	Carl J. Lorenzo	Robert J. Lounello
Carl J. Lupoli	Robert R. Lynch	Joel Marcus	Robert F. Marro	Marshall W. Mays
Robert J. McCafrey	Michael T. McCourt	Haze A. McDougal, III	Frederick H. McDougal	Kevin W. McGrath

David W. McKee	Roderick O. McLeod	Richard A. McQueen	Mervin Marx	 Michael Marchese
James Michos	William A. Miller	Peter J. Montalbamo	James E. Moore	 Gary F. Mousseau
 Thomas E. Mozinco	 Carmelo F. Munafo	 Robert F. Murdock, Jr.	 Thomas C. Myers	 Rafael M. Nieves
 Michael P. Notery	 John J. Nortz	 John A. O'Rourke	 Robert A. Orlando	 John H. Ornberg

George Pachter	Louis Palermo	Lewis J. Palumbo	Ronnie J. Parent	Arthur Patch
Nicholis A. Paul	Joseph Pelham, Jr.	Ivan V. Persic	George Phillips	Jophis A. Picarrello
Roy E. Pierce	David S. Porter	Michael A. Primicerio	George E. Razoyk	Robert L. Richardson
Dustan M. Rine	Stephen J. Rosinski	Raymond J. Roy	Robert W. Roy	Williams Rutski

Jerry A. Salter	Daniel Salvbtore	Thomas R. Scanlon	Ronald G. Schauwecker	Josef L. Schmidt
Elrico C. Seymour	John L. Shepard, Jr.	William L. Simonson	Gregory E. Sinibaldi	Kenneth A. Skitt
John M. Sleasman	Glendon Smith	Jeffrey P. Smith	Ralph D. Smith	Thomas H. Sprague
George J. St. Cyr	Dwayne Stanley	John J. Starkey	Bruce A. Stokes	Gary Stotz

Michael Swieczkowski	Ronald Tefft	Patrick F. Tierney, Jr.	Mati Toom	William J. Toth
Richard P. Toy	John H. Tripp	William Troller	Paul Tunis	Emmett Vinson
William Walsh	Thomas F. Ward	Earnest B. Ward	John Washwell	Morris Waters
 Stephen R. Watrous	 Richard H. Weckerly	 Gerald R. Weibly	 David W. Westley	 Richard L. Wighard

Albinc Wilcenski  Richard M. Williams  Terrance Woodfield  Kevin R. Wyman  Harry P. Yelle

Robert J. Zabrowski  David L. Zodl

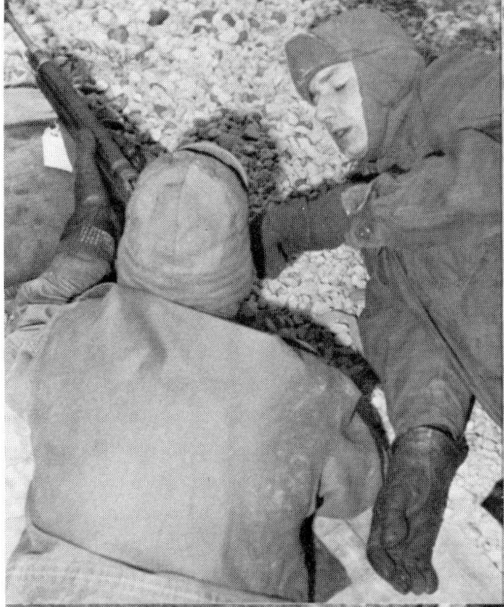
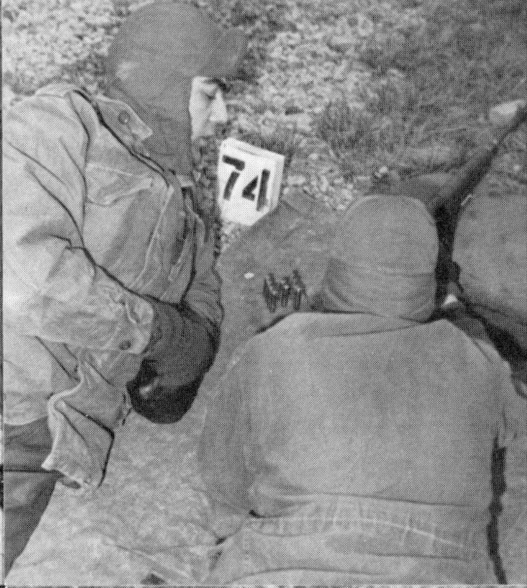
74
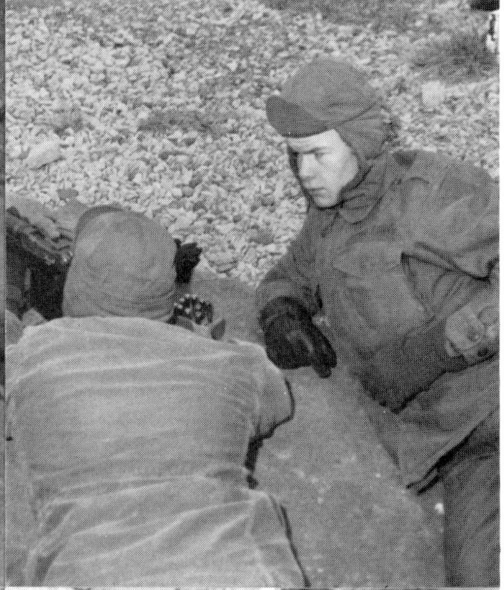
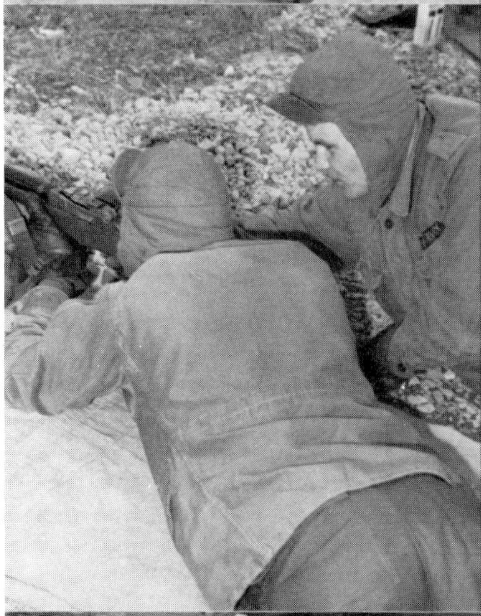
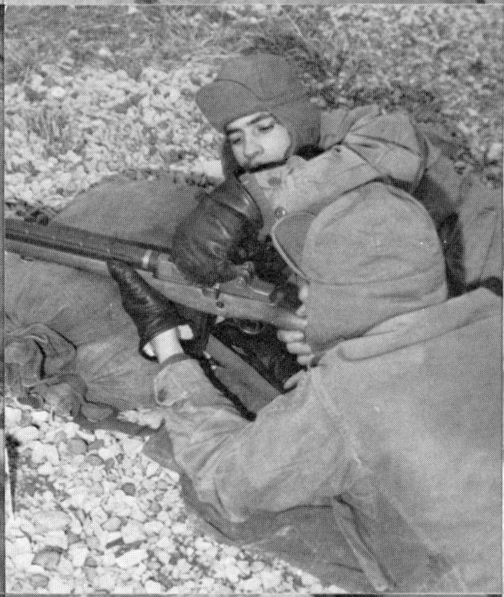
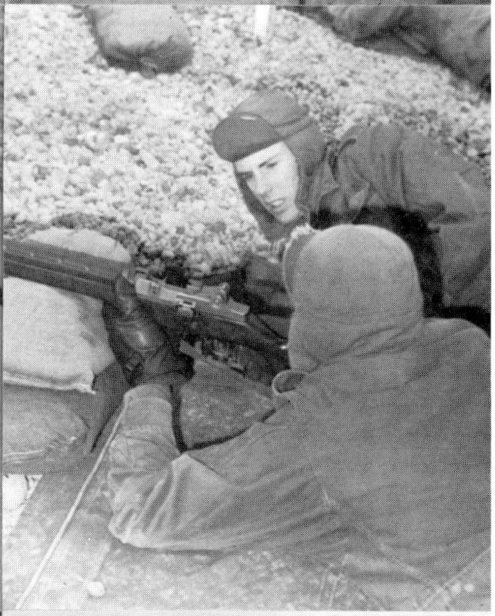
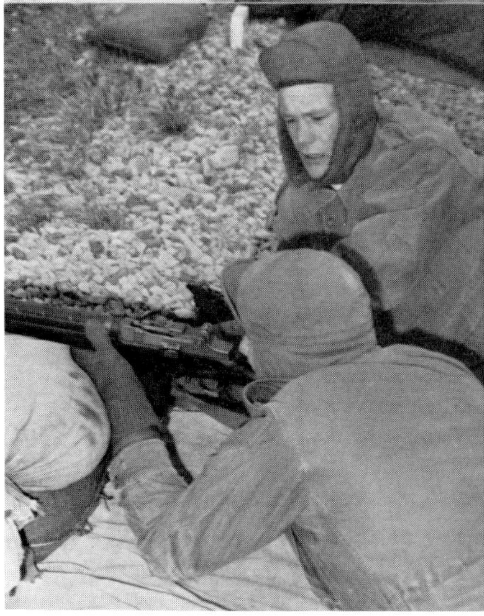
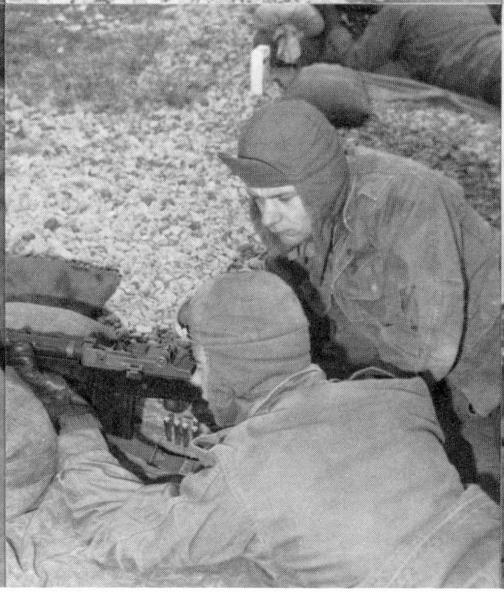
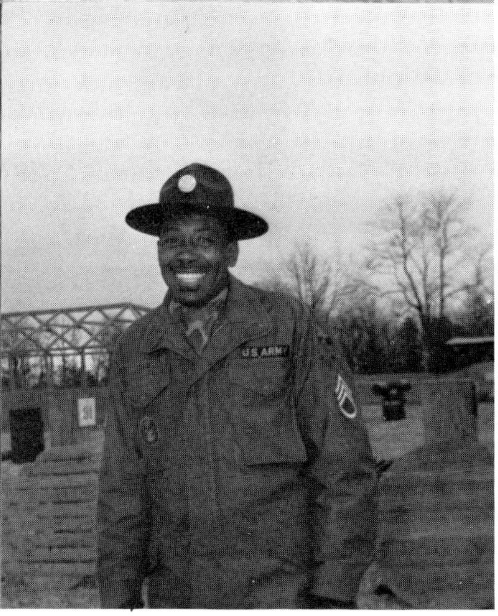
U.S. ARMY

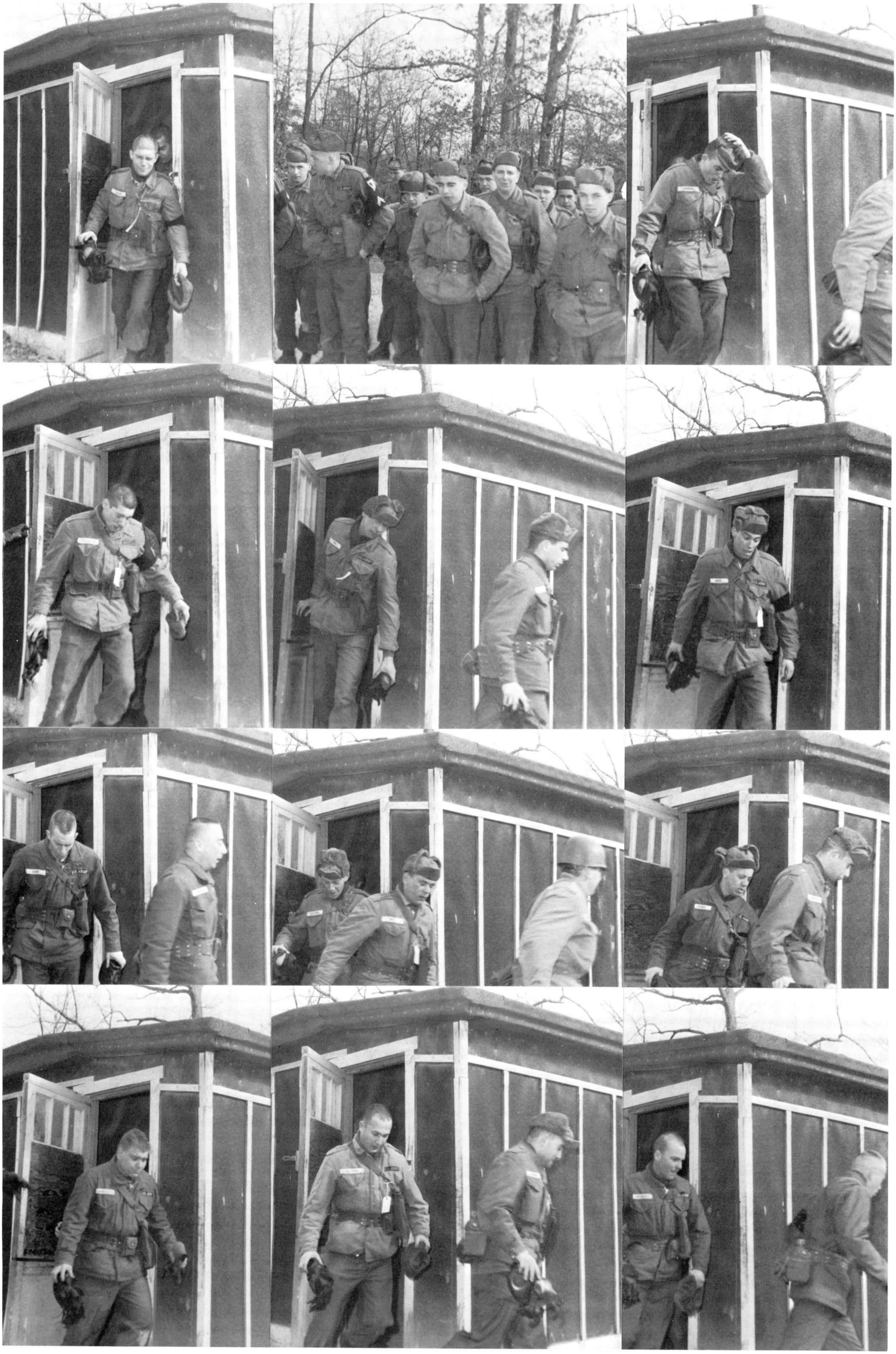

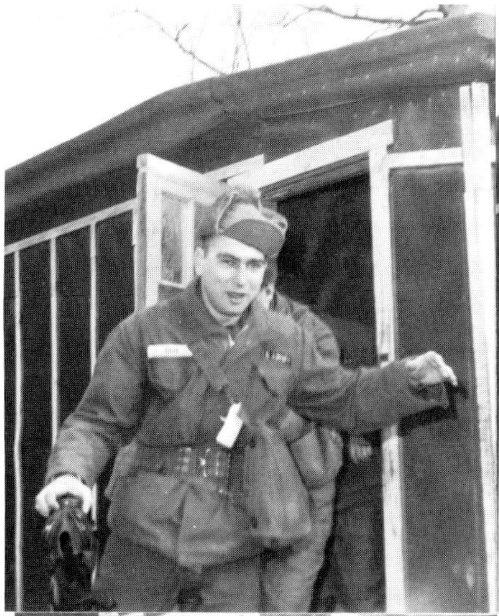
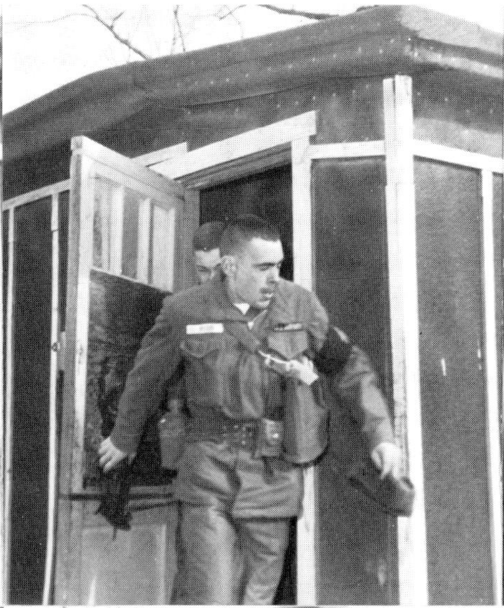
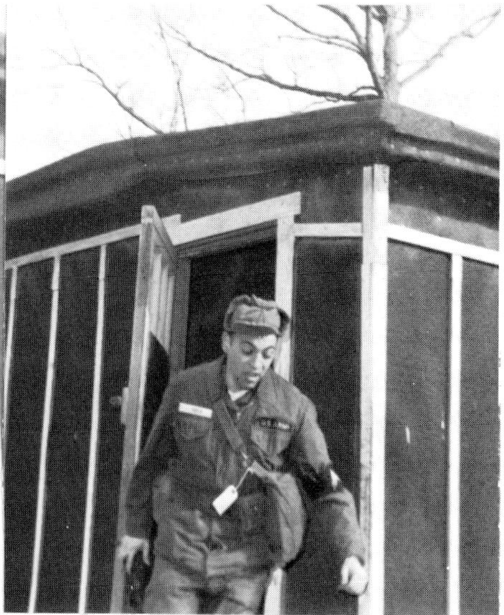
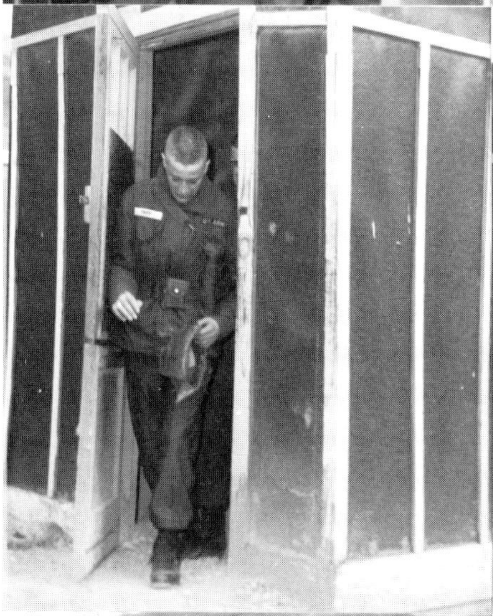
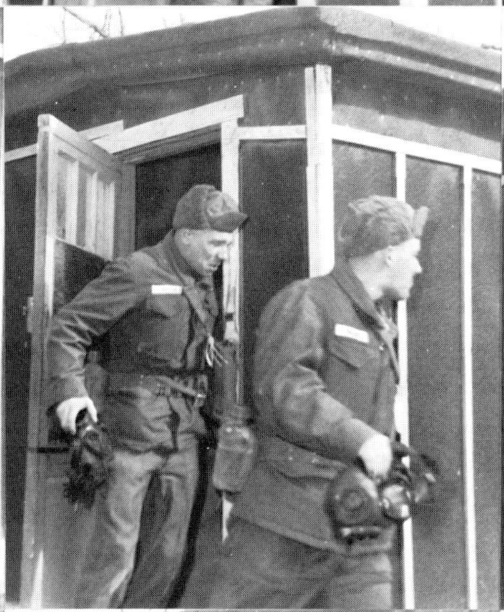
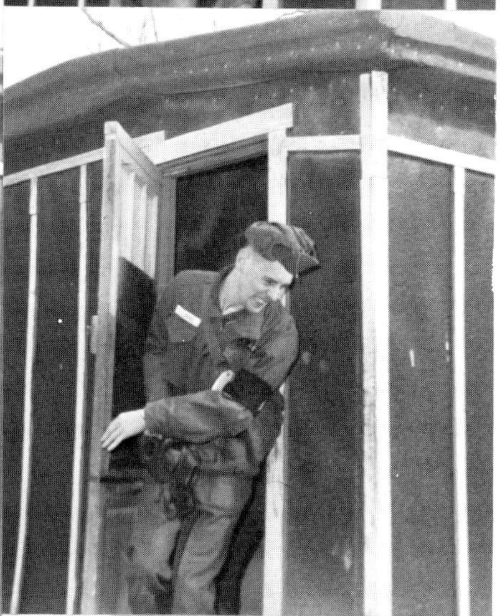
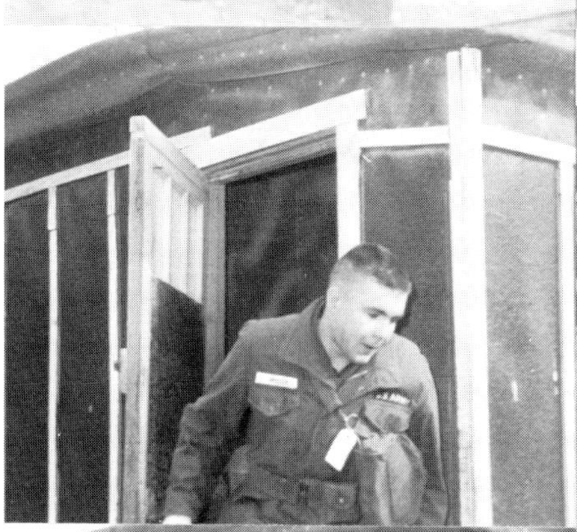
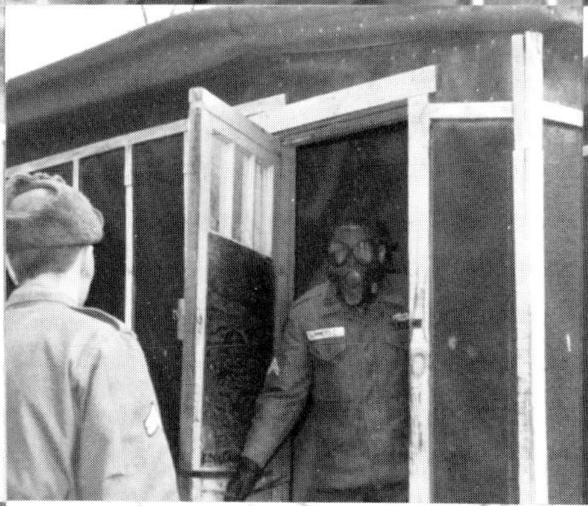
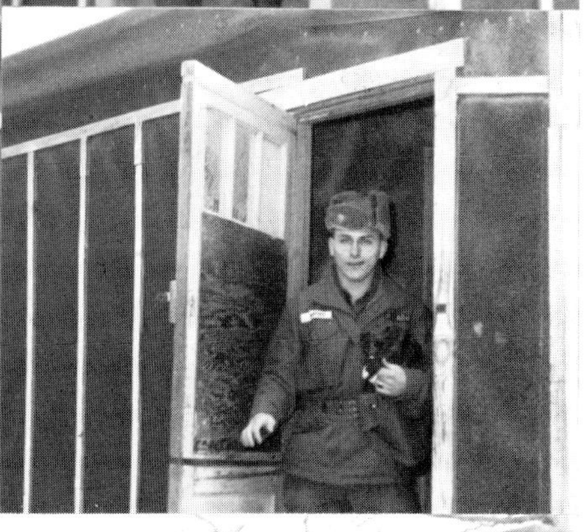
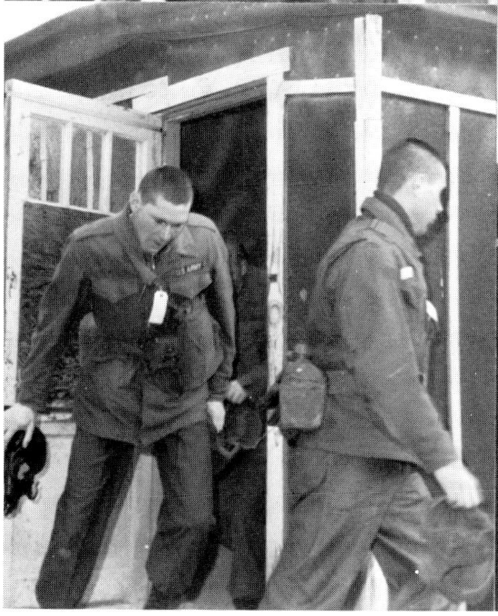
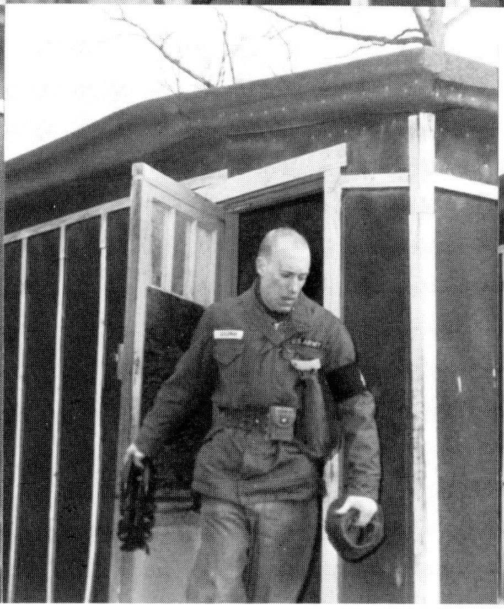
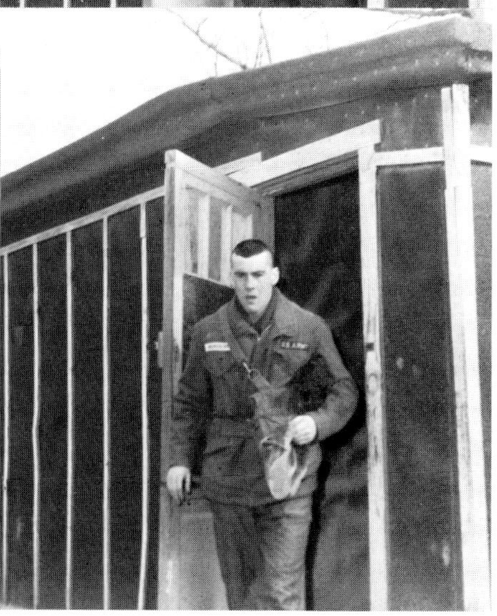

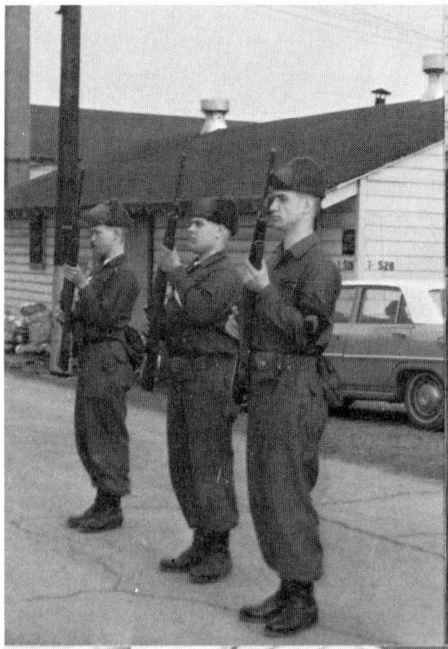
528
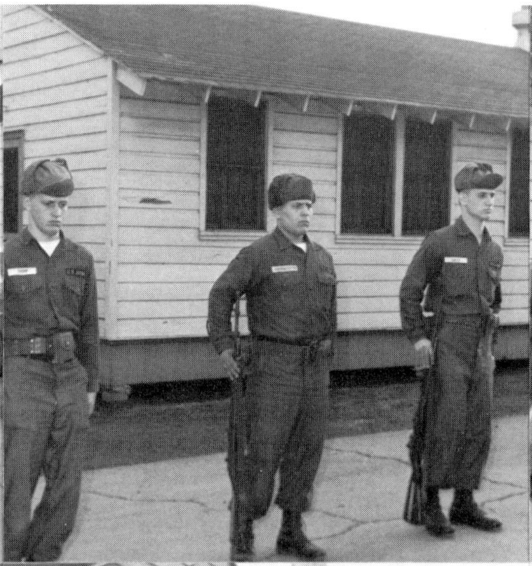
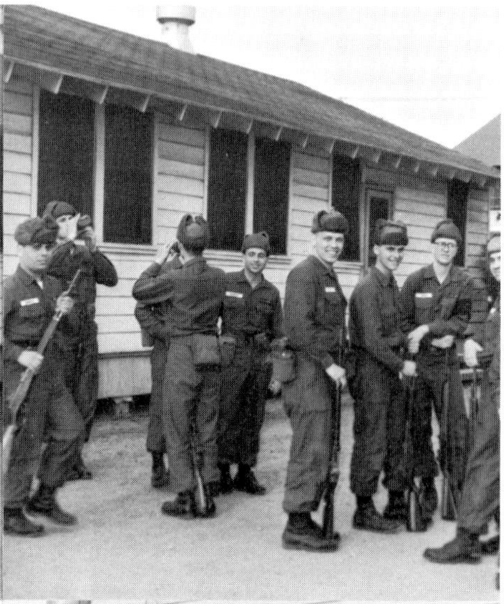
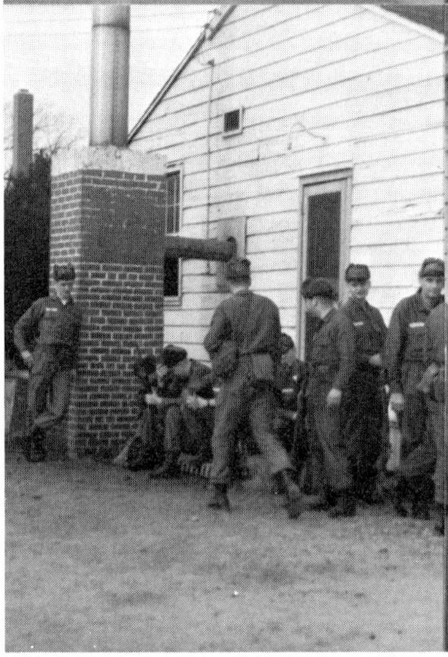
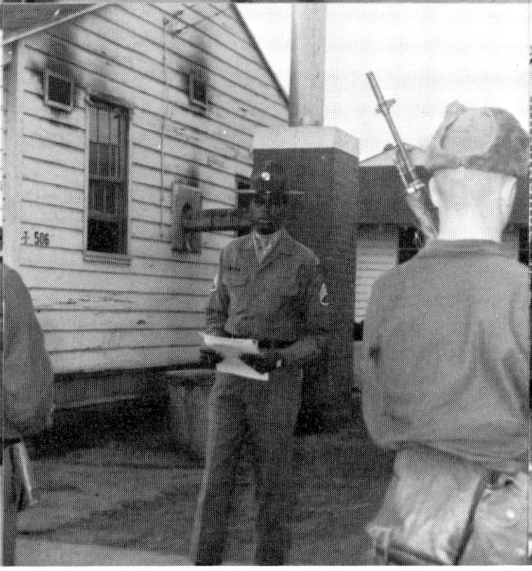
506
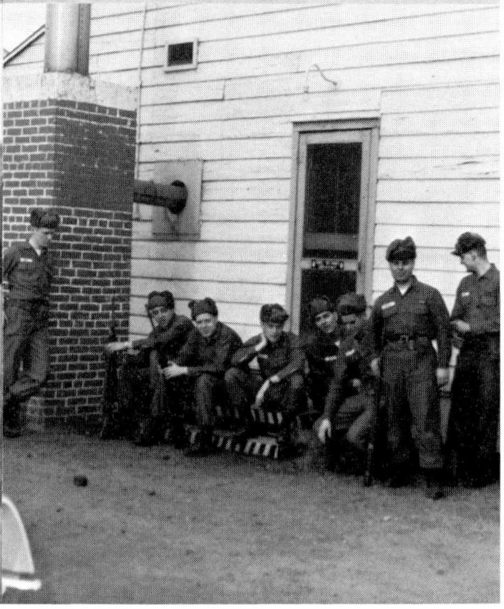
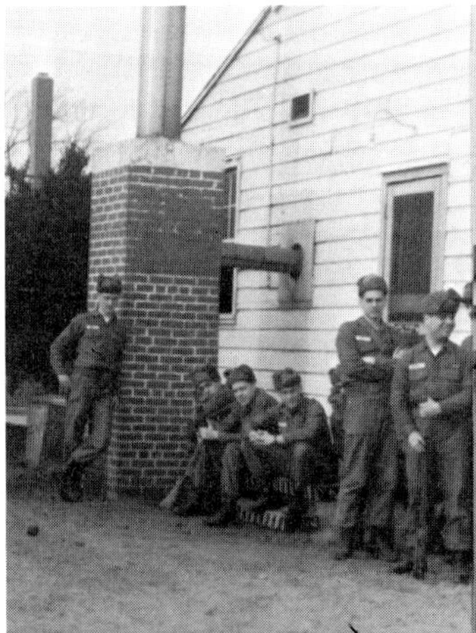
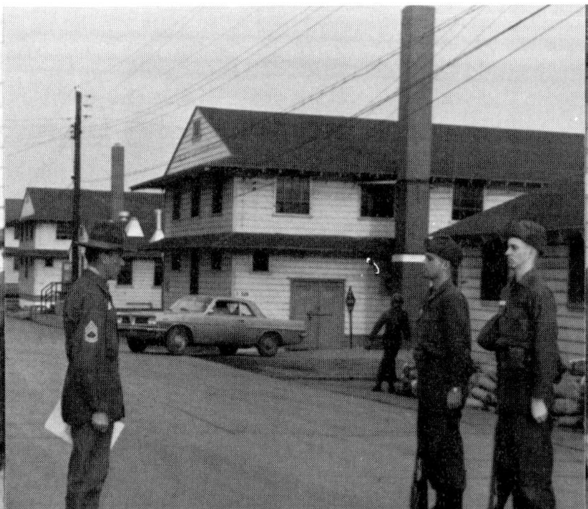
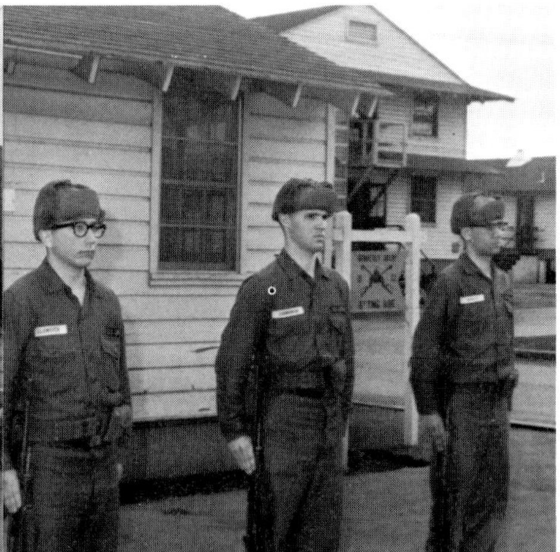

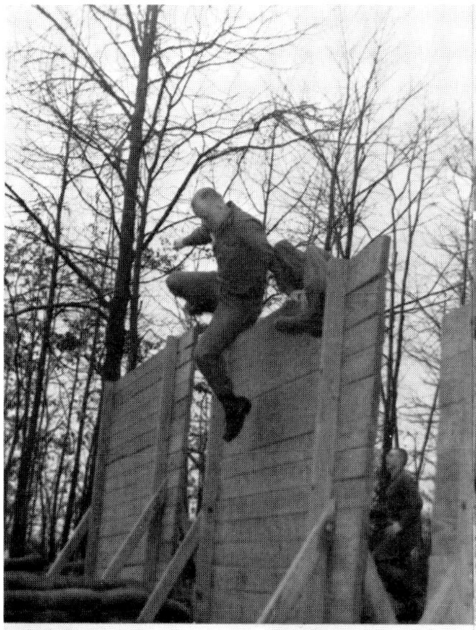
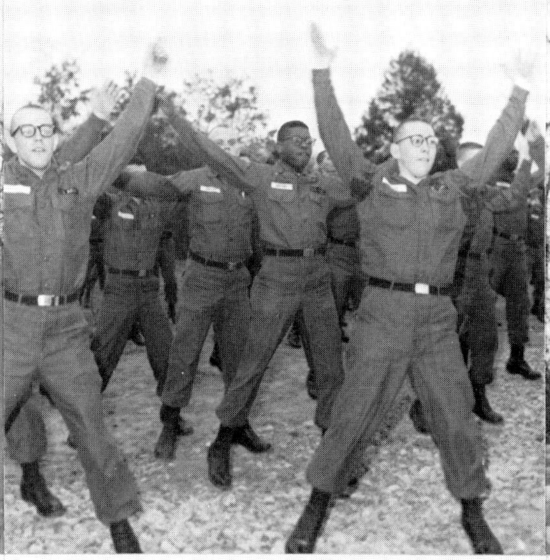
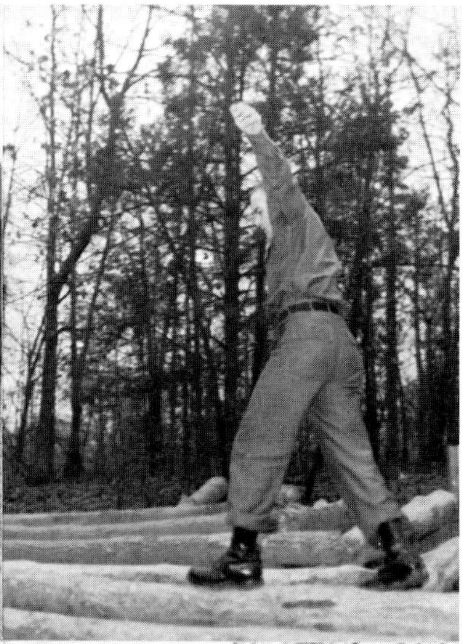
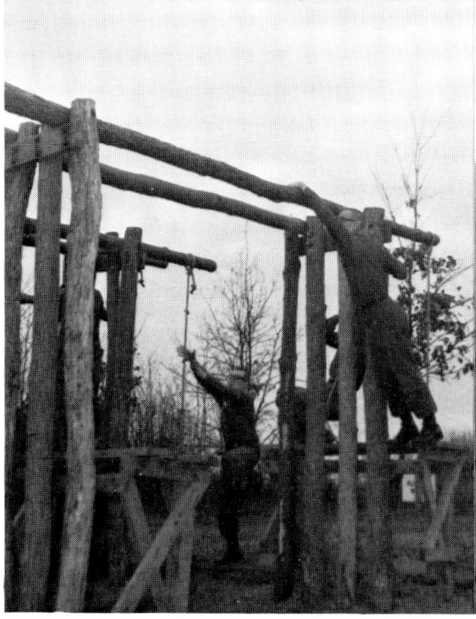
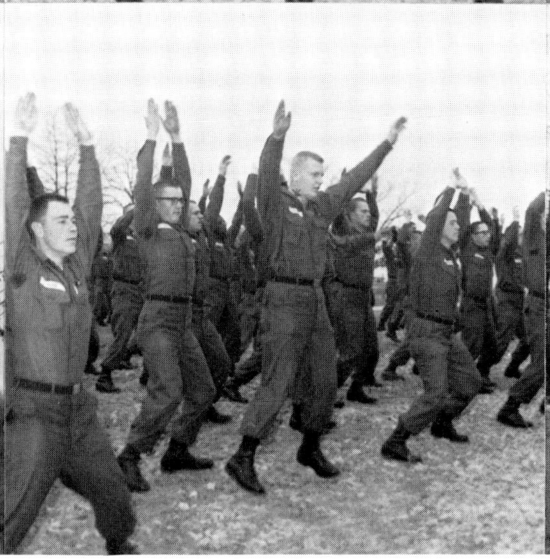
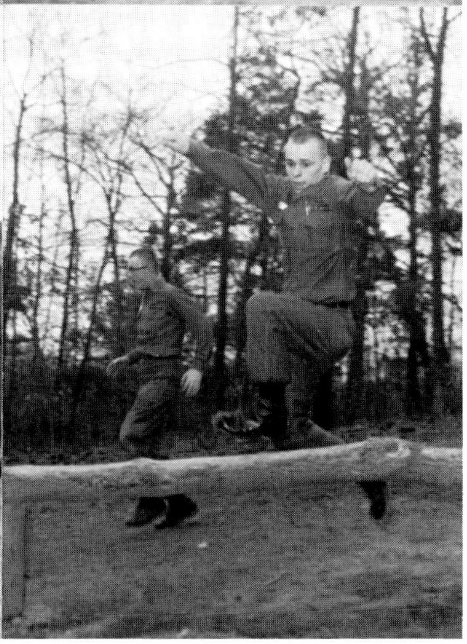
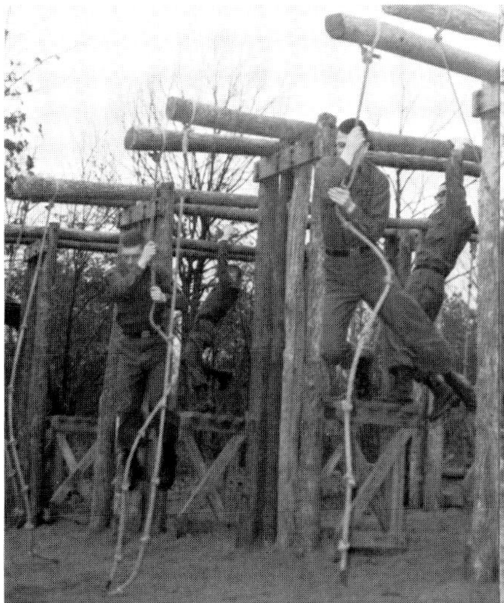
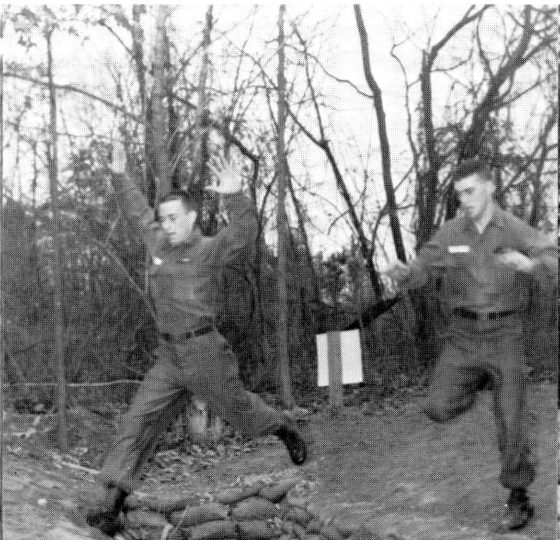
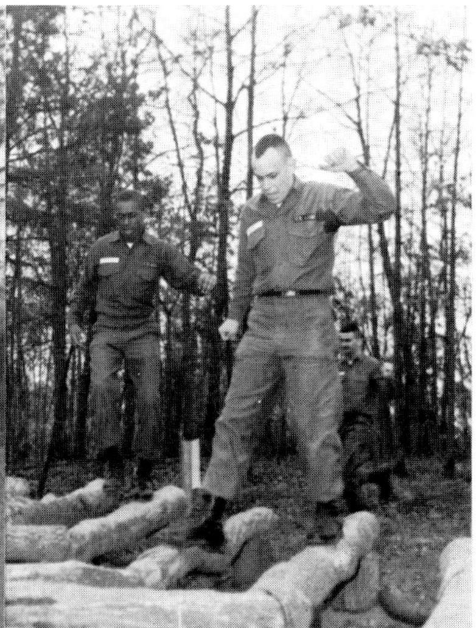

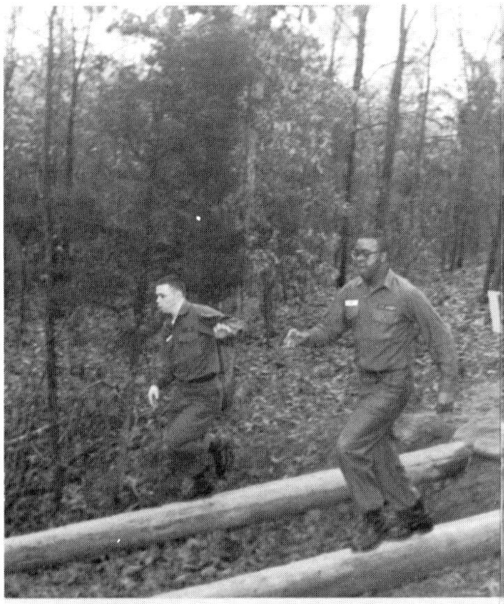
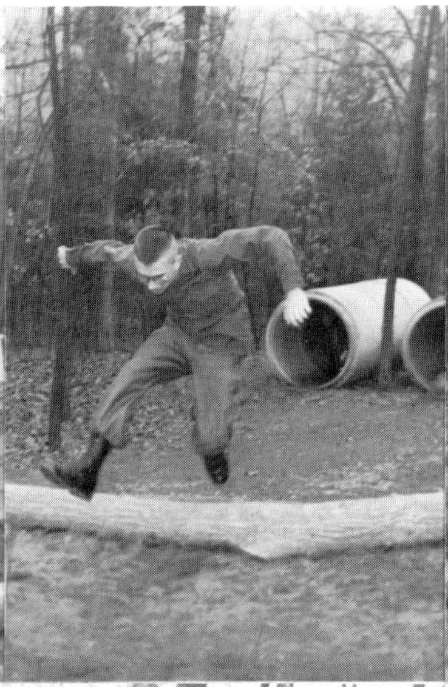
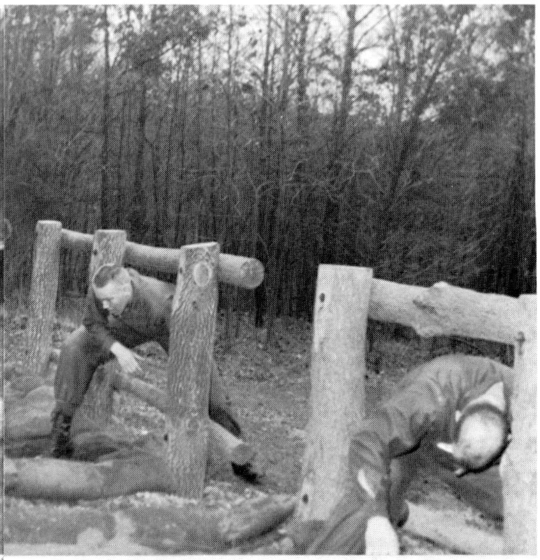
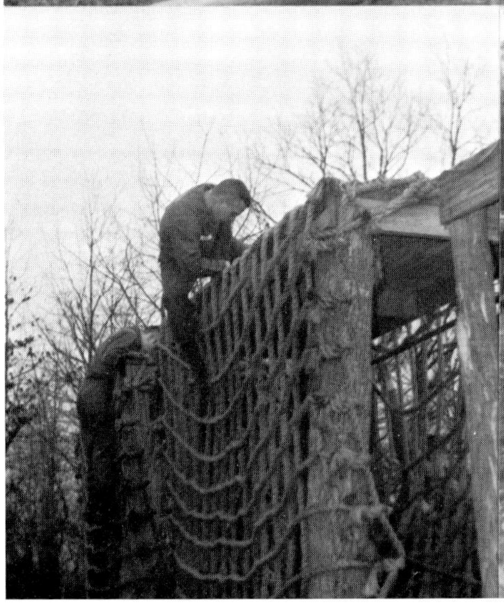
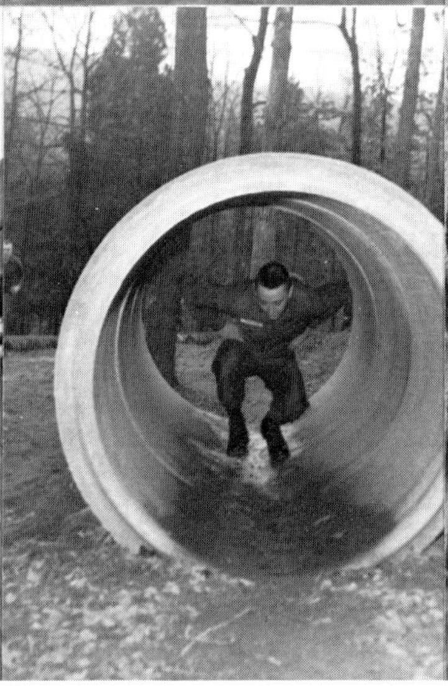
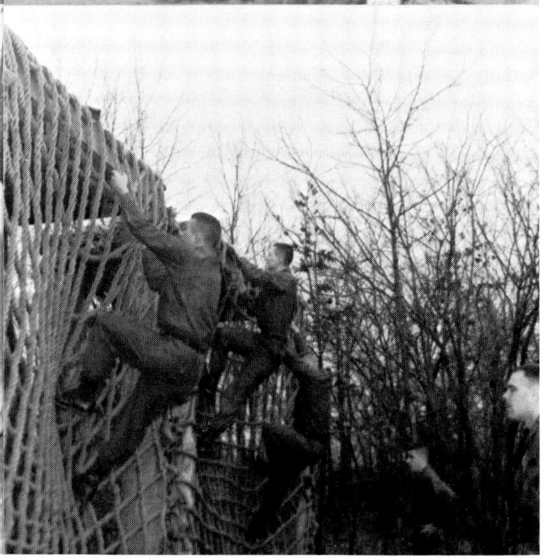
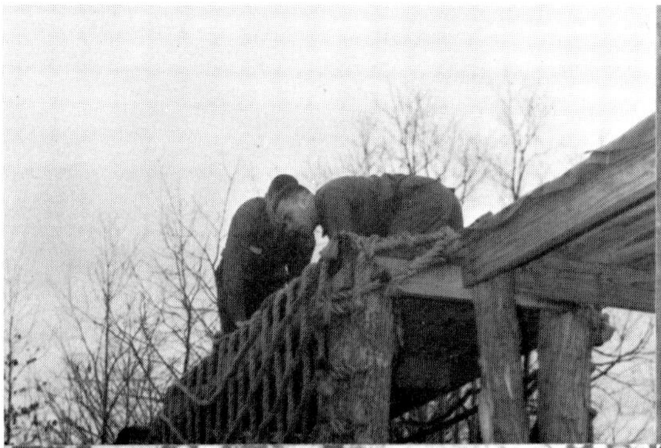
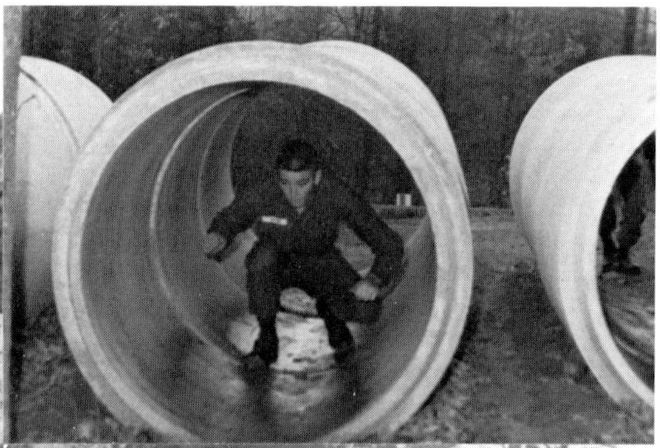
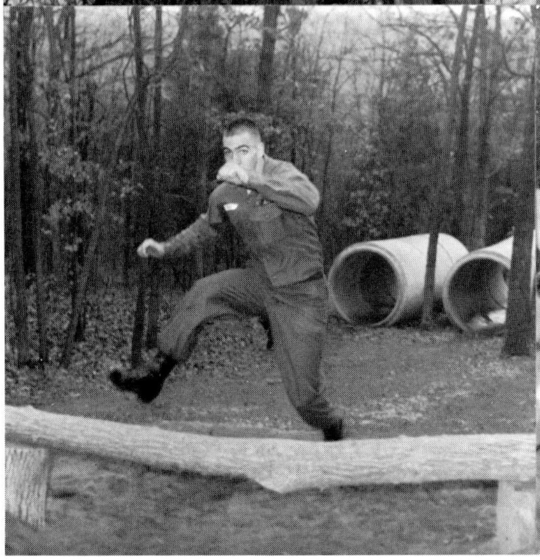
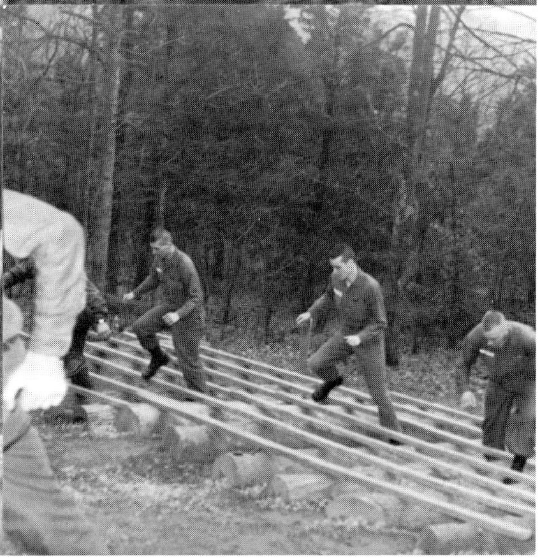

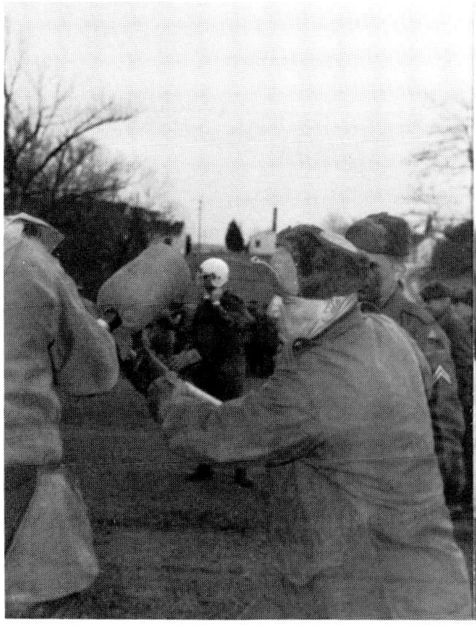
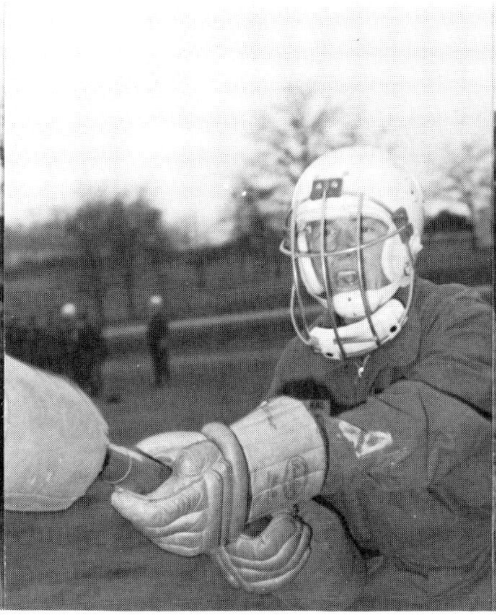
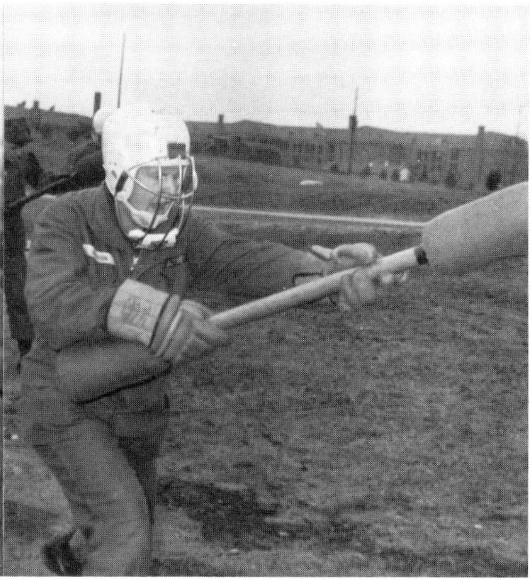
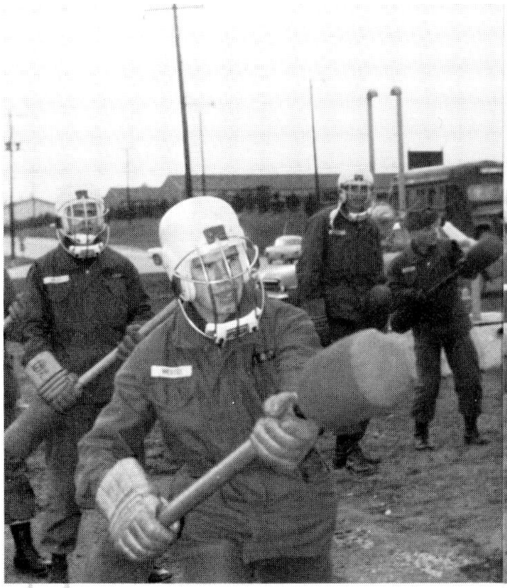
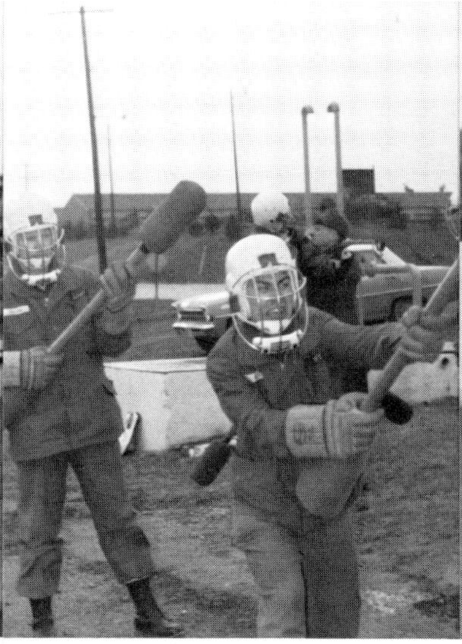
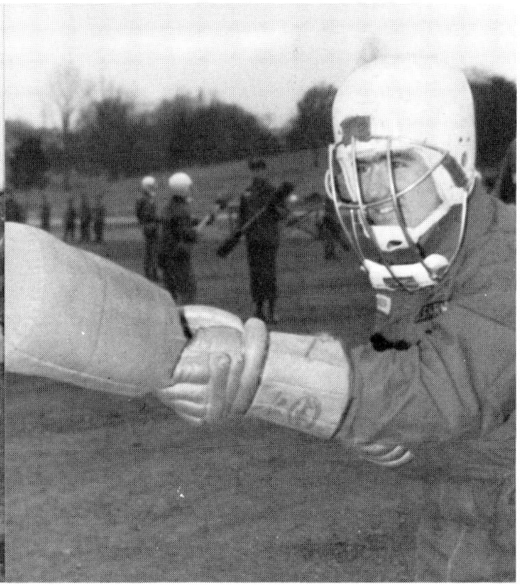
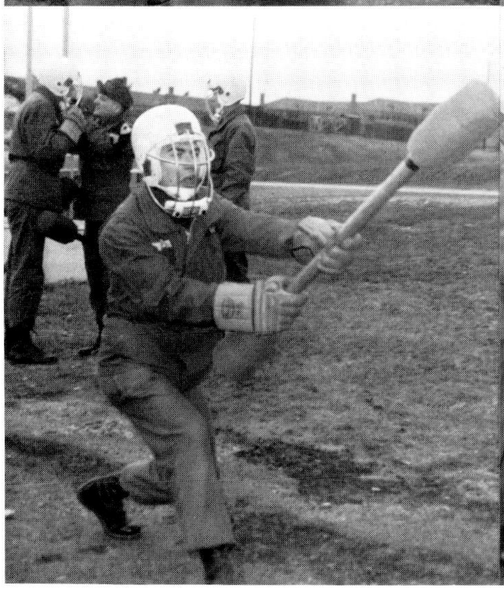
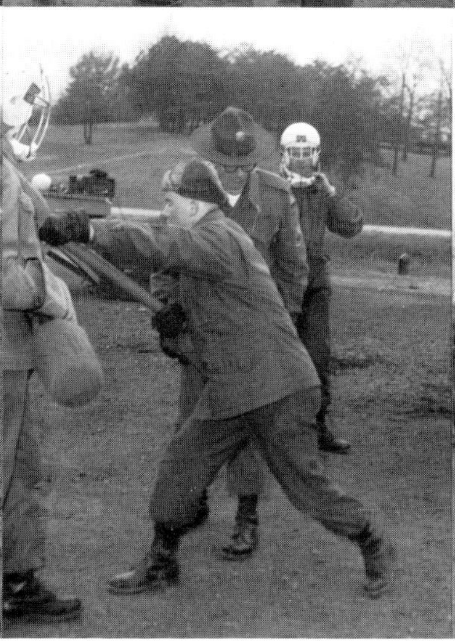
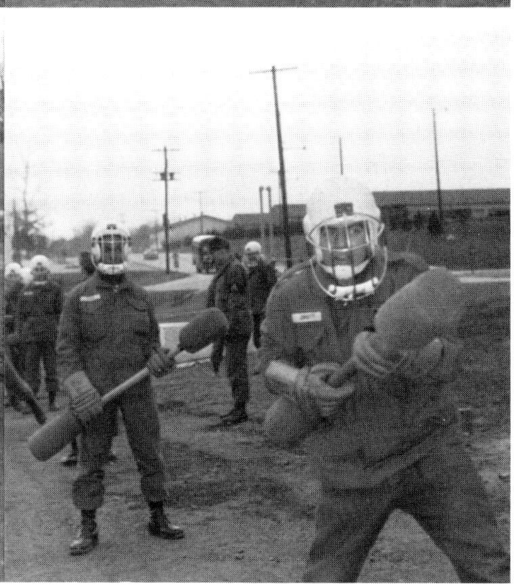

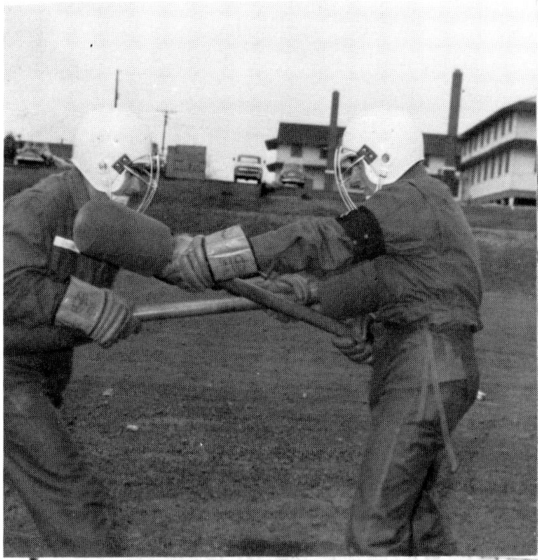
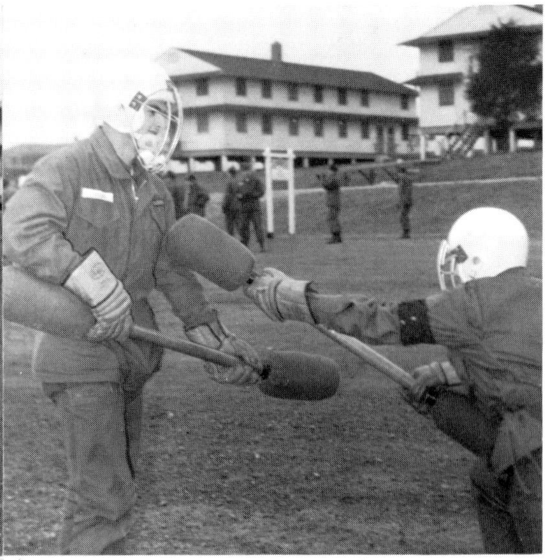
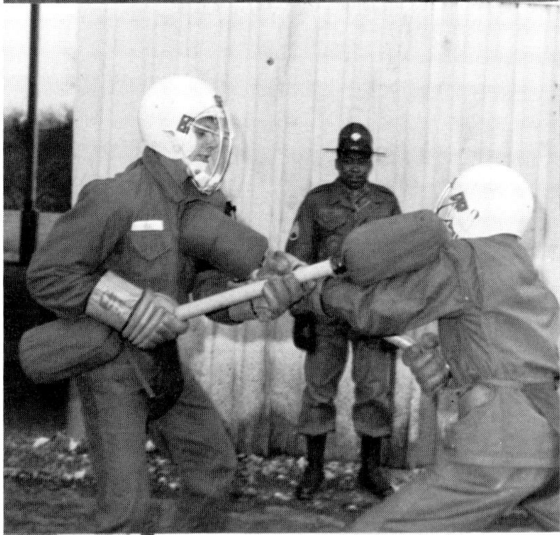
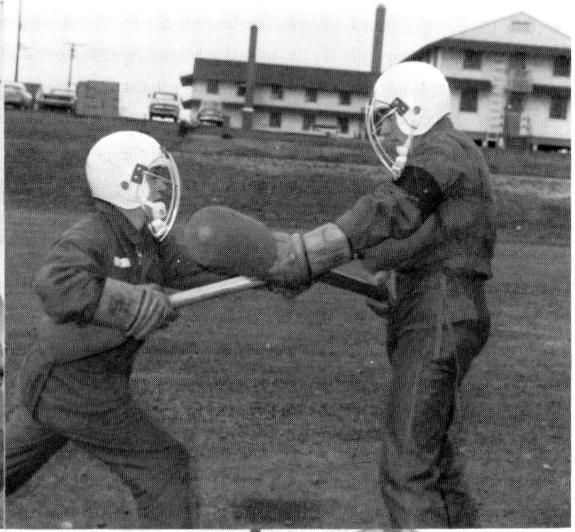
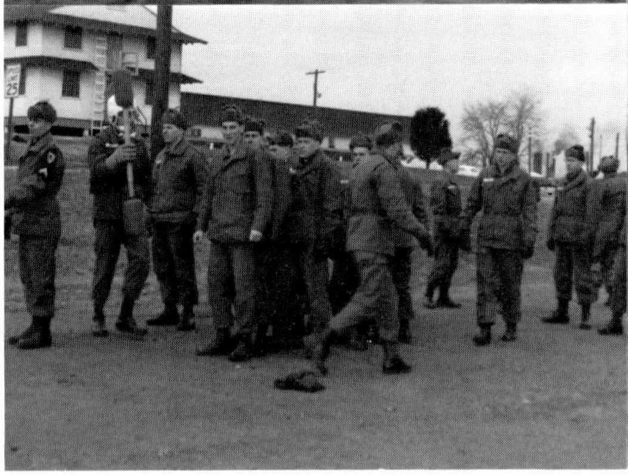
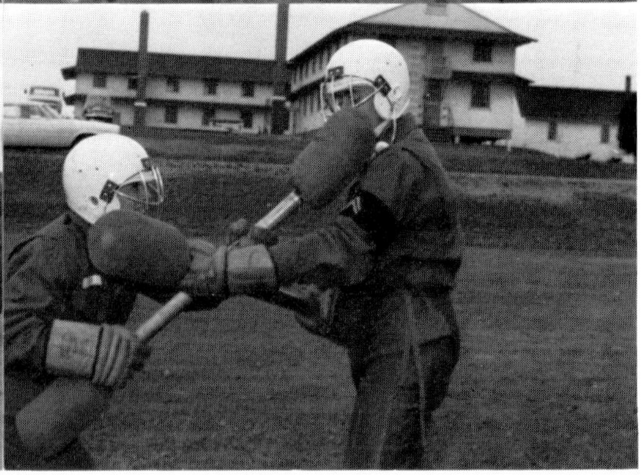
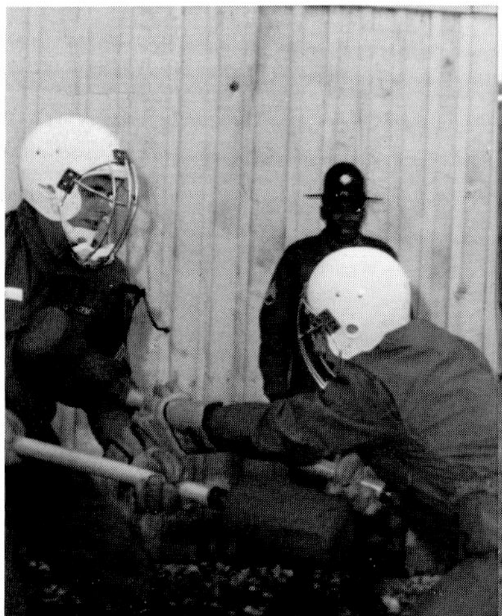
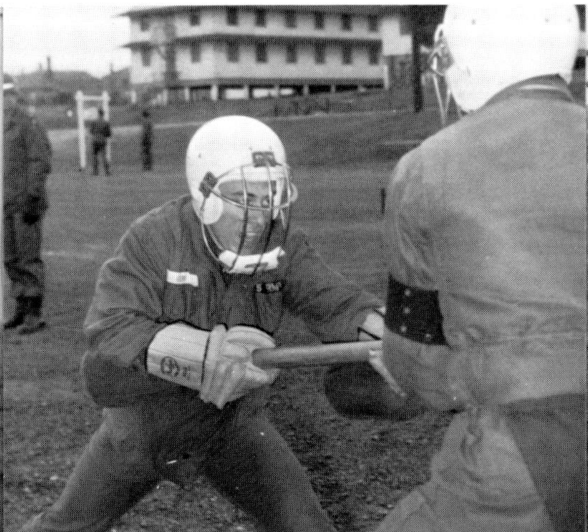
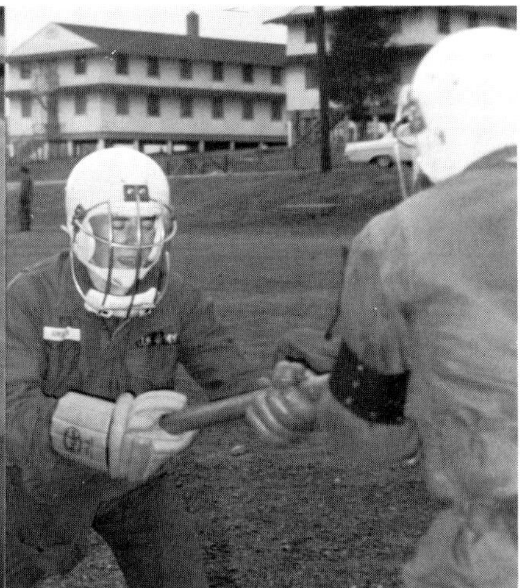

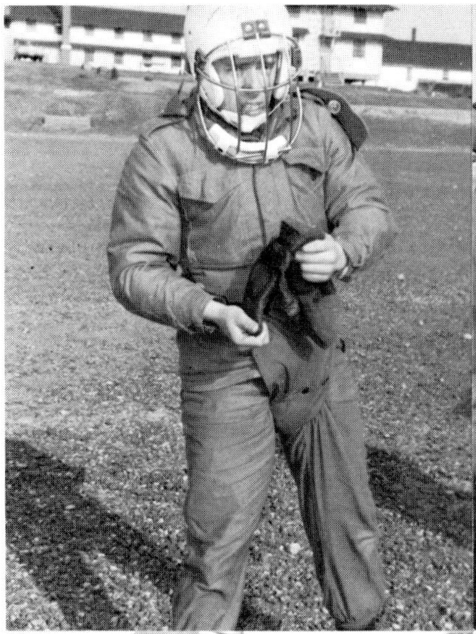
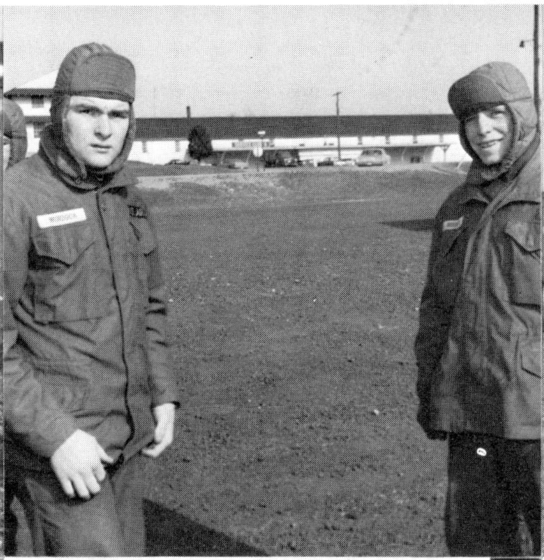
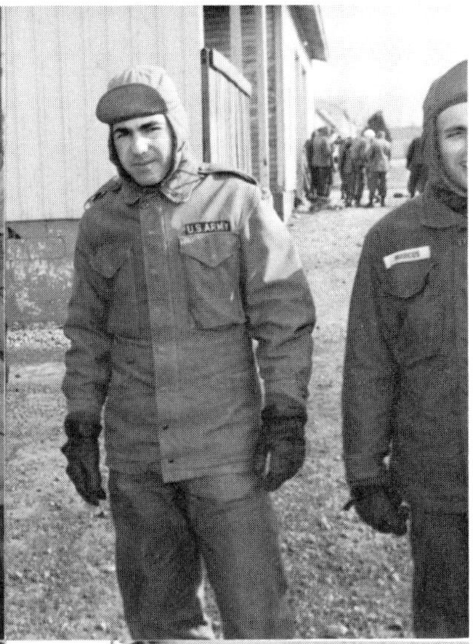
U.S. ARMY
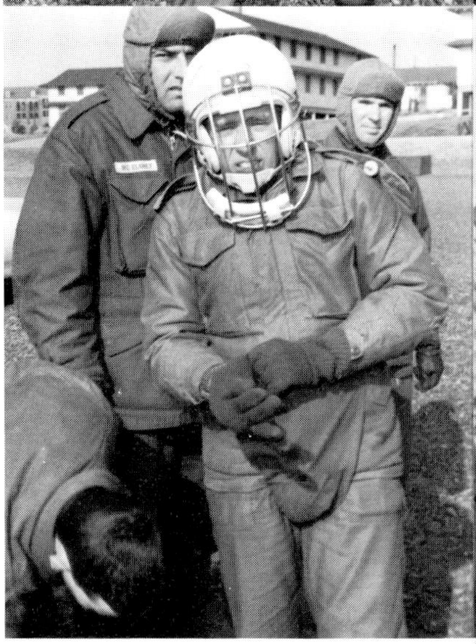
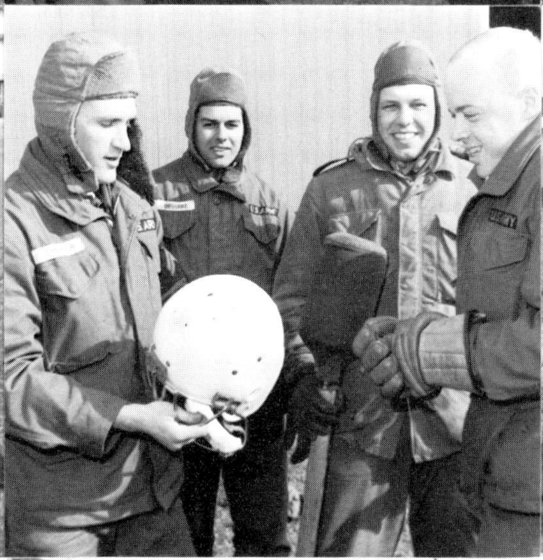
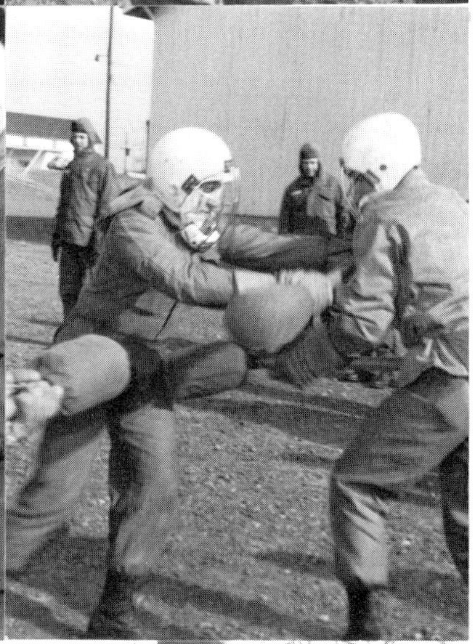
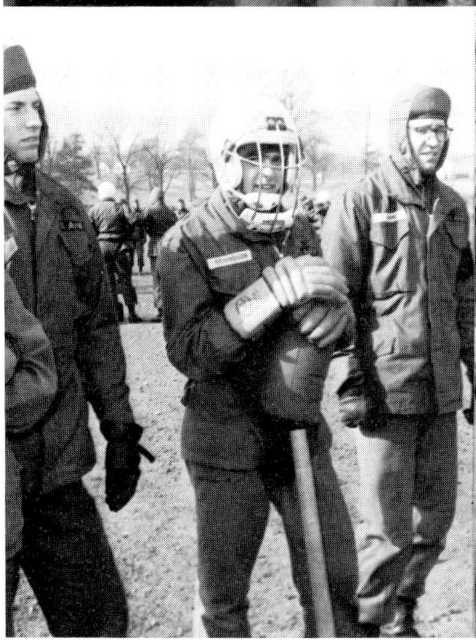
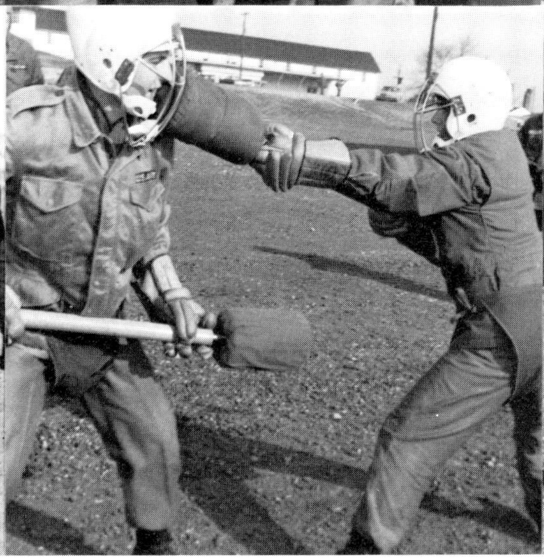
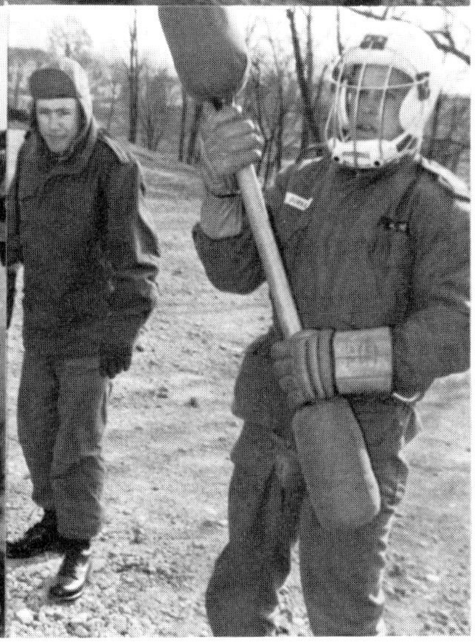

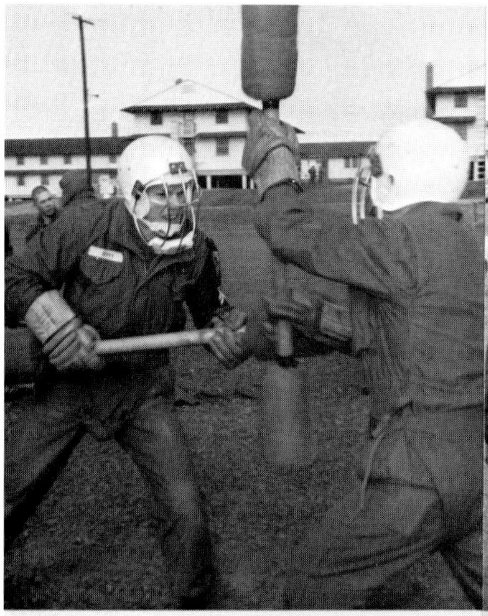

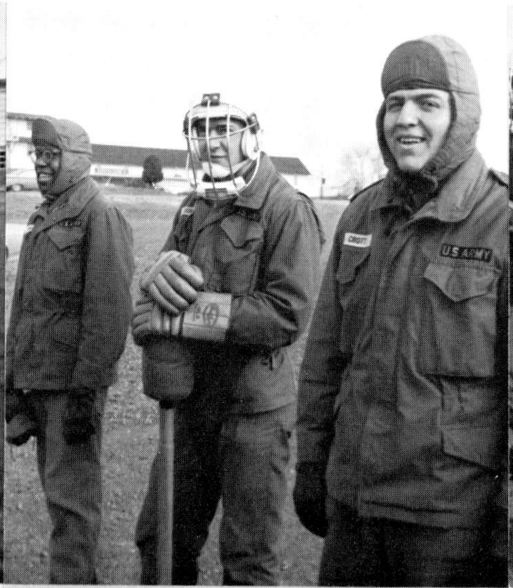
U.S. ARMY

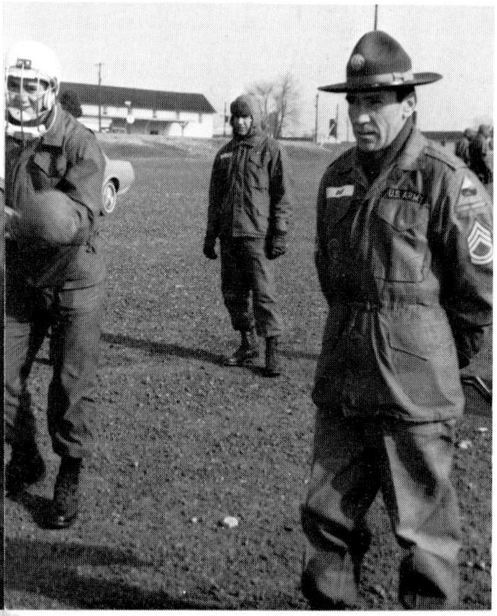
U.S. ARMY

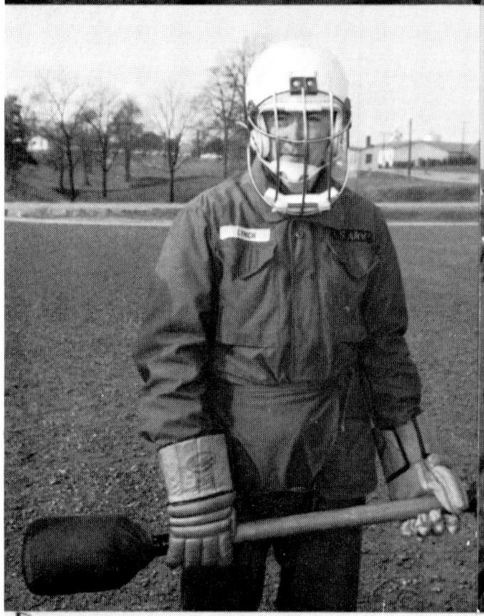
U.S. ARMY

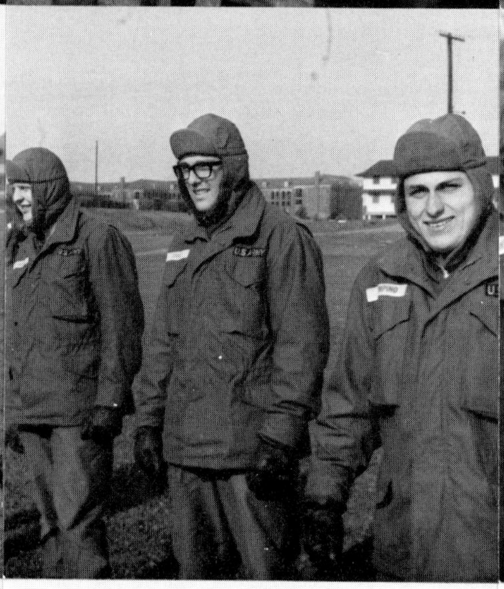

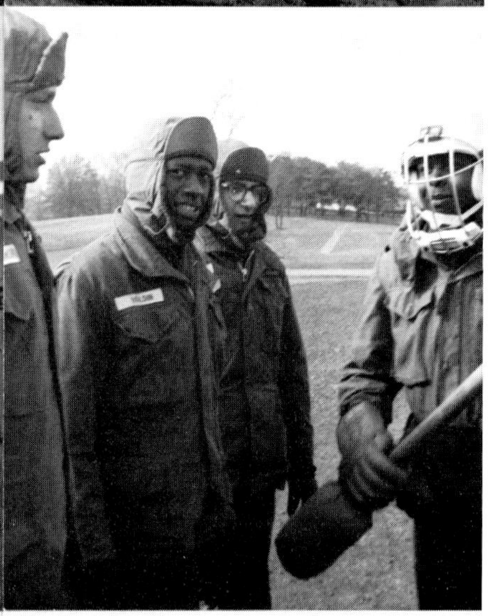

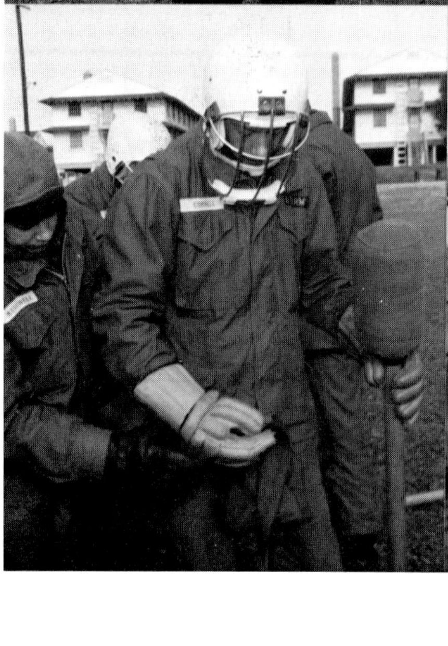

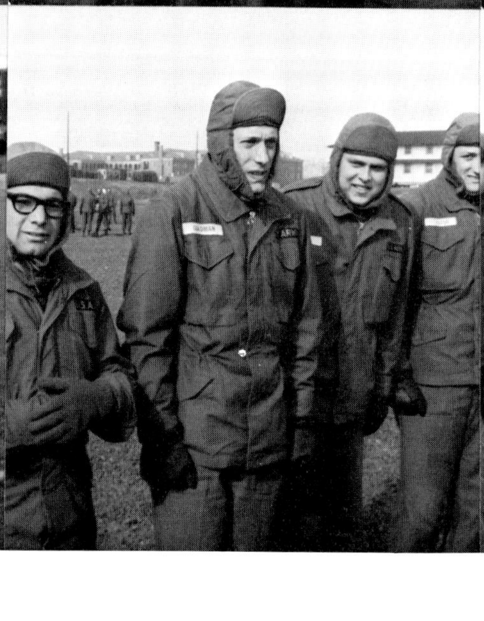

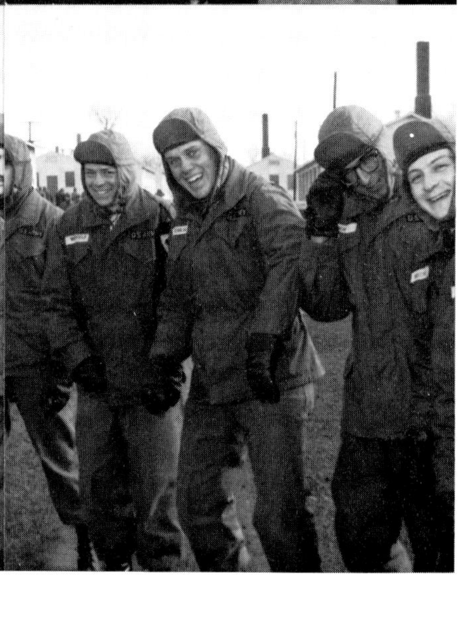

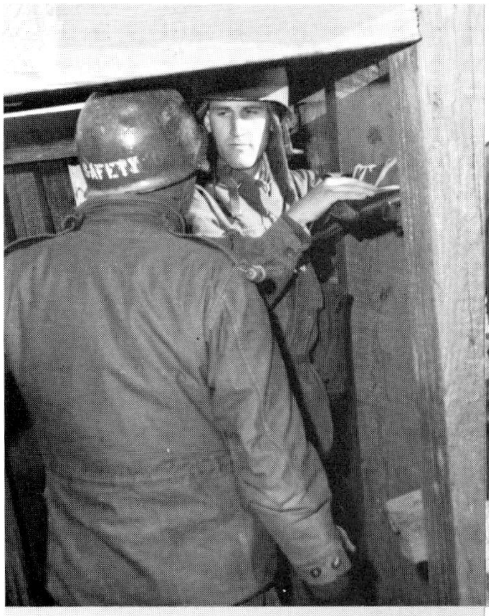
SAFETY

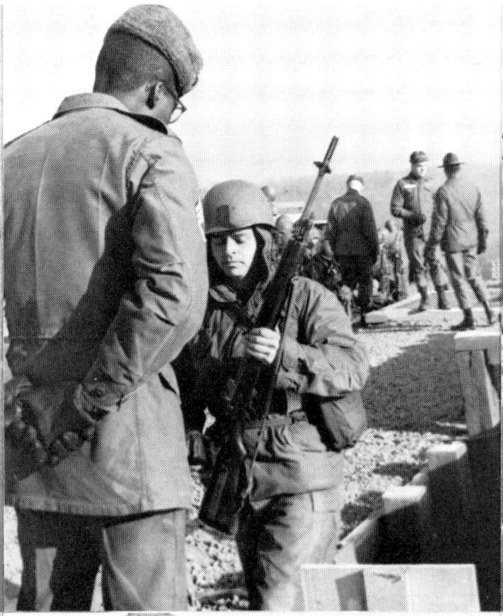

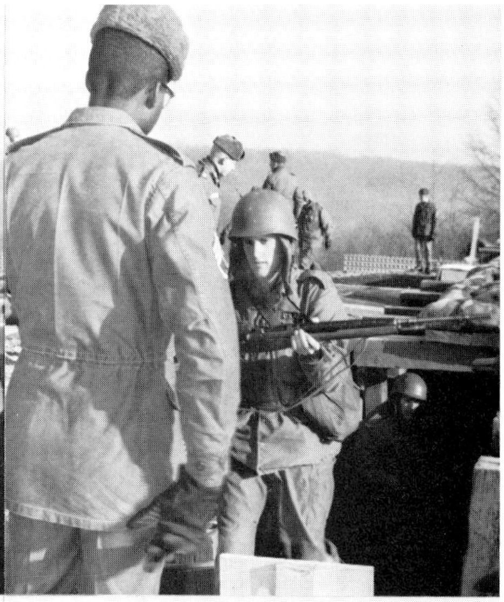

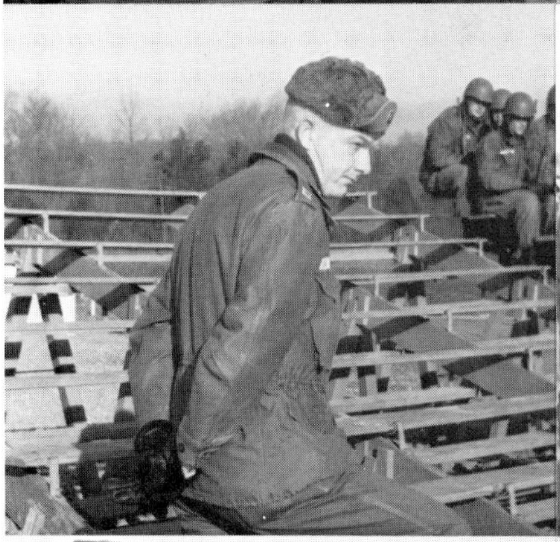

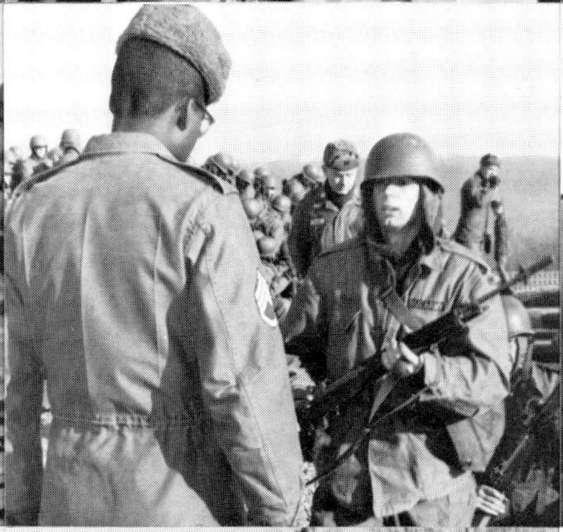

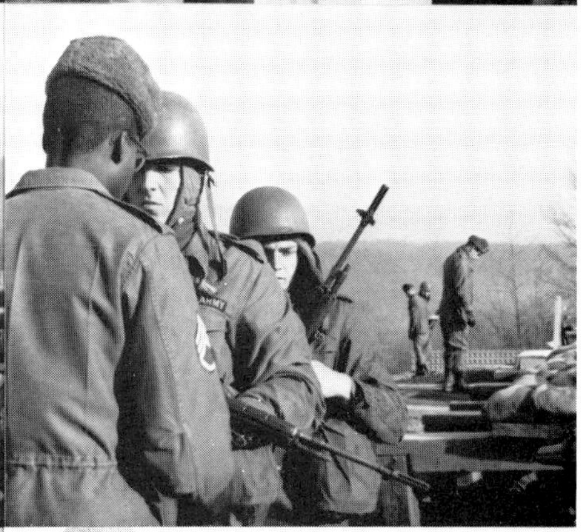

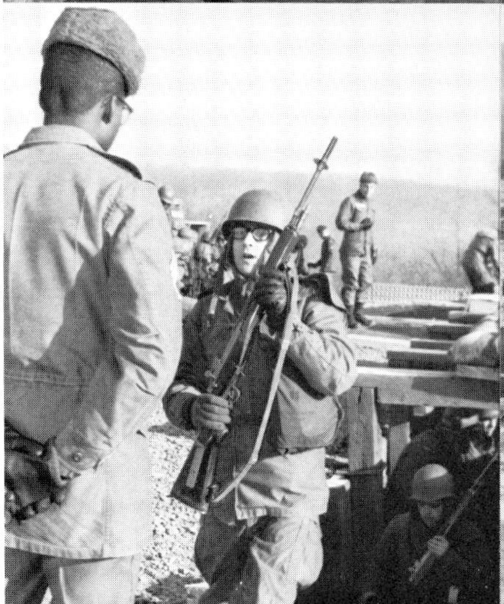

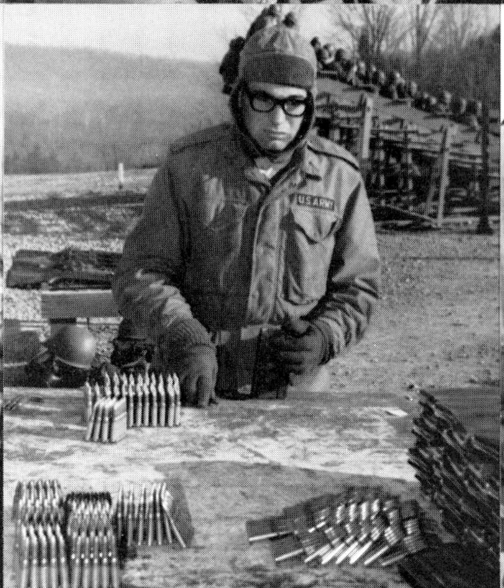

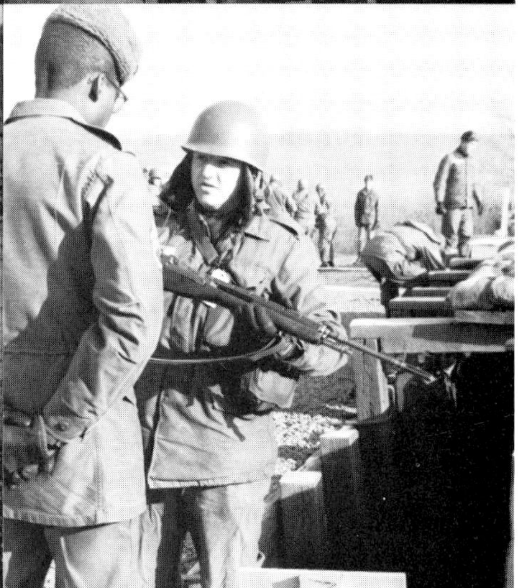

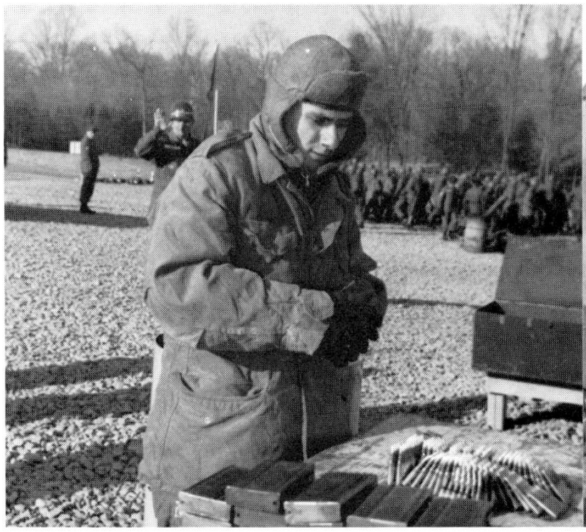

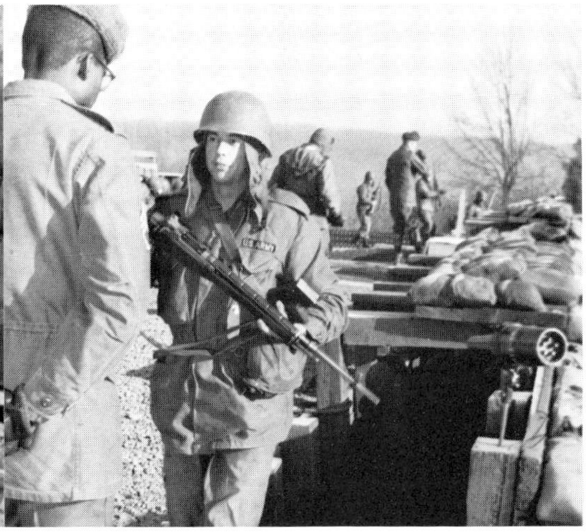

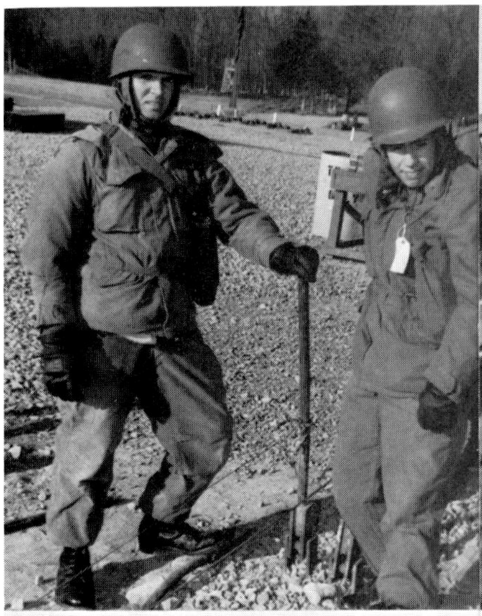
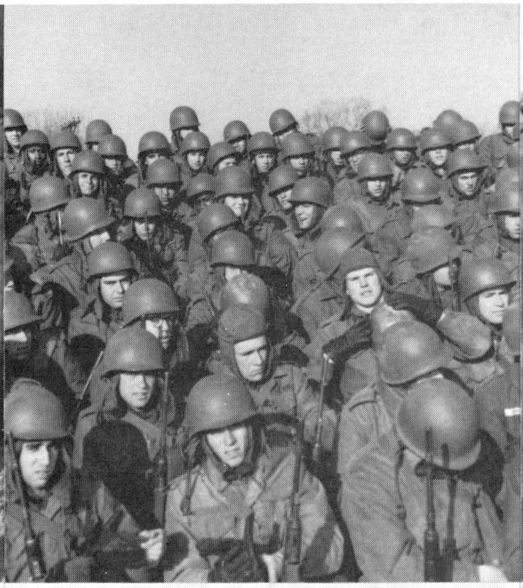
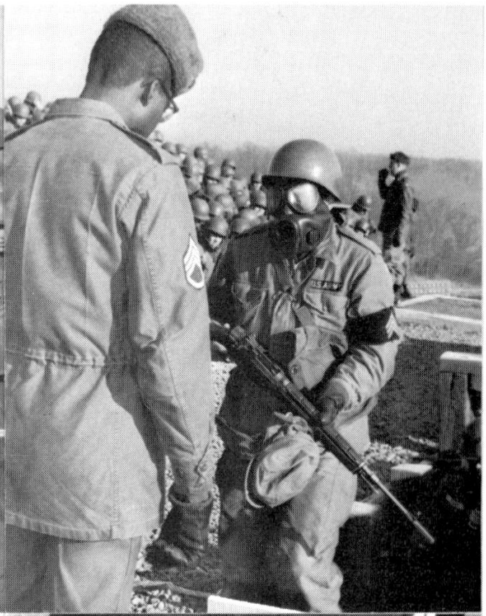
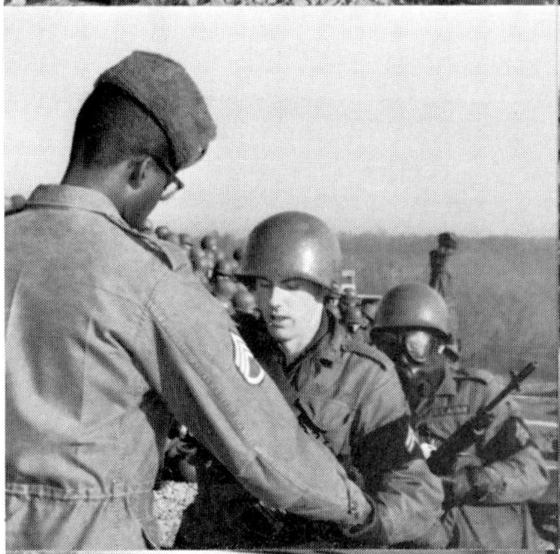
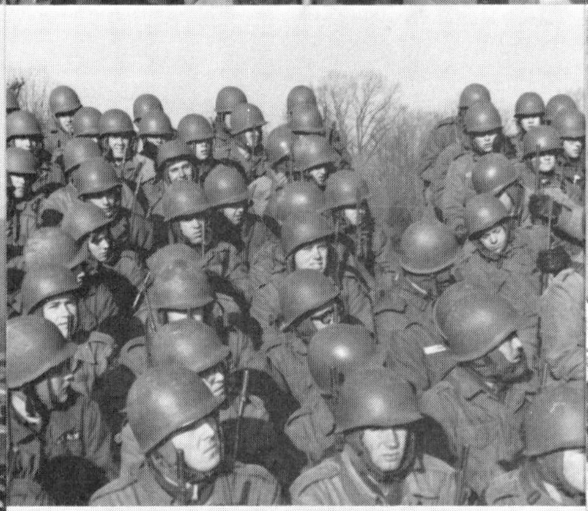
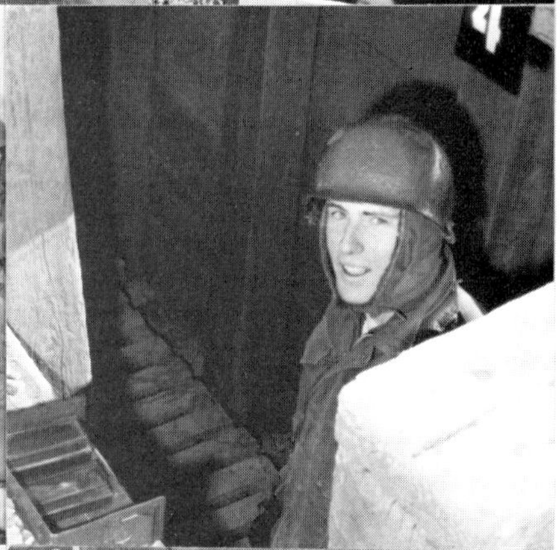
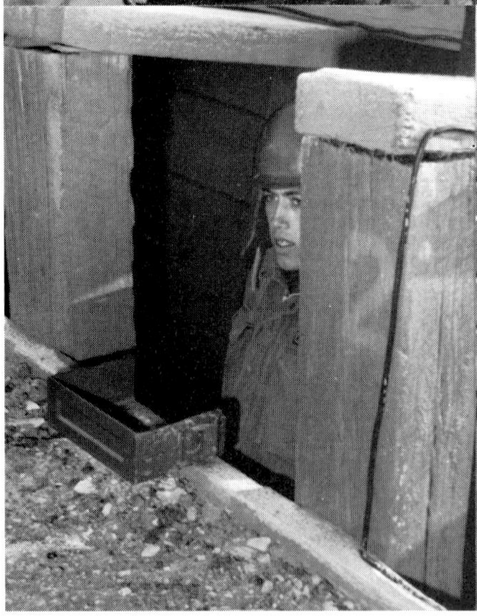
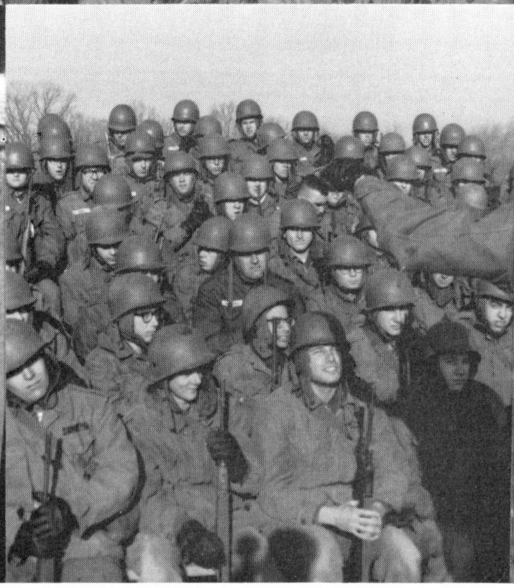
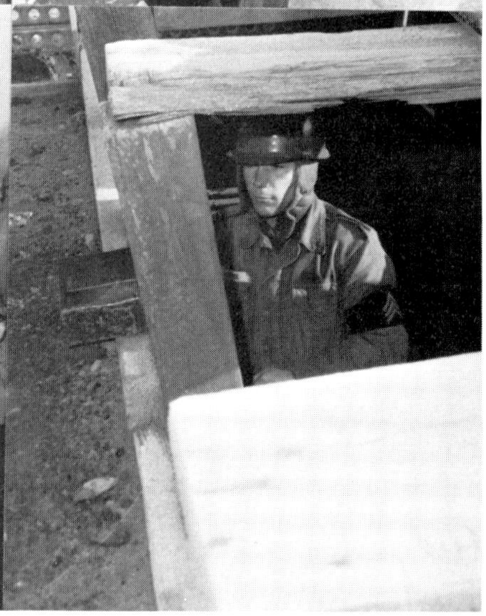
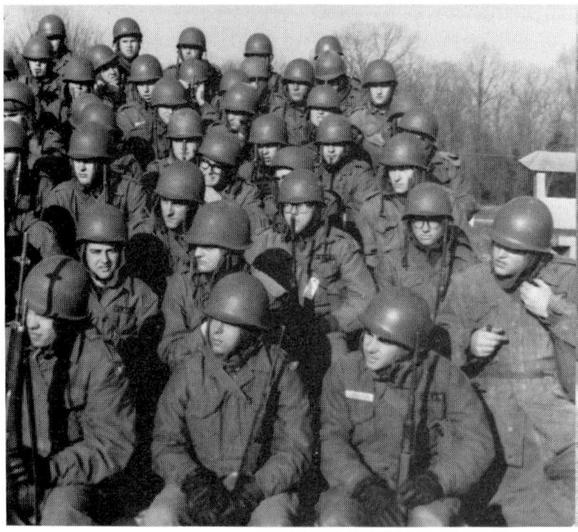
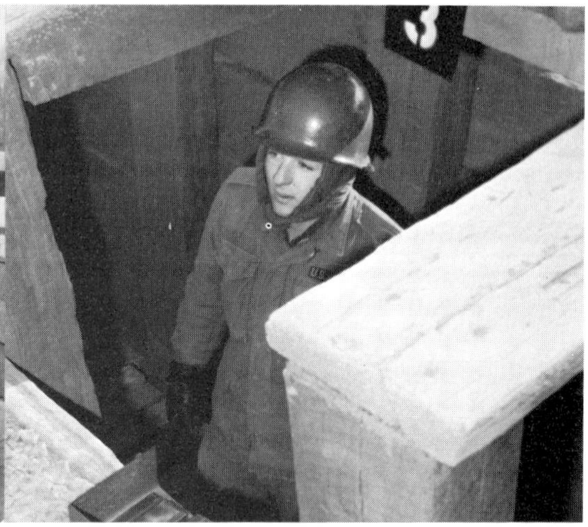
3

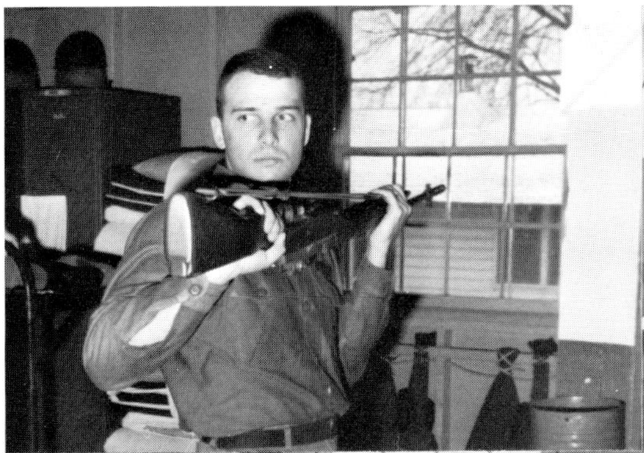
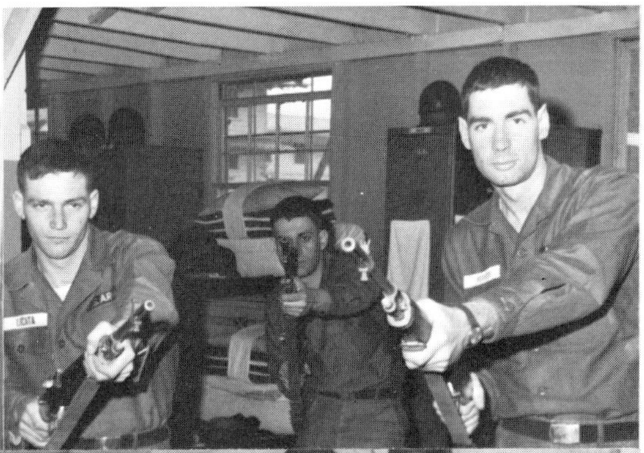
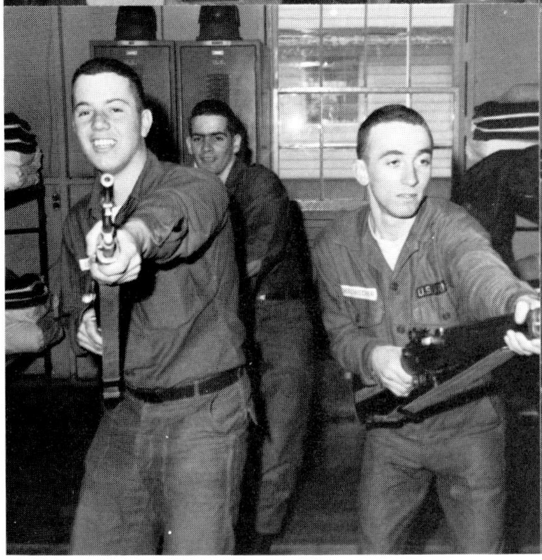
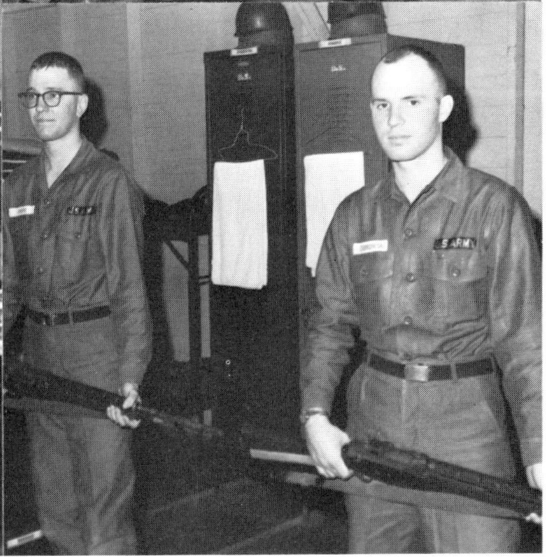
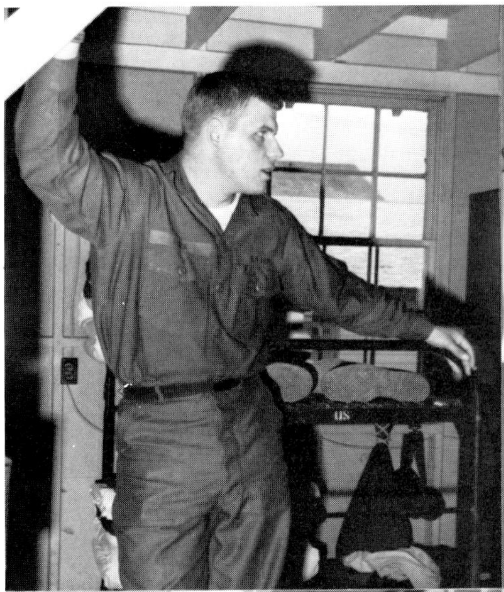
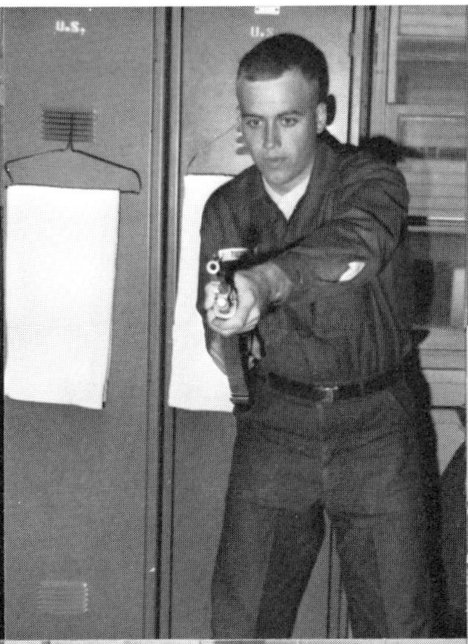
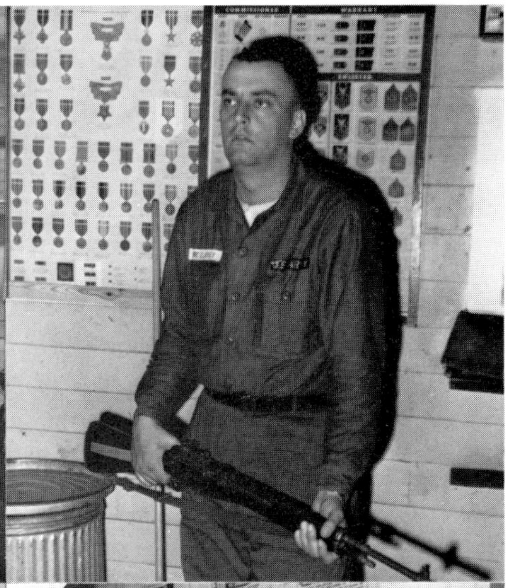
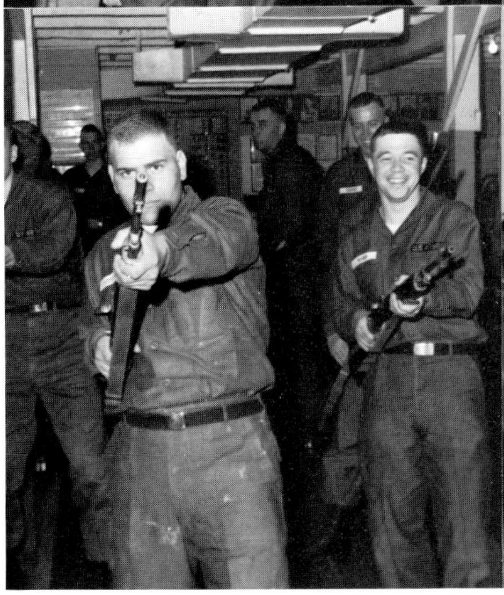
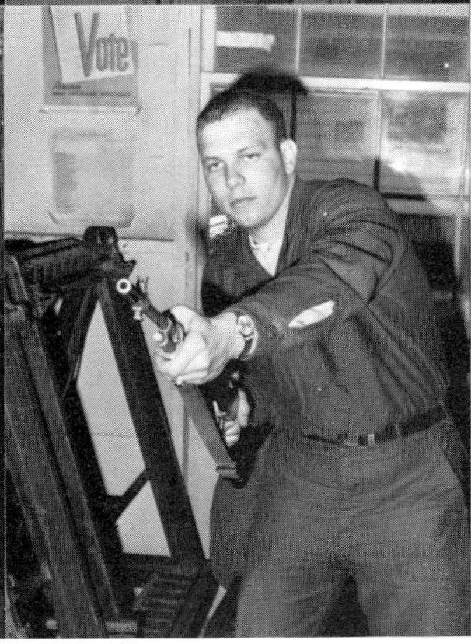
Vote
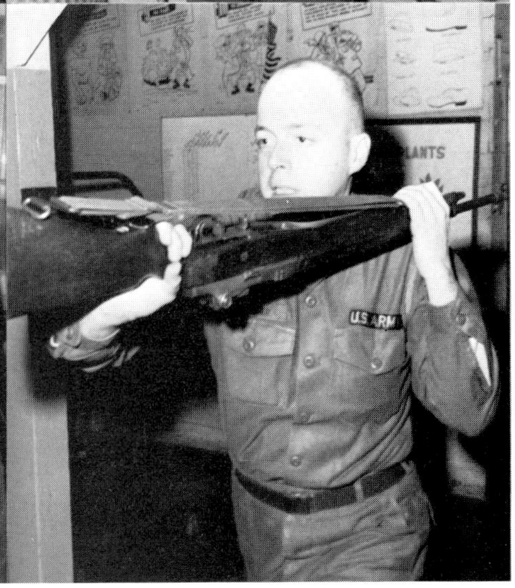
U.S. ARMY

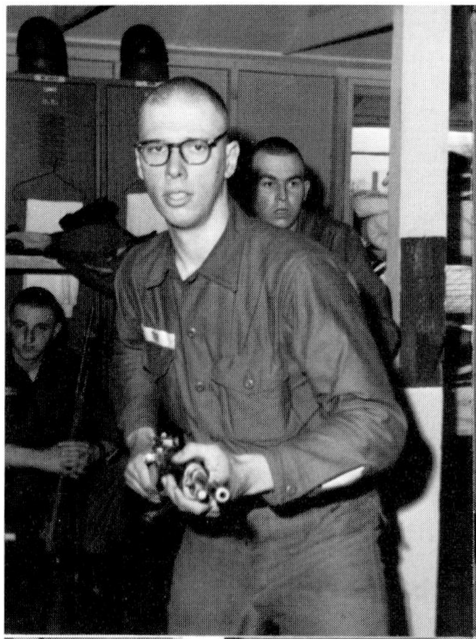
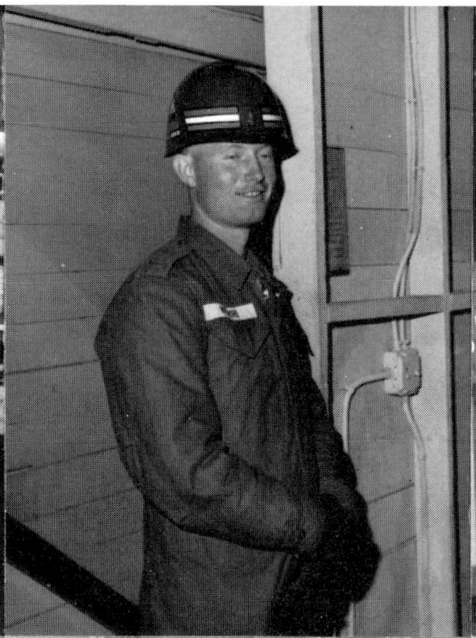
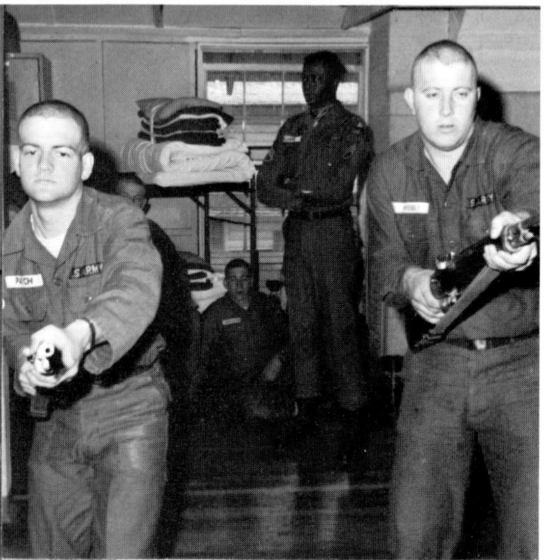
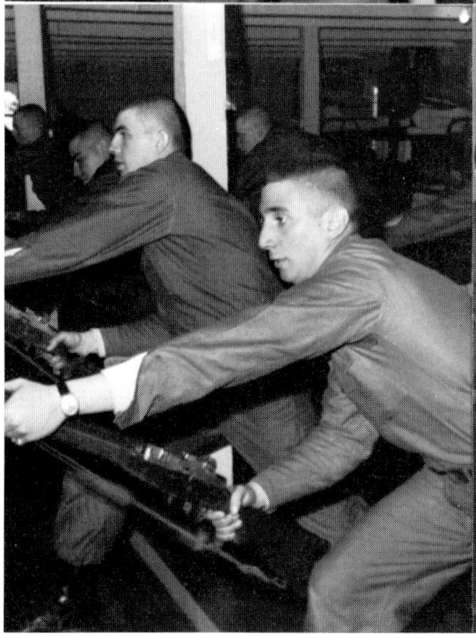
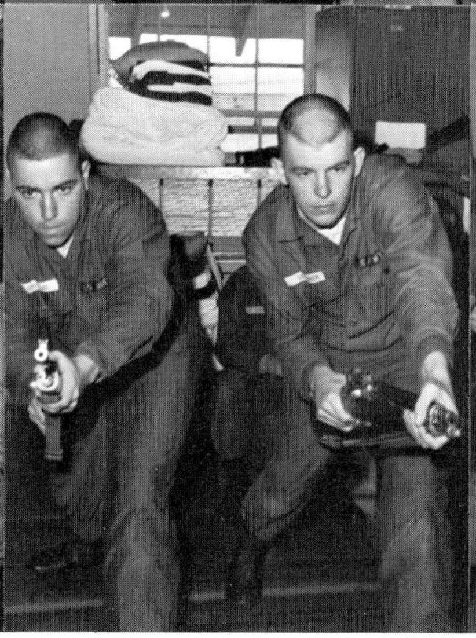
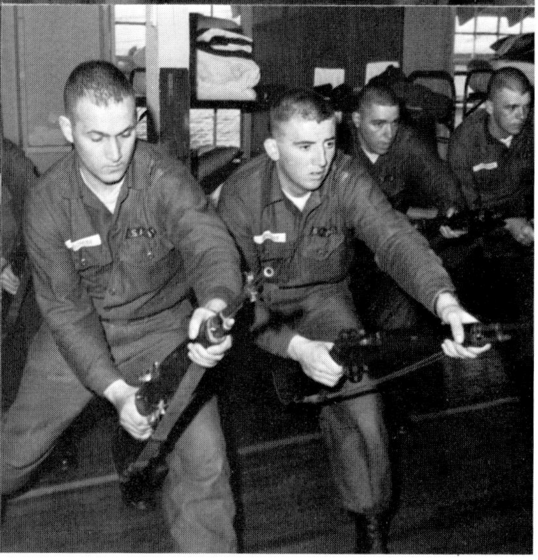
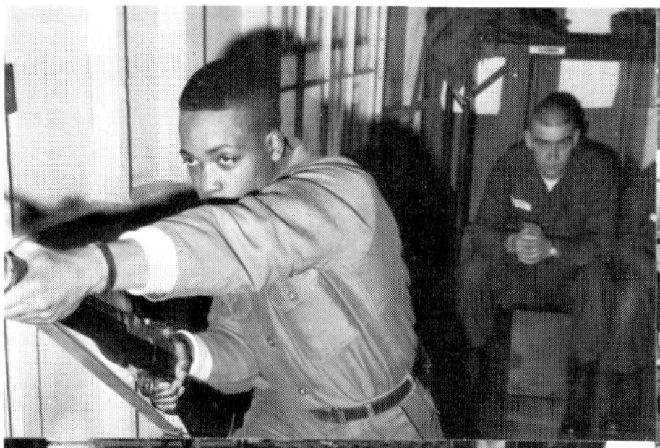
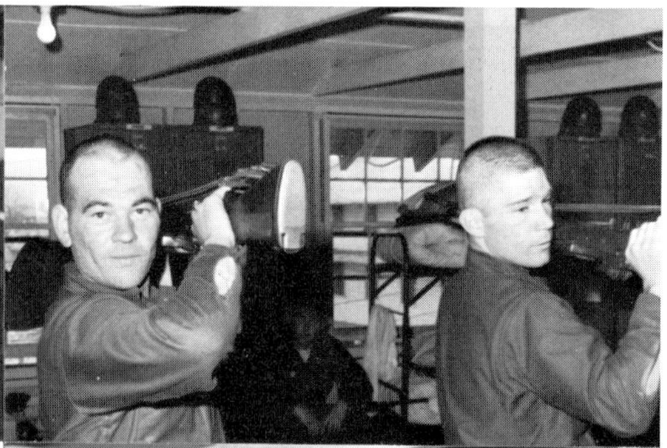
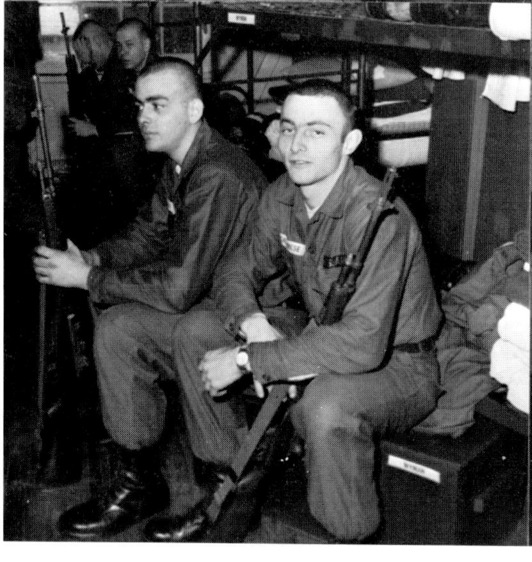
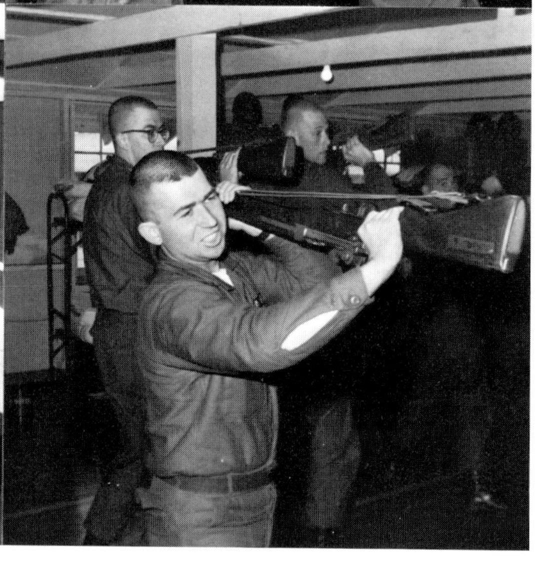

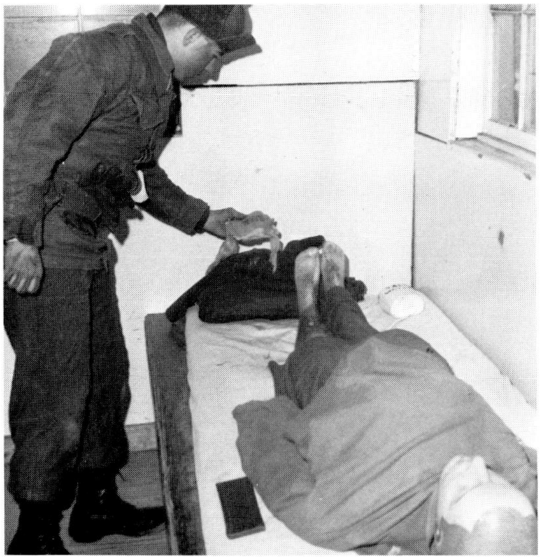

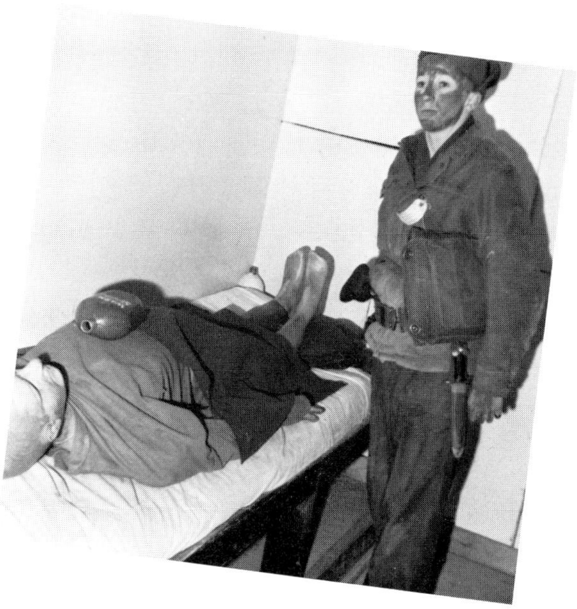

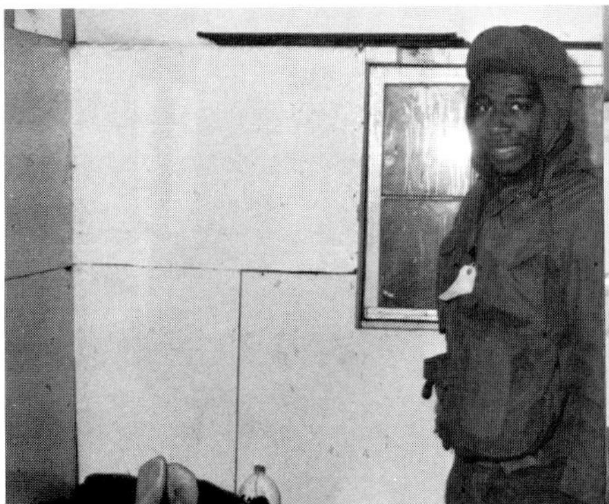

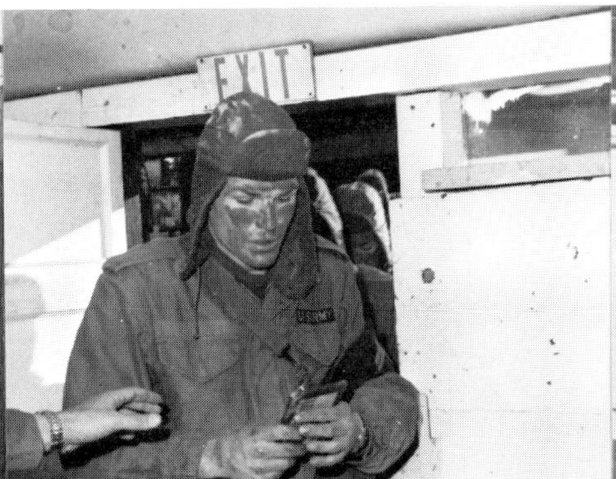
EXIT

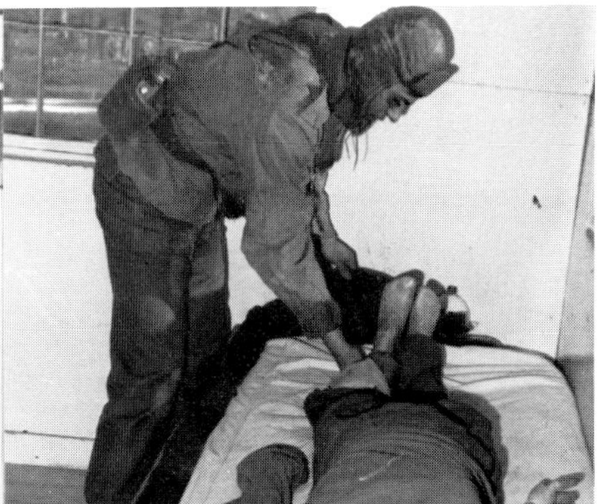

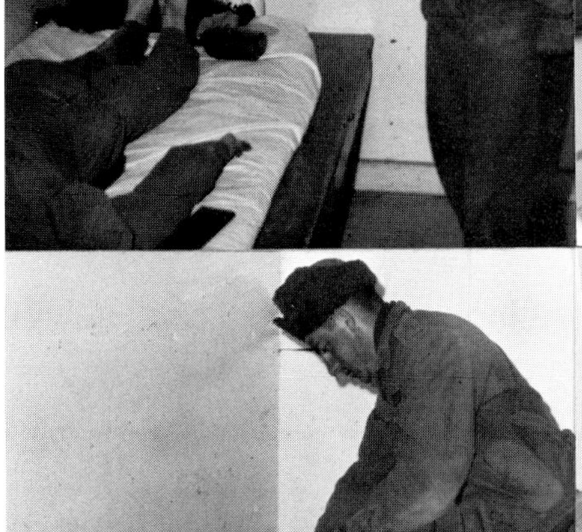

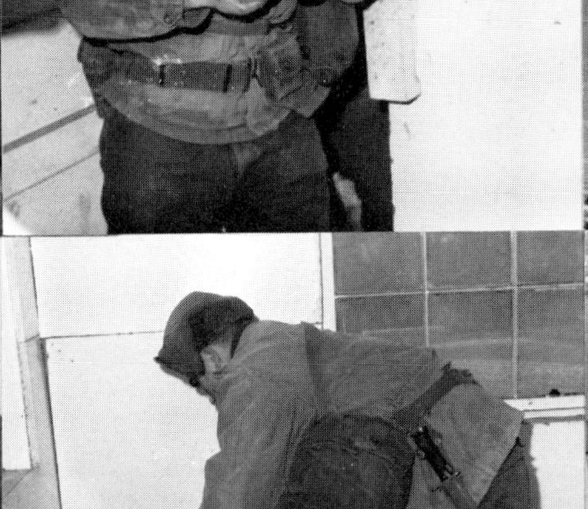

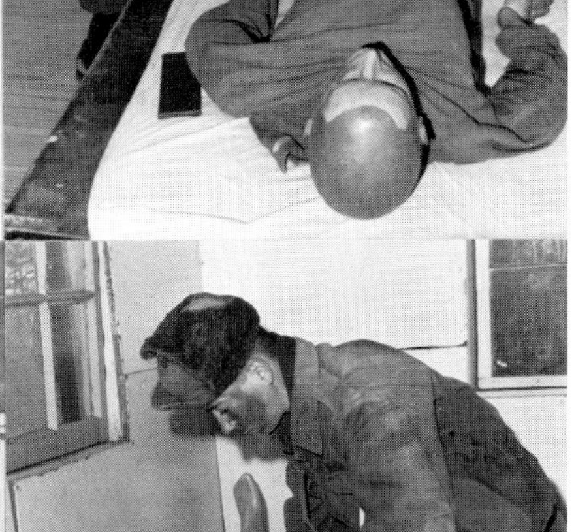

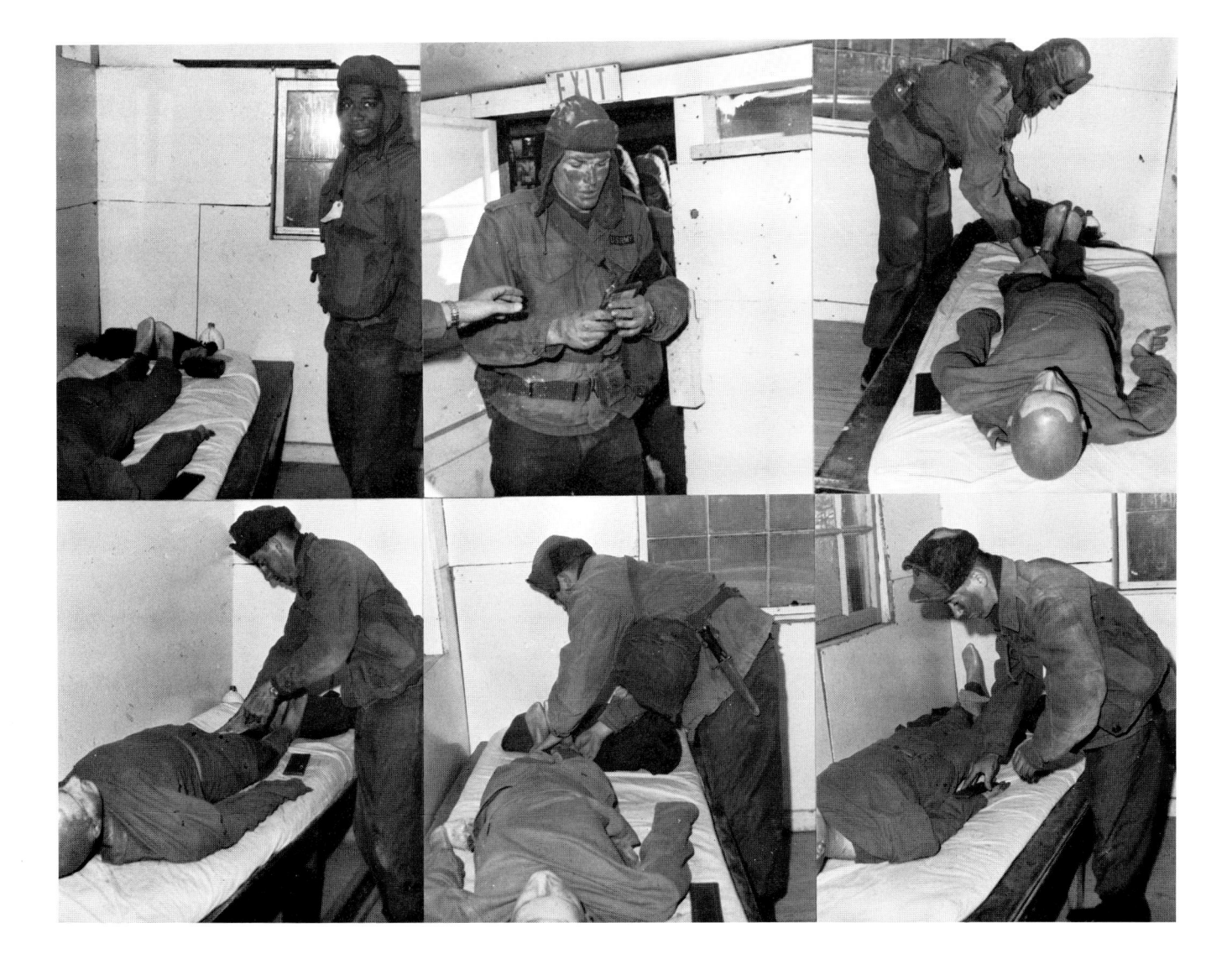

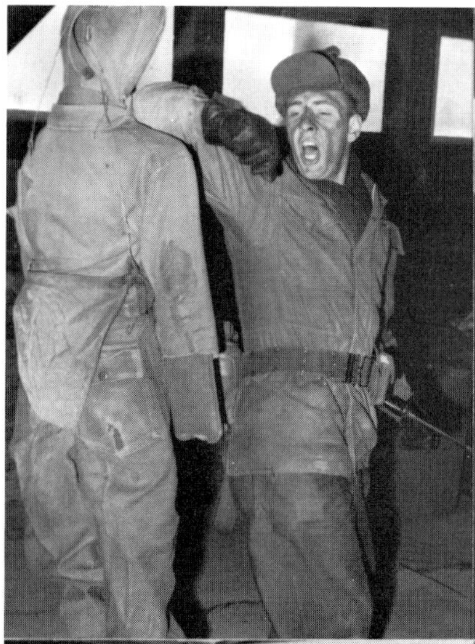
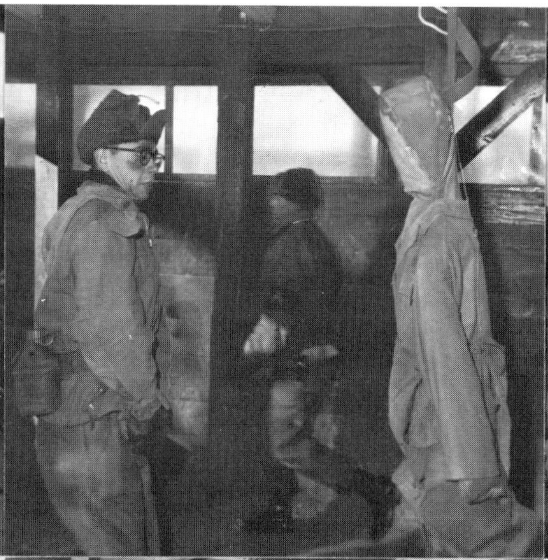
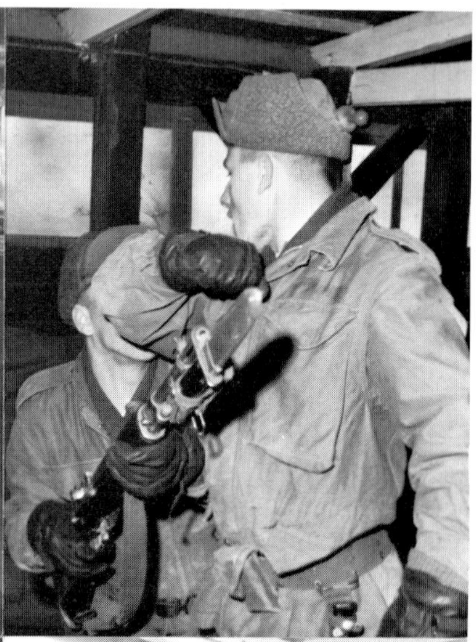
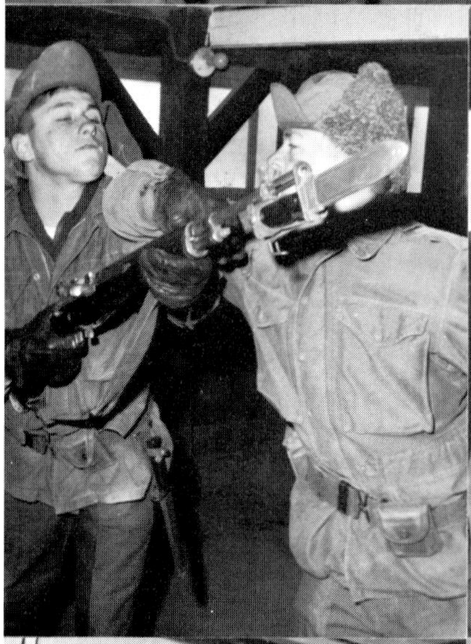
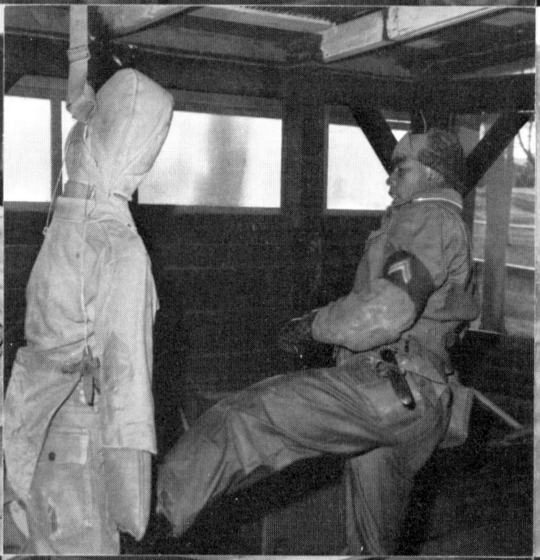
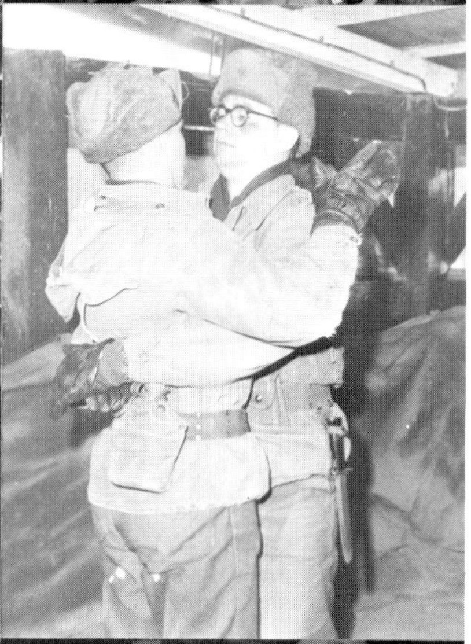
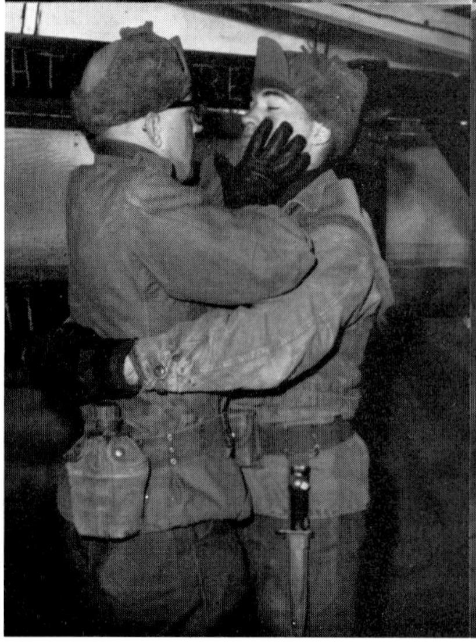
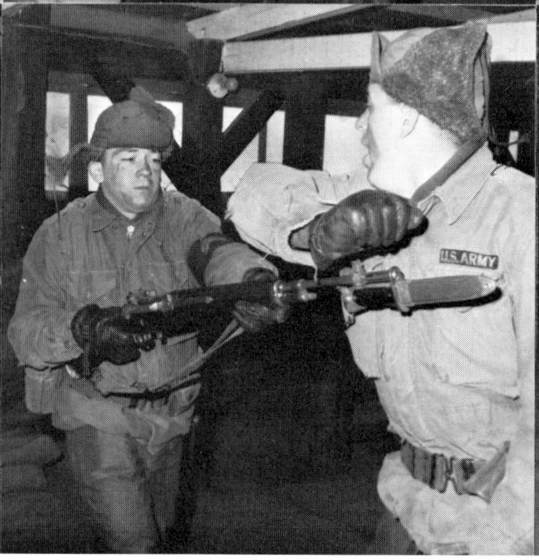
U.S. ARMY
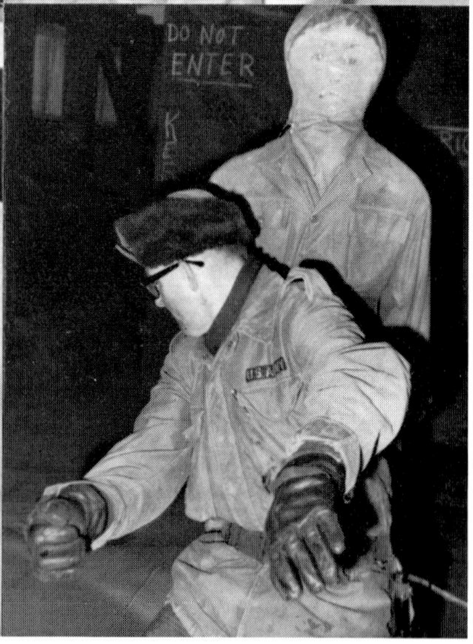
DO NOT
ENTER

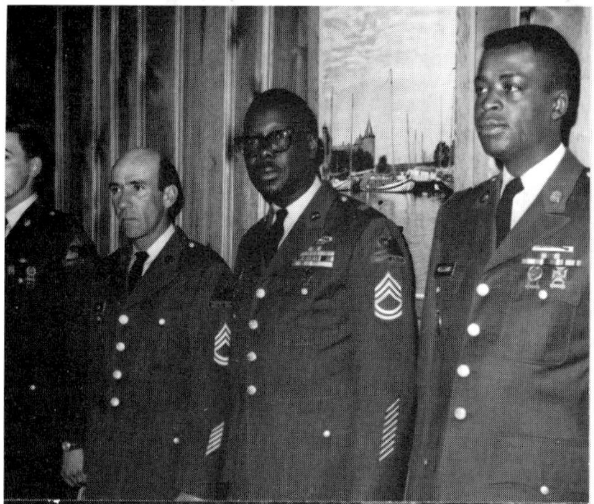
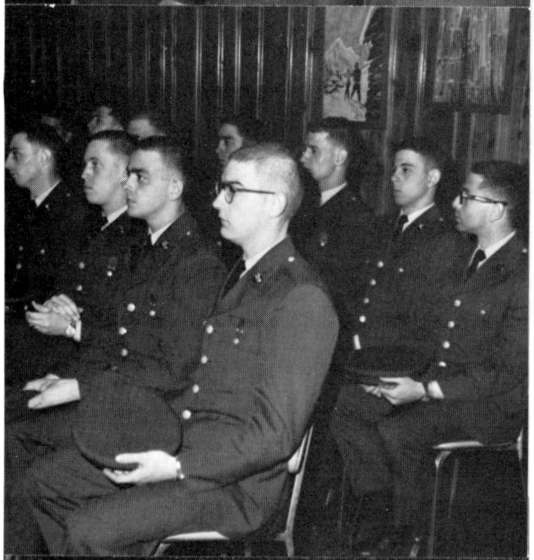
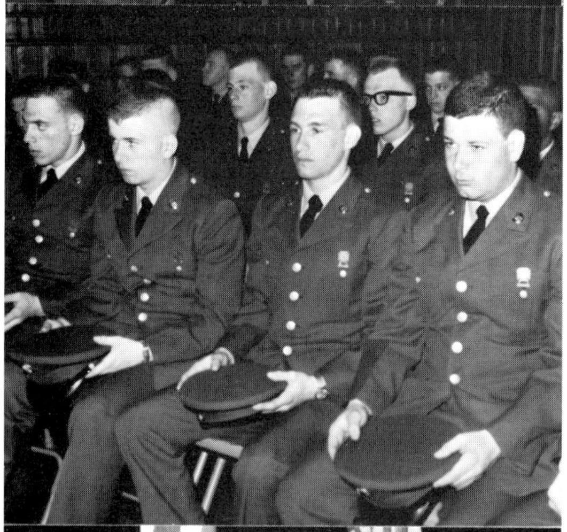
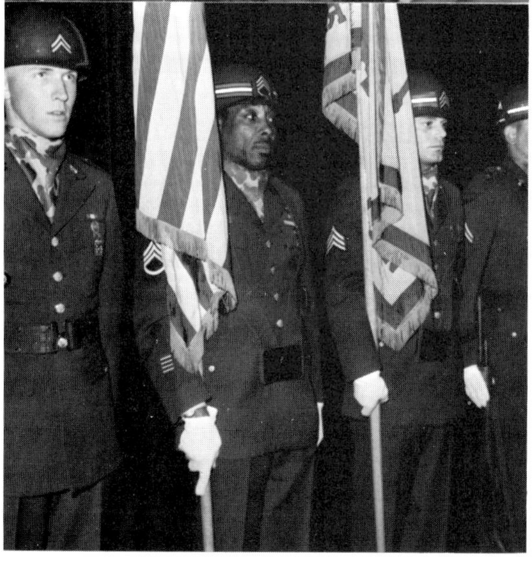
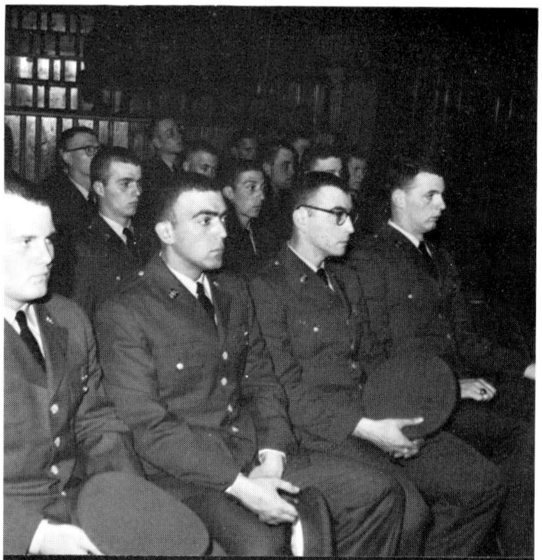
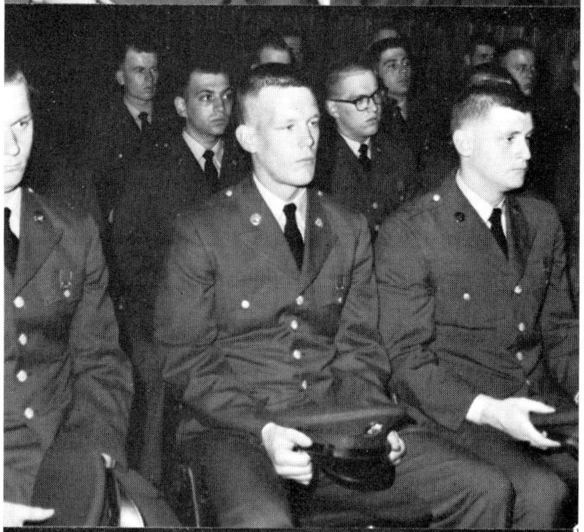
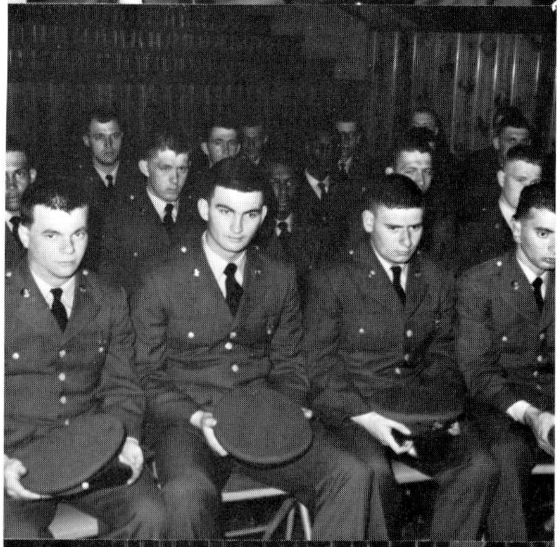
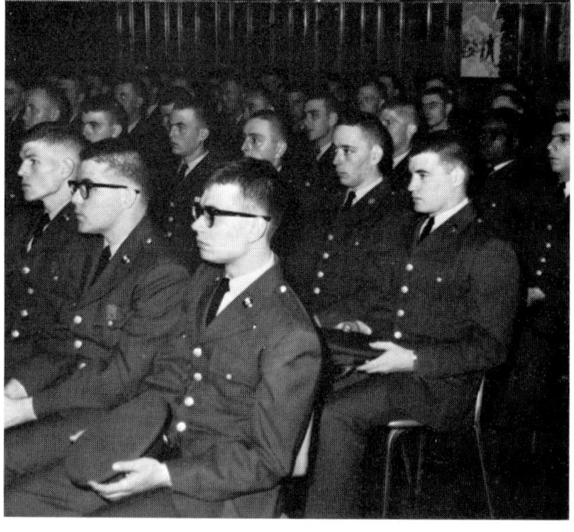